Sales and Marketing
for
Travel and Tourism

by
Philip G. Davidoff
and
Doris S. Davidoff

Illustrated by Carole Stokes, Cartoonist

National
Publishers
of the Black Hills, Inc.

Design, editing: Jean Babrick
Production: John Babrick
Editorial assistant: Claudette Bailey
Typesetting: Typesetters, Rapid City, South Dakota

ISBN 0-935920-09-9
Copyright © 1983
Philip G. Davidoff and Doris S. Davidoff

CONTENTS

Acknowledgements

This book would not be complete without acknowledging the help given to us by many people in the travel and tourism industry. We would particularly like to thank the following people who took the time and made the effort to send us material to use in compiling this text: John Zeeman of United Airlines, Guy Mitchell of American Airlines, Harry Dunham of Delta Airlines, Jeff Warner and Tim Carey of Trans World Airlines, Bob Dickinson of Carnival Cruise Lines, Lars Lindblad of Lindblad Travel, Patrick Sheridan of Gray Line, and James Host of the National Tour Association.

In addition to these industry representatives, we would also like to thank two travel agents who have given us much help and encouragement throughout our years in the industry. Without their encouragement, we might never have become as involved in industry education as we have. These two outstanding representatives of the travel agency segment are Andy Spielman, CTC, and Larry Frommer, CTC.

We must also thank Bob Blanchard of National College for his help and comments during his field testing of the manuscripts, and his students, who worked with the early versions.

Last, but certainly not least, we must thank our children, Donald, Douglas, and Dana, for their patience and the sacrifices they have made during this past year as we worked on this project.

Preface

The purpose of this book is to provide a practical application of sales and marketing theory to students and practitioners of the travel and tourism industry. We also want to give persons considering travel and tourism careers an understanding of the real world, and to give them specific techniques that can be used on the job as well as a broad understanding of the interrelationships of the sales and marketing processes in a diverse, segmented, yet interacting industry.

The book is divided into two sections. The first section gives the theory of sales and marketing along with practical examples in the field of marketing as it relates to this industry. The second section is a carefully selected readings section. The varied articles and case studies reprinted here will help enrich the text material by giving true life illustrations of the principles discussed earlier. Readers will have an opportunity to study the writings and experiences of a variety of people involved in the industry.

Given the dynamic nature of marketing and of the travel industry in particular, we recommend that readers of this book monitor both the trade press and the general press for new information and articles relating to the concepts discussed in this book. In this way, they can remain current on the topic and reinforce the concepts developed in *Sales and Marketing for Travel and Tourism*.

May 1983

Philip G. Davidoff, CTC
Doris S. Davidoff, CTC

1
INTRODUCTION

buyer's market
consumer-needs strategy
consumer-oriented marketing
marketing
mental-state strategy
problem-solving strategy
product-oriented marketing
seller's market
stimulus-response strategy
tour package
wholesale tour operator

Marketing is a very broad topic, and when travel industry practitioners are asked to define it, they usually give a wide variety of answers. Merchandising, advertising, promotion, a plan for selling products, salesmanship, meeting customer needs, media planning are all thought (by various people) to be marketing itself. While all of these activities can be considered part of marketing however, no one of them is marketing itself.

Before offering a definition, let us point out that two conditions must be met for marketing to be possible. First, there must be a person or company that desires to sell a product or service. Second, there must be potential buyers for this product or service. It is not important which comes first, but both must exist. When both factors do exist, *marketing is the total process or series of activities that brings the potential buyer of the product or service together with the product or service*. If a concern can sell its product or service at a profit, marketing is successful. If the concern fails to earn a profit, marketing fails as well.

It is important to recognize, then, that marketing is the sum of all the activities related to bringing buyer and seller together profitably. In our exploration of marketing in the tourism and travel industry, we will look closely at the tourism product itself (it's really a service) as well as at the potential consumers of tourism—travelers. In addition to the needs of the individual traveler, we will look at the travel market, its demographics and segmentation. We will also look at the sellers of travel and how the image of a selling company or a destination affects its marketing. We will concentrate on practical marketing tools that must be understood by anyone planning a career in the field of travel and tourism. We will review advertising and promotion and analyze various media and specific techniques for advertisement planning. We will study the sales function in the travel industry, including all components, and provide a thorough analysis of the sales process, together with a step-by-step method that can and should be applied on the job. Finally, we will look briefly at probable future developments in this important topic.

AN HISTORICAL PERSPECTIVE

This book is a practical approach to bringing buyer and product together in the travel industry. However, a brief history of the development of marketing in this century is important to an understanding of today's processes. We must begin by understanding that manufacturing in the first half of this century basically served a seller's market. Consumer demand for goods generally exceeded the ability to produce the goods. With the exception of the Great Depression of the 1930s, when both production and consumption were down, the marketing process was one of developing a product and getting it to the customer.

This product-oriented marketing was based on the old cliché: "Build a better mouse trap and people will beat a path to your door." This style of marketing began to fade in the 1950s when supply began to exceed

INTRODUCING THE 1957 EDSEL

"I don't understand your attitude, sir—our market research indicates you're going to love this car."

demand and a buyer's market developed. Now people had choices. They did not have to buy one type of product—they could choose from many. With the change in supply, the marketing process also changed. Instead of building a better product and hoping people would come to the door, executives began to ask: "What does my customer really want?" Thus began the development of consumer-oriented marketing. This style of marketing is very sound economically because, if a producer knows what a customer wants before production begins, there is less chance of producing the wrong product. The secret here is accuracy in determining what the consumer wants.

TWENTIETH CENTURY MARKET STRATEGIES

The Automobile Industry

From the 1930s to the 1970s, market strategy changed from product orientation to consumer orientation. In the heyday of the famous Model A and Model T Fords, industrialist Henry Ford said, "You can have any color car you want as long as it's black." And people bought black Fords and more black Fords. The producer was clearly in the driver's seat. After World War II, automobile colors started changing, but consumer demand then was so great that almost any car built was sold.

By the early 1950s, automobile production was at a peak. The number of manufacturers was much greater than today. Kaiser-Frazer, Crosley, Studebaker, and Packard automobiles were being produced, along with more familiar names such as Ford, Oldsmobile, Buick, Chrysler, and Plymouth. Supply began to exceed demand, and consumers were able to choose the brands and models that appealed to them most. The V-8 engine gained preference over the straight 8 cylinder engine. Packard, a major producer of straight 8 cars, became history. Other consumer choices governed the survival of some manufacturers and the downfall of others.

Ford Motor Company was one of the first to recognize that consumer choices were affecting the market place. As a result, Ford decided to determine what prospective buyers wanted in a car. Ford's management believed that if consumers were given what they wanted, they'd buy it. Thus began the earliest and most primitive market research. Unfortunately, the result was a total failure—the 1957 and 1958 Edsel. According to *Business Week* (Nov. 28, 1959) Ford spent $250 million to bring the Edsel to market, and lost about $200 million more in the two-

and-one-half years the car was in production. Ford was the laughing-stock of the automobile industry, but executives recognized what Ford had tried to do. They determined that in this case the execution of market research was faulty, not the concept itself.

The development of market research continued. For the last twenty years, no major automobile manufacturing decision has been made without strong attempts to determine what the consumer really wants. By 1970, management consultant and graduate business professor Peter Drucker observed that General Motors was not in the business of *manufacturing* motor cars, it was in the business of *marketing* motor cars. Today, successful marketers determine what product or service a client wants before developing the product or service. This approach is valid in all industries, including the travel and tourism industry.

The Airline Industry

Marketing within the airline industry is another parallel in our historical perspective. Through the 1950s, airline marketing was product-centered. Almost all advertising described the features of airplanes, including comfort, safety, and speed. Little was done to recognize the fact that different people travel for different reasons (primarily business or pleasure) until the 1960s. Jet airplanes began to be used in the late 1950s. By the early 1960s, jets were in widespread use in the United States and overseas. The jet vastly increased the capacity or supply of available airplane seats. It could carry more people per flight than propeller aircraft and fly almost twice as far on a given day. Thus, with supply exceeding demand, consumer-oriented marketing began within the airline industry.

After World War II, first-class and coach fares developed with differing levels of service. For example, the Boeing Stratocruiser used by Pan American World Airways and others featured a lower deck with sleeping accommodations. (It is interesting to note that in 1980 sleeperette seats were reintroduced in the first-class sections of Boeing 747 jumbo jets.)

By the 1960s, airline marketers began looking at reasons for travel. They determined that business travelers had certain needs (flexibility, speed, and last-minute planning capability) while vacationers had other needs (low cost, reliability, but usually much time for advance planning).

The business and vacation travelers are really purchasing different products. Frequency of service was established to meet business needs.

Special excursion fares began to be offered to attract the vacation traveler. Restrictions were placed on these fares so that the business traveler who needed to plan travel at the last minute still paid a higher "regular" fare. Today, passengers on the same flight between two cities may have paid many different fares depending upon the conditions under which they are traveling. The lower fares are established to attract vacationers away from their cars and fill empty seats on the frequent flights that business travelers need.

The Steamship Industry

The steamship and cruise industry provides an interesting contrast in our view of the historical perspective of marketing. From the beginning of the century until the 1960s the steamship was a major form of transportation. The growth of our nation can be traced to immigrants traveling in "steerage" class across the North Atlantic. Steamships also had one other class of service—first class. First-class service was exceedingly elegant and expensive and only available to the rich. First-class travelers and immigrants never saw each other because the ships did not permit movement between classes. Shipline marketing was definitely product oriented through the 1950s.

In the late 1950s, however, an event took place which had grave implications for the steamship market—and nobody noticed. This was the year that more people crossed the North Atlantic by airplane than by

"Thanks for all that information on cruises, dearie—now, which ship has the best table scraps?"

sea. By the early 1960s, with the introduction of jet airplanes, it appeared that the death knell was sounding for ship transportation.

However, just as the United States Cavalry rode to the rescue in old Western movies, customer orientation rescued the steamship industry. In the 1950s, some steamship lines had experimented with cruises—winter vacation trips where a steamship sails from one city, visits a number of ports, and returns to the city of origin. North Atlantic travel was at a low ebb during the winter because of poor weather and normal vacation patterns. The cruises were quite successful and provided some degree of income when ships would otherwise be idle.

With the decline of the steamship transportation market, shiplines introduced cruises on a year-round basis and found almost instant success. With the addition of air/sea packages and special ships designed specifically for cruising, the cruise market has developed into an important part of the tourism package. The development of the cruise was a reaction to changing consumer needs.

Hotel Industry

The hotel industry has also modified its marketing plans and, in reality, its product, to meet changing customer needs. The first hotels of the modern world were inns at critical points of stagecoach lines. With the advent of the railroad, hotels developed near central city railroad stations in large cities throughout most of the world.

Later, railroads sometimes created cities, as well as other destinations. Henry Flagler, developer of the Florida East Coast Railroad, invested heavily in the development of resorts in Miami Beach. He did this to provide a market for his rail services, and the first wave of winter tourism in Miami Beach, around the turn of the century, was promoted to fill both railway seats and hotel rooms. By the 1920s and 30s the rich routinely traveled to Miami to spend the winter on the beach. Other resorts for the wealthy, such as Greenbrier in Virginia and Asbury Park in New Jersey, were connected to major cities by railroads.

Shortly after World War II, a Memphis businessman and his family took a trip to Washington, DC and back by car. This man, Kemmons Wilson, was appalled by the lack of facilities for family travelers. The roadside cabins and tourist courts existing at that time were, with few exceptions, very poor in quality. They usually consisted of only a bedroom, a bathroom, and a parking space outside the door. Standards were not consistent and the traveler could not be assured of a pleasant experience. Hotels in cities were expensive, charged high rates for children, and had no parking facilities. Kemmons Wilson decided to do something about this. He and a few fellow investors were the founders of Holiday Inns, now the world's largest hotel chain in terms of number of rooms.

Holiday Inn was the first to recognize the needs of the family traveler. Free parking, swimming pools, and no charge for children sharing a room with parents were the initial sales features of the chain. The chain was also one of the first to use franchising as a major method of expansion. Holiday Inn franchises were expected to meet strict operational standards and pass periodic unscheduled inspections. Other hotel chains soon adopted similar methods.

Gradually, the distinctions among hotels, motels, and resorts have faded. Previously, hotels were commercial in nature, offering just rooms and restaurants, and were usually located in cities. Motels (motor hotels) were located near well-traveled highways, provided free parking facilities, and usually had a swimming pool. Resorts emphasized facilities for rest and relaxation, such as pools, tennis, golf, shuffleboard or other activities. Today, also, many downtown hotels offer health clubs, swimming facilities, tennis courts, and other types of recreation. While parking is not always free, it is generally available. Today, downtown hotels compete with resorts for conventions and business meetings. The roadside motel, which previously depended upon vacation travelers, today competes for business travelers—especially where companies have established major facilities in suburban areas. Motels also seek their share of the meetings market.

"In years to come, Margaret, we'll look back on this vacation as one of our happiest moments."

Today all accommodation facilities market to the traveler and also to the local community. While the local community does not provide many room nights of business, local residents make hotel restaurants and catering facilities profitable. Such family gatherings as weddings, anniversaries, and bar mitzvahs have helped many hotels to be profitable—especially on weekends when business travelers are not usually on the road.

The Tour Package

Tour packages are a relatively new marketing strategy of the tourism industry. By definition, a tour package is any combination of two or more travel service components put together and sold as a single unit. Before the development of packages, travel agents had to make individual arrangements with each service supplier for each client. If a couple traveling to London requested a hotel, transfers to and from the airport, theater tickets and a city tour, the agent would make separate contacts with the hotel, transfer service operator, theater ticket agency, and sightseeing tour operator. Or else, the agent would contact a receptive service operator in London for arrangements. The process would be repeated for each point on the tour itinerary. For overseas destinations, agents would establish "foreign independent tours" (FITs); for domestic destinations the agents established "domestic independent tours" (DITs).

"And to top off your visit to Paris, my associate, Mr. Quasimodo, will escort you on a personally guided tour of Notre Dame."

With the development of the jet airplane and the consequent boom in middle-class travel came the need for easy-to-sell vacations. Destinations wishing to encourage the development of tourism (such as the Caribbean Islands, Hawaii, or Europe) needed inclusive programs that were easy to advertise and promote and also easy to book. Travel agents handling the new wave of travelers needed programs that were easier to explain to prospects than FITs and DITs, and also priced lower than the custom-tailored independent programs. The package tour was developed to meet these needs.

The package tour also brought a new class of business operation into the travel and tourism industry—the large wholesale tour operator. These companies assemble a range of travel service components into package tours. The programs are described in detail in brochures that are often elaborate and printed in full color. The brochures are distributed to travel agents and airlines for use in soliciting travelers. These folders and brochures have become essential for selling travel, and most prospective travelers expect and want to see them. The brochures help make an intangible service more tangible.

Tour packages are marketed in all sizes and shapes and in all price ranges. The package may be a one-day sightseeing tour, a city or resort package including hotel and transportation, or a long escorted tour with many features to several destinations. Costs may range from a few dollars to thousands of dollars. Several points will be common to all, however. The package will be designed for a target market segment. It will be described in reasonable detail in a brochure, and it can be booked with a single phone call to a tour operator or airline.

SALES VERSUS MARKETING

Many who are involved in the sales function in many industries believe that sales alone is marketing. They concentrate their efforts on the skills and techniques of selling and believe that this alone will produce results. While the sales function may certainly be considered the most important part of the marketing process, it is not a substitute for marketing itself. Although sales skills and techniques will help generate sales, they are better used as part of an overall marketing plan.

Sales is only part of the process. The identification of potential markets, development and pricing of products and services to meet the needs of these markets, and advertising and other promotional efforts are important parts of marketing. When matched with proper sales techniques, this overall marketing process will make all the components of marketing as effective as possible. However, since selling is the marketing component most often confused with marketing itself, a brief consideration of sales strategies may be helpful here.

SALES STRATEGIES

As marketing concepts have developed, four types of sales strategies have also developed. Stimulus-response, mental-states, consumer-needs, and problem-solving strategies are the primary descriptors of popular sales methods.

Stimulus Response

Most advertising is based on the stimulus-response theory. Originated in the last century by the Russian scientist Ivan Petrovich Pavlov, the basis of the theory is that a person may be conditioned to respond to a stimulus. Pavlov conditioned a dog to begin to salivate (as if food was in front of him) when he heard a bell. In advertising and sales, stimulus response is based upon repetition. Repeat something often enough and, if it has any impact, people will respond to it. "I can't believe I ate the whole thing," conditioned people to think of Alka Seltzer in a famous advertising campaign. In sales, stimulus-response theory stresses the use of repetitious canned speeches by the salesperson. While this strategy may be effective in a simple sales process, we do not believe it is an effective sales strategy in the travel industry. It does not consider the needs of the prospective purchaser nor does it provide for much interaction between salesperson and customer.

Mental States

The mental-states strategy is based on thorough preparation of the salesperson. This is the preferred strategy of the high-pressure salesperson who can "sell refrigerators to Eskimos." This strategy features a complex, but "canned" presentation technique with the salesperson convincing the purchaser to purchase the product or service. Many marketers consider this strategy to be unfair to the consumer. While initial sales may be generated, repeat business is rarely achieved because such sales do not meet real consumer needs.

Consumer Needs

The consumer-needs sales strategy was developed as a byproduct of the customer-oriented marketing system that characterizes current marketing theory. The role of the salesperson under this strategy is to find a need and fill it. This is a highly interactive process in which complex interviews of prospective customers by a salesperson are required to determine the customer's real need. The salesperson then provides the product or service to meet the need. Much successful selling in the travel industry follows this strategy.

Problem Solving

The problem-solving strategy is really a refinement of the consumer-needs strategy. It is most used in the sale of expensive or "high-ticket" items. The strategy requires much preparation on the part of the salesperson to understand the activities of the prospective customer. The salesperson helps his prospect identify problems, analyze alternatives to solve the problems, and, of course, provides the products or services necessary to solve the problems.

Chapter 11 provides detailed discussion of sales processes in the travel industry. Techniques for identifying client needs, making recommendations, overcoming objections and closing travel industry sales are provided in detail. At this point, it is important to recognize that selling, while important, is only a part of the larger marketing process.

CONCLUSION

Anyone involved in the tourism industry is involved, somehow, in the marketing process. An understanding of the history of marketing in the various segments of the industry will help you to understand this process, as will an awareness of all the components of marketing. This book is intended to help you gain that understanding and awareness.

SUMMARY
The prerequisites of marketing are: a person or company wishing to sell a product or service, and potential buyers for that product or service. When both these prerequisites exist, marketing is the total process that brings these two factors together profitably.

In this century, marketing has generally moved from a product-oriented to a consumer-oriented approach. Examples of this shift can be seen in the history of marketing in the automobile, airline, steamship, and hotel industries. As this shift took place, market research—used first in the automobile industry—has become more and more important. The products, also, have changed.

The tour package is a relatively new marketing strategy that has also created a new class of travel business—the wholesale tour operator who assembles a variety of travel service components into packages.

Although most important, sales is not the sum total of the marketing process. However, knowledge of the four major kinds of sales strategies is necessary. These four are:

- stimulus response, based on repetition;
- mental states, depending on intensive, high-pressure sales presentations;
- consumer needs, in which the salesperson interacts with the customer to discover and fill needs (an especially appropriate strategy in the travel industry); and
- problem solving, a refinement of the consumer-needs strategy, most often used in selling "high-ticket" items.

QUESTIONS FOR THOUGHT AND DISCUSSION

1. *What is marketing?*

2. *Describe the differences between product-oriented and consumer-oriented marketing.*

3. *Discuss the role of sales or selling in the marketing process.*

4. *Compare and contrast the histories of the airlines, steamship, hotel, and rail industries.*

5. *What is a tour package? Discuss the advantages and disadvantages to the traveler of such packages.*

6. *Discuss the consumer-needs and problem-solving sales strategies and how they can be used to sell travel.*

2
THE NATURE OF THE TOURISM PRODUCT

discretionary travel
intangible
nondiscretionary travel
off-season
on-season
parity product
perishability
quality control
seasonality
timeliness

Travel is one of the broadest, most diverse products imaginable. Travel is everything from getting in the car and driving 200 miles to visit the grandparents to the couple taking an around-the-world cruise. However, although travel encompasses so many activities, it has two primary divisions that must be marketed and sold differently because the motivations of the traveler in each of these divisions are quite distinct (see Chapter 3 on the psychology of the traveler).

NONDISCRETIONARY AND DISCRETIONARY TRAVEL

The first division of the travel product is nondiscretionary travel. This is the travel that is done out of necessity. These travelers go because they have to—not because they want to. The business traveler, the family going home for a wedding or a funeral, the student flying back to college are all examples of nondiscretionary travel.

Discretionary travel, on the other hand, is voluntary. These travelers can choose between staying home, driving somewhere, or flying to the Caribbean for their vacation. The discretionary traveler is the one most influenced by differences in fares and the many advertisements showing the romance of travel.

Because these two divisions of travel serve travelers with very different needs and wants, marketing techniques must differ. For example, most of the advertising of low air fares and low season prices for hotels is directed to the voluntary, discretionary traveler. In contrast, most of the frequent flyer and other brand loyalty types of promotion are directed toward the nondiscretionary business traveler.

INTANGIBLES

When considering the nature of the tourism product, we must remember that travel is different things to different people. Take the purchase of an airline ticket. To businesspeople who must buy a plane ticket to get to a meeting in a distant city, it is a necessary part of getting the job done. These travelers are most interested in the airline's on-time performance and efficiency, and in being able to get their baggage quickly or even carry it on board. To someone buying a ticket to get home because of a family crisis, buying a plane ticket is a stressful purchase. This traveler needs understanding and efficiency to make a difficult time easier. To the many vacationers, however, who are deciding how to spend their discretionary income, travel is quite different. To them, it is the purchase of a dream—an intangible.

The 55-Plus Club Hawaii Trip

Before   After

For example, a young woman buying a vacation package to Cancun does not get something tangible that she can take home, look at, and enjoy. Instead, she buys the use of some tangible items such as an airplane seat and a hotel bed for a brief time, but, even more important, she buys the culture and friendliness of Mexico, the beautiful beaches, the exposure to new and different things. She buys memories. About the only tangible items left after her vacation may be the pictures she took, some souvenirs, and the receipts for the money she spent. As this example shows, in the purchase of the travel product, we are looking primarily at the purchase of intangible services.

QUALITY CONTROL AND STANDARDIZATION

The marketing of a service differs from the marketing of a tangible good that can be held and examined. True, there are some similarities, but there are also many differences.

One primary difference is that of quality control capability. General Electric can institute quality control procedures to ensure that all its toasters are identical. These toasters will all carry the same warranty. The price may vary at different stores, but GE's marketing approach can focus on the quality of the product, which can be kept uniform. Consumers can buy safely at a cash and carry discount store, basing their decisions on price only, because they know GE will stand behind the toaster if it is defective.

This is not true in a service business. In most businesses within the travel industry, the product is service. You cannot return a defective trip. Travel employees can be trained to perform their jobs in a somewhat similar manner, to reflect the image of the company. However, because the service is so personal, no standard, uniform quality control is possible. The same employee can and will act differently on different days.

A hotel can be sure that the rooms have the same furniture and are clean, but the actions of front desk personnel will vary. It is possible for General Electric to discard an inferior toaster; it is not possible for the manager of a service business to discard a hasty and inappropriate remark made by a desk clerk to a guest. Any service business must train its people to act in a proper and desired manner all the time, but training is not always remembered, and instructions are not always followed properly.

Similarly, an airline may be able to standardize its aircraft and its food, but it cannot totally standardize its flight attendant crews. Anyone who has flown frequently knows that a flight can be made a very enjoyable experience or a very difficult one by the attitude of the flight crew. The crew is on the front line of the airline's marketing because they influence travelers to continue using that airline or to look for another.

PERISHABILITY

In addition to the problem of quality control and standardization, service products have other differences. One of these is perishability of the product. If a dress store does not sell the inventory it has stocked by a certain date, the management has several choices. It may reduce the price of the dress to the level of cost or below to avoid a total loss; it may keep the dress on the rack for a longer period of time; or it may put the dress away until next season. The store may not make the profit it had hoped to make, and may even lose some money on that item, but at least some money will be retrieved. The dresses will not be thrown out. Even the so-called perishable products of a produce department in a supermarket have some life and hope left after their ideal date of sale.

In contrast, an airplane, train, or bus seat or a hotel bed must be sold in a timely manner or it will have no value. A seat or a bed for May 10 can only be used on May 10. If it is not sold before that date, it is literally "thrown out." When the plane leaves the gate or the night is over, that May 10th seat or bed can no longer be sold, even at a greatly reduced price. It can never be put back into the inventory of the company. The company cannot recoup one cent of its cost for that seat or bed.

"We will now circle JFK for the next three hours, at no extra charge to you."

This is the reason for a practice of the airline and hotel industries that receives much bad publicity—that of overbooking. When a hotel or airline knows that historically some of the people with reservations do not show up on that date, it will sell a number of seats/beds over the number that actually exist. The company is gambling on the historical odds. Usually, this practice works out well and fills seats or beds that would otherwise go empty.

But, occasionally, the airline or hotel misjudges and loses the gamble. Fewer "no-shows" occur than expected, and more people arrive than can be accommodated. In these cases, the manager has to decide what to do with the overflow. He cannot put on additional seats or beds, so airline passengers are "bumped" and hotel guests "walked." Newspaper reports in early 1983 showed the problems Mexican hotels faced when the devaluation of the peso suddenly made Mexico a travel bargain. Rooms that they had expected to be empty were suddenly filled, and overbookings led to confusion, disappointment, and "walks" to other accommodations for many vacationers. Coping with the perishability of the travel product creates these situations.

TIMELINESS

A tangible good is manufactured at one time and used at another. It can be warehoused, saved, and analyzed for quality before it is sold. A service, on the other hand, is produced as it is used. The product of use of a room at the Sleep More Hotel on February 15 is produced and used on February 15. The room on February 14 is a different product entirely. The services of a travel agent—those of consulting and advising and selling—are produced as the agent is talking with the client. They cannot be produced and put on a shelf to be used and sold later.

PARITY PRODUCTS

In some components of the travel industry, competing companies market what is known as *parity products*. They actually sell the same basic product. The differences are not meaningful. A primary example is the airline industry. All the major airlines fly basically the same equipment, maintain it the same way (government regulations require this), serve the same food (even made in the same kitchens), and train the flight attendants on the same safety procedures. They all have equivalent safety records and virtually the same on-time performance.

With so many things the same, how can one line get the consumer to choose its product over a competing carrier? To be successful with a parity product, an airline will market small differences that under normal circumstances would not really matter. For example, in the 1960s Braniff achieved success by promoting its multicolored fleet of aircraft. Braniff also marketed the designer uniforms of its flight attendants. The color of a plane or a uniform does not really affect the actual product, but Braniff found that it made them stand out from the crowd. Marketing parity products is quite difficult, since the marketer must create a difference in the mind of the consumer when no meaningful difference exists.

Today, the airlines, car rental companies, and hotels are marketing in a new way. They are trying to build brand loyalty in the frequent traveler—a concept which has never really existed in the industry. Through frequent-flyer, frequent renter, and other programs, travelers earn free flights or other bonuses. These programs appear to be very successful.

In the case of hotels, restaurants, destinations, and other travel products, we do not have the problem of parity products. Here, the differences are actual and sometimes great. A Holiday Inn markets an image of "no surprises," while Intercontinental markets the image of each hotel representing the area in which it is located. The consumer has a choice here of safety and security (but little adventure) or of being able to sample the native spirit (but perhaps not liking it).

The small pension without private bath in Europe is quite different (but in a different way than the Holiday Inn) from the Intercontinental luxury hotel. The location of one hotel, the weather and facilities at one destination, the type of food and price at one restaurant may be quite

The Flying Carpet Bazaar

distinct from that of a competitor. Therefore, in those segments where differences are substantial, the job of marketing is clearer. Marketing managers in those segments can decide which market segment they want to appeal to and develop the appropriate marketing plan. They do not face the challenge of creating differences in the mind of the consumer.

COMPETITION FOR THE TRAVEL PRODUCT

There is a tendency on the part of marketing managers in the travel industry to look at other travel products as their primary competition. For example, the airlines look at the train as competition and the train looks at the bus. One destination sees another destination as its primary competition. A travel agency sees the agency down the street and the airline as its main competition.

Although it is true that one travel product competes with another, there is other, more threatening competition. The real competition is the nontravel product. The average consumer has a certain amount of "discretionary" income—that money left over after he has purchased his necessities. Every time he turns around, he sees products competing for that discretionary income. The color TV, the video recorder, the home computer, the swimming pool in the backyard, the local country club, the new car—these are the real competition. The travel industry must first market travel as the desired activity for the discretionary dollar.

The travel and tourism industry is currently one of the largest industries in the United States and the world—in terms of both dollars spent and number of jobs created. For this reason, it is important that this industry continue to grow. And there is much room for growth in this industry. In addition, since the travel product is so varied, this growth can continue even in times of recession when other industries are retrenching. The growth may slow, but there will still be growth if recent history holds true.

The industry must work together—all of its components—to continue to win the discretionary dollar for travel. This cooperation can have other benefits, also. When a community works to improve itself for the purpose of encouraging additional tourism revenue, it will usually improve itself for its local residents. When the local residents feel good about tourism in the area, they will welcome the tourists with behavior that encourages repeat visitors. This local reception is an important part of the image the destination portrays. An excellent example of this is the

Before (above) and after (below) views of Baltimore's harbor area, transformed from a dilapidated waterfront to an attractive area popular with both tourists and residents.

city of Baltimore. Baltimore has rebuilt its harbor area into a thriving convention and visitors' center with additional luxury hotels, interesting shopping, and museums in what used to be a decaying waterfront area. This development has brought in many tourists, but it has also proved to be a great attraction for residents within the local area.

Once again, it is necessary to realize that the travel product is broad. Many parts are included in both the travel sector and also in sectors meeting local needs. Many restaurants, amusement parks, museums, and sports facilities meet both touristic and local recreational needs. When both segments benefit, overall tourism is enhanced and marketing efforts made easier. Tourists generally like to mix with local residents and feel a part of the locale.

SEASONALITY

Travel is a product that often suffers from seasonality. The beach will attract many visitors when it is warm, but who will come to a northern beach in the winter? The southern beach attracts the northerner who wishes to escape the cold back home, but is not as attractive when the weather improves in the North.

For this reason, destinations, hotels, and airlines found that they could not market their product in the same way year-round. Many marketing devices have been developed to try to even out these peaks and valleys of use. One of the most common is that of on-season and off-season prices. In the Caribbean islands, the price in the summer is usually substantially lower than it is in the winter. This helps attract the bargain hunter, who would like to visit new places but will sacrifice time of year (and perhaps ideal climate) for price. As another example, due to school vacations, summer is a very crowded time in many areas. Therefore, many bargains are available at other times of year. European prices, for example, are substantially lower in winter.

Another way of evening out these cycles is to promote convention business. Since spring and fall were traditionally their slowest travel times, cities started promoting special convention rates and activities in these off peak times. This practice has been so successful that it has become very difficult to find rooms in large city hotels or space in good convention facilities during October.

Still another method for promoting off-season business is to develop special activities. Some of the Caribbean islands have introduced special summer activities so that visitors in the summer not only get a lower price but actually get more for their money. Nassau has its "Goombay" season; Jamaica its "Boonoonoonoos"; and Bermuda, where the cool winter is slow, its "Rendezvous" season. Hawaii Aloha weeks and Quebec Winter Carnival serve similar purposes. All of these promotional activities have helped to increase business in previously slow seasons. Concerts, marching bands, and cultural activities are featured during these times. The airlines and hotels cooperate by lowering prices. Therefore, a vacation during the slow season may be only one-half to two-thirds the cost of the on-season trip.

Airlines develop special "promotional" fares, which encourage the vacation traveler who does not have to fly. However, these promotional fares create other marketing problems with the second division of travel—the business travelers. In developing promotional fares aimed at vacationers, the airlines must also establish rules to try to avoid use of these fares by the businessperson who must travel almost regardless of price. That is why many of these promotional fares require that the traveler remain at the destination over a Saturday night—most business travelers want to come home for the weekend. The requirement of advance purchase also helps keep away business travelers, since they frequently must make plans at the last minute.

The differing needs of business and discretionary travelers can affect airline fares more directly also. On routes that are heavily business oriented, Saturday fares can be quite a value. On the other hand, on routes that are popular for vacations, Saturday fares may have a surcharge. On the vacation routes, Tuesday through Thursday travel may bring the best values since most vacationers prefer to travel on weekends if there is no price differential.

Another type of seasonality is seen when some resorts raise prices to extremes during special demand periods, such as the Christmas vacation. In many resorts this season has a surcharge and a required minimum stay of varying length. Since the properties will be sold out during that period, they increase prices to help pay for the slower seasons.

When an airline owns a plane, or a hotel has a certain number of beds, they own them all the time and must try to maximize their use all the time, not only on special days or times of the year. Therefore, the marketing and sale departments must find ways to bring in enough business in the slow times to cover expenses so that the high seasons will bring in a profit. One of the challenges of marketing is to continue to create new approaches to this problem.

CONCLUSION

The travel product is an intangible, where quality control is impossible, and which has the characteristics of perishability, timeliness, and seasonality. In certain parts of the industry, the challenge of marketing parity products also exists. Knowledge of these characteristics and challenges is essential for the travel professional.

SUMMARY

The travel product can be divided into nondiscretionary and discretionary components—travelers who travel because they must (for business or personal reasons) or those who travel because they want to. These divisions require differing market techniques. Also, the discretionary travel product must compete with other discretionary products, such as color TVs or country club memberships. The basic strategy of the travel industry as a whole must be to market the travel product as a prime contender for the discretionary dollar.

Discretionary travel is an intangible, and as such it is not returnable. This makes the people involved in providing the intangible the most important part of the service. However, quality control over people is virtually impossible. The travel product is also perishable; it cannot be warehoused for later sale. And it is seasonal—a Caribbean beach in December is not the same product as a Caribbean beach in July. Finally, the travel product is sometimes a parity product, lacking meaningful differences from one supplier to another.

QUESTIONS FOR THOUGHT AND DISCUSSION

1. *Discuss the differences between discretionary and nondiscretionary travel, and how this difference affects marketing.*

2. *Discuss the four major factors of an intangible product such as travel. How do these affect marketing?*

3. *Define* parity product, *give examples within the travel industry, and discuss some of the marketing problems associated with parity products.*

3
PSYCHOLOGY OF THE TRAVELER

allocentric
life stages
Maslow's hierarchy
motivation
motivational segment
need-satisfaction theory
needs
psychocentric

The human need for travel has persisted throughout history. However, until recent times, most travel was for necessity rather than pleasure. This was true because in early times travel was usually both dangerous and difficult. It is not coincidence that the root word for *travel* and *travail* (heavy labor) is the same. Travel was hard. Today, it is pleasurable (or at least it is supposed to be) and looked forward to by most people.

It is impossible to market a product or service effectively without knowing the psychology of the prospective consumer. What motivates potential buyers to take a particular action? What motivates them to avoid a particular activity? Why do they react in certain ways? What can one do to make them desire a particular product or service? Most of the following discussion of the psychology of the traveler will focus on motivations—the forces that cause a person to take a specific action.

Remember, however, that the travel market is extremely broad, and therefore the motivations and needs of various segments of this market will differ and will require different marketing plans.

DIFFERING TYPES OF TRAVEL

Travel is an activity that occurs in every income and educational level within our society. The differences are in the type of travel. In the lower income and educational segments, travel is primarily by automobile or intercity bus transportation, and lodging is primarily with family or friends. As we go up in the economic and educational levels, travel increasingly involves air transportation and lodging in hotels. Segments of the industry, such as airlines and luxury hotels, are primarily interested in marketing to the middle and upper income groups. Low-price motels, fast-food restaurants, and intercity bus companies will be more interested in the lower income groups.

The average business traveler or vacation traveler purchasing a trip involving paid transportation and lodging is an up-scale individual. Members of this group are usually better educated and more affluent

Table 1
CHARACTERISTICS OF TRAVELERS AND NONTRAVELERS

	Travelers				Nontravelers
	1978	1979	1980	1982	1982
Proportion of Population	(43%)	(52%)	(54%)	(53%)	(47%)
Male	49%	49%	46%	53%	49%
Female	51	51	54	47	51
18-24 years of age	18%	17%	20%	16%	17%
25-34	24	26	24	27	24
35-44	16	16	18	20	16
45-54	19	17	16	14	10
55-64	12	13	12	13	14
64 or older	11	11	11	9	19
Married	71%	69%	66%	67%	59%
Single/never married	17	16	17	19	19
Living together	2	2	3	1	1
Separated/divorced	5	7	8	7	9
Widowed	5	6	7	6	12
High school incomplete	18%	19%	23%	9%	29%
High school/technical school graduate	36	41	37	35	40
College incomplete	23	19	20	23	15
College graduate	13	11	11	19	10
Attended graduate school	10	13	8	13	5
Household income under $15,000	39%	36%	31%	17%	36%
$15,000-$24,999	34	36	28	21	25
$25,000 or more	27	28	40	44	20
$25,000-$34,999	NA	NA	21	21	13
$35,000 or more	NA	NA	19	23	7

Travel Pulse, 1982, Opinion Research Corporation, Washington, D.C.

than the average. The number of professional or white collar heads of households in this group is also above the average (See Table 1).

In Table 1 we can see that there are significant differences in certain characteristics when travelers and nontravelers are compared. In categories such as those over 65 years of age or those who are widowed, nontravelers considerably outnumber travelers. This is probably because people in these two categories often lack the physical wellbeing or discretionary income that would allow travel. In another comparison, as education and income increase, so does the proportion of travelers. Among those without a high school diploma, nontravelers significantly outnumber travelers, but as we get to high-school graduates, this difference becomes quite small. As we go on to those with some college education and those with graduate educations, the percentage of travelers increases steadily to a ratio of almost three to one.

The same kind of relationship holds true for the various income levels shown in the table. At the lower income levels, nontravelers outnumber travelers, but as we get to incomes above $25,000 a year, travelers become the larger group. In those families with incomes over $35,000, travelers outnumber nontravelers more than three to one. (One note to keep in mind in reading this table is that the household income is given in actual dollars. An income of $15,000 in 1978 was different in purchasing power than that same dollar income in 1982. In all areas except income levels, the differences among travelers from 1978 to 1982 are small. In income level, however, these differences are quite substantial. This is most likely due to the purchasing power differences rather than to real changes in life styles at different relative income levels.)

According to studies by Travel Pulse in 1978, 43% of the U.S. adult population were travelers. *Traveler* as defined in this study is one who purchases a roundtrip at least 200 miles from home that includes air fare or paid accommodations for at least one night, or that includes a cruise. By the 1980 study, this number had risen to 54% of the adult population (see Table 2).

This was a substantial increase in the number of travelers, and the number continues to grow, although at a slower rate. Although Table 2 does indicate a 1% decrease in 1982 (to 53%), this is not a significant difference. The economic recession created a flat, no-growth period for the year. However, all future indications are for continued, gradual growth. As the general population shows an increase in the number of college-educated adults and in higher average real incomes, this figure

Table 2

U.S. TRAVELERS AS PERCENT OF ADULT POPULATION

% Adult Population

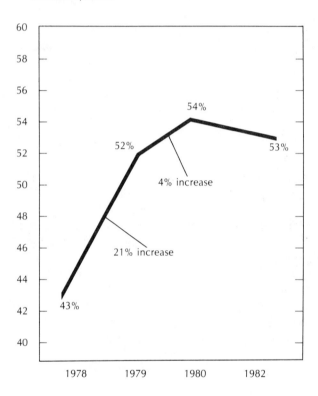

Travel Pulse, 1982, Opinion Research Corporation, Washington, D.C.

will most likely continue to grow. This means that the market for the travel product is also extremely large and growing.

Travel has been and continues to be one of the symbols of the good life for many people. It is important that it be marketed properly if this growth is to continue. Several theories have been developed that are useful in understanding consumer motivation, which is essential to successful marketing.

NEED-SATISFACTION THEORY

All consumer purchases are made to satisfy some need of the consumer. An individual has a desire for something. Depending on circumstances, the desire may grow into an actual need. A person doesn't buy a bicycle just to own a bicycle unless he is a collector of bicycles. The purchaser is fulfilling some need that the bicycle can satisfy. Perhaps he needs transportation but is too young to drive, or perhaps he wants exercise. If the desire becomes strong enough, it becomes a need. Perhaps a neighbor just bought one and there is a desire to keep up with the Joneses. Notice that in all cases the bicycle was the means to satisfy a particular need.

The same is true of travel. People don't travel just to travel. Travel fulfills some need in each consumer. The needs may differ just as the needs for the bicycle differed, but in each case travel can be the satisfier. Some of the most popular reasons given by people for why they travel are:

• To visit friends and relatives

• To see new places and learn new things

• To do things they can't do at home (skiing, for example)

• To get away from the weather

• To relax

REASONS FOR NOT TRAVELING

In addition to knowing why people travel, it is necessary to understand why some people do not travel. There are many reasons. Some of those most commonly heard are: "I can't afford it," or "I don't have the time."

Frequently these reasons are just excuses. They hide other underlying fears of travel. Fear of flying is quite common and accounts for many people who insist on driving on a vacation or other trip when they could fly. Fear of the unknown keeps many people from leaving their own country or even their own city. Many travelers travel frequently domestically but are afraid to go where they cannot understand the language. Some potential travelers are afraid of the unfamiliar decisions they will have to make in a strange place, such as how much to tip, how to get around a strange city. All of these fears are valid deterrents to travel. When a seller of travel meets an objection to the purchase of travel, it is necessary to interview the consumer to determine the *real* reason for the objection. People hesitate to discuss their fears. Frequently, they are unaware, themselves, of their real reasons for resisting a new experience. "Too little money" or "too little time" are convenient, nonembarrassing excuses that can hide the real fears.

It is also important to realize that about 13% of the population, according to a 1977 Travel Pulse study, say that they like traveling but end up doing other things instead because of the hassles of traveling. This group seems to be increasing recently, because an increased number of people see this as a problem.

TRAVELERS' EXPECTATIONS   One of the major motivations for travel is the desire to get away from it all for a little while. Thus, travel should be a pleasant experience. If travelers expecting a pleasant experience meet delays in transportation, missed connections, lost baggage, overbooked hotels and conditions different from what brochures show, they will decide that it is better to stay home. Travel must be enjoyable to succeed. When problems do occur, how they are handled is critical.

In the 1978-79 Travel Pulse survey, about two-thirds of the respondents agreed with the statement "I love to travel and do so whenever I can." By the time of the 1980 survey, that number had dropped to less than one-half. In addition, in the 1980 survey, almost

"Nervous? What makes you think I'm nervous?"

twice as many respondents (approximately one-fourth) said that although they like to travel, they end up doing other things because of the hassles involved.

Travelers must feel that they are important and that people care about them. They must find travel conditions to be what they were led to expect by the salesperson, the brochures, the advertisements, and all the other components of travel and tourism marketing. If these expectations are not met, travelers will be unlikely to repeat the experience.

Tourism USA Vol. I *Appraising Tourism Potential* (University of Missouri, 1978), a study done for the United States Travel Service of the United States Department of Commerce, describes eight different motivational segments of tourism. They are:

- Ethnic tourism—a desire to visit one's roots and learn about the culture from which one has come.

- Cultural tourism—a desire to learn about other cultures. This includes the desire to visit museums and other cultural places.

- Historical tourism—the desire to learn about the past.

- Environmental tourism—the desire to concentrate on the environment, to see beautiful scenery, fall foliage, the ocean, to get away from bad weather.

- Recreational tourism—a desire to participate in activities such as skiing, golfing, or tennis.

- Entertainment or sensual indulgent tourism—a desire to be entertained; for example, to see shows, to gamble, or indulge in gourmet dining.

- Social status or ego enhancement tourism—the need for recognition, to go where one's friends have been and be able to take part in their discussions of the world. These travelers will usually bring back many souvenirs to prove their status.

- Interpersonal tourism—the desire to visit friends or relatives. This travel motivation accounts for the largest number of personal trips.

As Peter Drucker states in *Managing for Results* (Harper & Row, 1964), the Cadillac competes for the customer's money with mink coats, jewelry, "the skiing vacation in the luxury resort, and other prestige satisfactions." What this demonstrates is that a purchase satisfies a need—one that could be satisfied in several different ways. Travel, as pointed out in Drucker's example, is a satisfier of general prestige needs. One must understand what is actually motivating the consumer to consider travel and answer that need in selling the travel product.

Drucker also points out that there are actually two consumers. One is the ultimate purchaser—the user of the product or service—and the other is the distribution channel—in the case of the travel product, usually a travel agency. The supplier of the product must convince both of these customers of the product's worth. Frequently, the consumer is not aware of the variety of suppliers available and relies on the travel agent to choose the actual travel service that meets the need. Therefore, it is necessary for travel producers—airlines, hotels, cruise lines, sightseeing companies, etc.—to market to both travel agents and their clients.

NECESSITIES, CONVENIENCES, AND LUXURIES

In a survey taken for the *Boston Globe*, the public was asked to rate several items as necessities, conveniences, or luxuries. The results of this survey are very enlightening. Travel was rated quite high in the necessity

Table 3
CONSUMER CLASSIFICATIONS OF
NECESSITIES, CONVENIENCES AND LUXURIES

	Necessity	Convenience	Luxuries
Black and white television set	35%	55%	8%
An air conditioner in your bedroom	9	38	53
Automatic dishwasher	6	40	54
Color television set	9	40	51
Two cars	31	28	39
Automatic clothes washer	63	30	7
A refrigerator	96	4	—
A Hi-Fi or stereo system	8	45	47
A home freezer	23	44	33
Automatic clothes dryer	30	48	22
A vacation trip of a week or more every year	40	31	29
Buying a pair of shoes that cost 35 dollars or more	31	20	48
Buying at least two new outfits of clothing each year	62	25	12
Buying fire and smoke detectors for your home or apartment	78	17	5

Reprinted with permission of the Boston *Globe*.

and convenience categories and quite low in the luxury category. Many items (such as a dishwasher) that make life easier for more days of the year were given lower priority than travel. Human beings have a need to travel. In fact, even when times are hard travel usually continues. Perhaps people need to be able to "get away from it all" through travel and will sacrifice other purchases to be able to relax even for just a few days. The only items considered more of a necessity than vacation travel were a clothes washer, a refrigerator, at least two outfits of clothes a year, and fire and smoke detectors—most of which are taken for granted by a large segment of our society.

MASLOW'S HIERARCHY OF NEEDS

A study of travelers' motivation would not be complete without a discussion of Abraham Maslow's theory of the hierarchy of human needs as proposed in his book, *Motivation and Personality* (Harper & Row, 1954). This classic theory has been the basis for most modern studies of human behavior and motivation.

Maslow believes that the human being proceeds through five stages of motivation. It is impossible to move to a higher stage until the needs of lower stages are met (see the diagram below). An individual does not

Maslow's Hierarchy of Human Needs

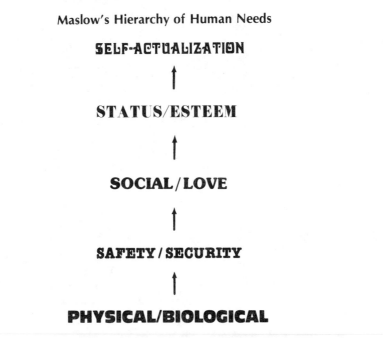

SELF-ACTUALIZATION

↑

STATUS/ESTEEM

↑

SOCIAL/LOVE

↑

SAFETY/SECURITY

↑

PHYSICAL/BIOLOGICAL

function on only one level in all aspects of life, but operates on different levels for different activities at different times. One must be comfortable at a lower level before moving to a higher one.

Physical and Biological Needs

The lowest level of human needs is physical and biological. These are the needs for food, shelter and clothing sufficient to protect against the elements. Individuals functioning on this level are not generally involved in tourism. They do travel, but usually as refugees seeking shelter and food or escaping from absolute poverty or war.

Safety and Security

The next level of need is that of safety and security. People who prefer escorted tours are looking for security. They do not want to have to handle their baggage, worry about tipping, or have to find activities on their own. They want the safety of a leader to whom they can turn if a problem arises. They want to be sure that a translator is available if needed.

Another aspect of the human need for safety and security that affects the travel product is that of political conditions at the destination. In the late 1970s Jamaica and the Virgin Islands suffered great tourism losses because the consumer perceived these destinations as unsafe. Northern Ireland and much of the Middle East suffer from these same problems. People will not travel for pleasure to a location they believe to be unsafe.

Social Needs

The human being has a need to belong, to feel wanted and loved. These are the social needs. Satisfying this level of human needs is a major motivation for choosing a product such as travel. It is one of the main reasons for the popularity of group travel. People are more comfortable

"Perhaps you'd like to re-think your itinerary, Mrs. Simpson— eight of these destinations are having revolutions and four others show signs of political unrest."

when they are with other people with whom they feel compatible. The success of tour operators who specialize in singles tours focus on this need. The individual traveling with such a group has both security and social needs met by this product. As another example, cruises also cater to the social needs of people with an abundance of planned activities.

Status or Esteem Needs

This level in the hierarchy of needs is also important in marketing the travel product. When a destination is newly popular, such as China today, many people will travel to China so they can say they have been there. The movie *If It's Tuesday, This Must Be Belgium* is symbolic of a popular type of trip. See seventeen countries in fourteen days. Travelers cannot really learn too much about any one country and probably do not remember where they saw what, but they *can* talk about seeing seventeen countries to their friends. Travel is one of the primary status symbols in today's society. This is reflected in the home movies of vacations that have been the target of comedians for many years. The home movie is a way to impress one's friends with one's travel experiences and sophistication. In the same way, being able to mention one's stay at a popular resort or hotel is important to many people.

Self Actualization

The last and highest level of Maslow's hierarchy refers to the person who is above the level of needing to impress friends and associates. Self actualizers have reached a high level and their motivations are higher yet. They work for such goals as having a hospital named for themselves. The average seller of travel does not often work with people at this level of motivation.

Although Maslow's hierarchy is a simplification, as are all models, it does serve an important purpose. It shows that an individual does not operate on one level all the time but on varying levels, depending on circumstances. The businessperson staying at an exclusive hotel to fulfill status needs may drop very suddenly to the safety/security level after calling home and learning that a robbery has taken place. If you are an employee of that hotel, you must now treat this person differently as you help him get in touch with home and take care of the problem. The traveler who is having a great time on a social level and is confronted with hostility in a foreign city will drop quickly to the safety level also. When talking to a potential consumer who is a high level business executive, you may assume a high level on the hierarchy scale, but this executive may be afraid of dealing with a different language in a foreign culture. This traveler must be treated on the security level, just as you would treat the blue-collar worker who doesn't know how much to tip on a cruise ship.

LIFE STAGES

In a study done for the United States Travel Service (*Tourism USA* Vol. II *Development: Assessing Your Product and the Market,* 1978) nine different stages of life are depicted. Each has an effect on travel motivations. These cycles are:

Stage 1 - Bachelor stage. Young, single people not living at home
Stage 2 - Newly married couple. Young, no children
Stage 3 - Full nest I. Youngest child under 6
Stage 4 - Full nest II. Youngest child 6 or older
Stage 5 - Full nest III. Older couple with dependent children
Stage 6 - Empty nest I. Older couples, no children living with them.
   Head in labor force
Stage 7 - Empty nest II. Older couples, no children living at home.
   Head retired
Stage 8 - Solitary survivor, in labor force
Stage 9 - Solitary survivor, retired

Today other stages have become important, such as the single parent household or divorced parent with children visiting periodically.

Although this list is not the only one for life cycles, it does show some important divisions. Stages 1 and 2 are important elements in the travel market since they generally have adequate money with few responsibilities competing for those dollars. Stages 3, 4, and 5 have the greatest number of budget items competing for the discretionary dollar. People in these stages of life most often travel by car or camper and visit grandparents or other friends or relatives. They make less use of air travel and paid accommodations for vacations. This age bracket, however, is highly represented in business travel.

Stages 6 and 7 frequently return to the pleasure travel market and will buy air transportation or cruises. They are tired of driving from all the years of doing so with the children. Stages 8 and 9 find travel important if health permits in order to meet people and feel less alone. These persons, usually elderly, often prefer to travel with a compatible group.

It is important to realize that the "empty-nester," the couple whose children have grown, is different from the "never-nester," the couple who never had children. Given the same age bracket, the couple who never had children is probably much more experienced in travel than the couple who start to travel after the children have grown. The product that will appeal to each couple, and their level on Maslow's hierarchy, will differ.

ALLOCENTRIC VS. PSYCHOCENTRIC PERSONALITY

Travelers, like all people, have differing personalities. Some are leaders and some are followers. Allocentric personality types are leaders and psychocentric personality types are followers. The allocentric person is a trend-setter—the first in the community to go to a new destination. The psychocentric person doesn't go anywhere until sure of what the destination is like. The psychocentric waits for friends to go, and then follows what is in fashion. It is necessary to judge a consumer's place on this personality scale in order to provide the proper travel experience. Most people, of course, fall somewhere in the middle (see figure 3-1).

Figure 3-1

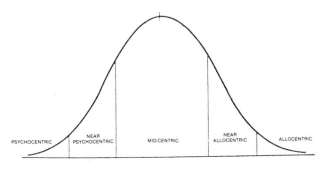

| PSYCHOCENTRIC | NEAR PSYCHOCENTRIC | MID-CENTRIC | NEAR ALLOCENTRIC | ALLOCENTRIC |

Figure 3-2

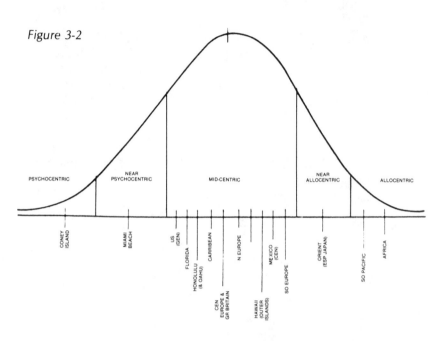

From an article originally published in the February 1974 issue of *The Cornell Hotel and Restaurant Administration Quarterly.* Reprinted here with the permission of the Cornell University School of Hotel Administration. © 1974.

Each season, different destinations come and go in popularity. When selling travel to an allocentric person, the salesperson would want to emphasize the new and exciting destination. On the other hand, when a salesperson is working with a psychocentric client, it is necessary to go with the "tried and true" destination. The traveler will be frightened by anything too unknown. This person doesn't want to experiment and is more comfortable with the well-known. Figure 3-2 shows destinations popular with the range of personalities from psychocentric to allocentric.

"Hey, Fred! Here's a note from those people who went around the world on a tramp steamer."

CONCLUSION

Although no two travelers are identical in their psychological makeup or motivations, they do fall into certain patterns. When a salesperson has the ability to judge and properly categorize the consumer, the sale is made much easier and the consumer will ultimately be more satisfied. It is necessary to understand the consumer's true needs, not just what he or she says they are. It is necessary to know what travel consumers expect to obtain from a travel experience in order to fill their needs adequately.

When all these factors are understood and the proper product is offered, the result will be a satisfied consumer. Any salesperson must be part psychologist to be successful, but the result of a happy consumer is well worth the effort of understanding needs and motivations.

SUMMARY

A knowledge of human motivation is essential for successful marketing. Travel products must be marketed to a wide variety of market segments. As incomes and educational levels rise, so does the possibility of up-scale travel.

Understanding consumer motivation must also include understanding motivations to avoid travel, such as fear of flying or of strange situations. People who do travel expect pleasant experiences, and every effort should be made by travel professionals to see that the promises made in the marketing process are fulfilled in the actual experience.

Human motivations in general, and motivations for travel in particular, have been described in a number of ways. These include:

- need-satisfaction theory—needs to be satisfied may range from the desire to see new things to the desire to escape bad weather.

- Maslow's hierarchy of needs—five stages of motivation, ranging from physical/biological to (successively) safety/ security; social; status; and self-actualization.

- life stages—nine parts of the life cycle that range from the young single person on his own to the solitary retired individual.

- allocentric/psychocentric personality theory, which divides people into allocentric (leader) and psychocentric (follower) groups.

QUESTIONS FOR THOUGHT AND DISCUSSION

1. *Why do some people who can afford to travel choose not to do so?*

2. *Describe five reasons why people travel, with examples of possible trips for each.*

3. *Discuss Maslow's hierarchy of needs and relate this concept to travel motivation.*

4. *Choose three of the life stages described in this chapter and discuss their similarities and differences as they relate to travel potential.*

5. *Describe the characteristics of an allocentric person. What type of travel might appeal to this individual?*

4
MARKET RESEARCH

demographic information
external market segmentation
historical research
internal market segmentation
market research
primary research
psychographic information
questionnaire
secondary research
survey
target market

Market research is the attempt to systematically gather and analyze information about potential consumers to aid in properly understanding and meeting their needs. This research can be very formal and expensive or informal and inexpensive.

Information gained from market research is statistical in nature and describes factors such as income level, attitudes (likes and dislikes), and desires for new products and services.

**PRIMARY VS.
SECONDARY RESEARCH**

There are two sources of market research information. The first is *primary research*. This is research that you do yourself through questionnaires, personal interviews, phone surveys, or other similar means.

Secondary research is research that had been done by someone else. Examples of secondary research are census bureau studies, information from sources such as the Louis Harris Poll, or research published by the United States Travel Data Center. Secondary research is generally inexpensive to obtain. However, it frequently is not applicable to specific needs. If the product being sold has a broad market, much secondary research can be useful. In almost all cases, it can be used as background for primary research.

Properly used, secondary research can save time and money. For example, census data is broken down into very narrow segments, even as small as specific zip codes. Therefore, if an organization wishes to conduct primary research in a small specialized area, it is a good idea to obtain the census information on that area in order to know the income level, the age level, and other such data. There is no reason to take the time and spend the money to rediscover data that already exists.

In most cases, primary data is expensive to obtain. If sophisticated results are necessary for large organizations, the expense may be justified. For organizations such as airlines, hotel chains, steamship companies, amusement parks, and other large enterprises, the information needed generally covers a rather broad area and the results will be used to determine future marketing directions that will involve large expenditures. Therefore, it is usually conducted by professional market research organizations.

On the other hand, this is not normally the case for small organizations in the travel industry, such as travel agencies. A small travel agency generally does not have the budget to contract for major research. For the small company, research can be as simple as driving around the neighborhood to see the type of people that live there and how they seem to spend their money. A neighborhood with lots of campers and station wagons in the driveways will signify a neighborhood of families with growing children. Conversely, neighborhoods of apartment houses and primarily small cars would signify either a community of young people who have not yet started their families, or of older people whose children are grown, or a combination. Even information as simple as this

"Uh—have I got this down right, then? When vacationing, you prefer Palm Springs for the holidays, Rio at Carnival, and Club Med for an occasional weekend?"

can be helpful to a company in determining the needs of the market. The travel needs of a family with young children are quite different from the travel needs of the other two groups.

Many travel organizations conduct primary research. Airlines continually contract for surveys, both of people flying on their airlines (in which case the traveler may be handed a questionnaire to fill out and return by mail) or of people at the airport. An airline may even survey the general public to obtain information on the attitudes of nontravelers as well as travelers. It is important to realize that the information returned from a person who is at an airport or on an airplane may be quite different from information returned from a sample of the general community in a shopping center.

Hotels also conduct frequent research, as do restaurants. Most hotels leave a form in the room to be filled out by the guest. This is done to obtain the guest's opinion of the service. Here it is important to remember that people fill these forms out and return them primarily when they have something specific to say (in most cases a complaint to make or, in some cases, a compliment over extraordinarily good service). The middle group of people who are satisfied but saw nothing particularly wrong or right generally do not bother to complete these forms. Therefore, the person analyzing the information on these returned forms must keep in mind that it is not a representative sample of all people who have stayed

Response card courtesy of Perkins, Memphis, TN

To Our Guests:

Thank you for selecting Howard Johnson's. Because we sincerely value your patronage, we want to provide and maintain the most comfortable of accommodations and the finest in travel services. In this interest, would you please take a few moments of your time to let us know your comments and suggestions using this postage paid postcard. Just drop it in the nearest mail box.

Thank you

Howard B. Johnson

Howard B. Johnson, President

MOTOR LODGE LOCATION (*MOTOR LODGE MAY PLACE LOCATION STAMP HERE*)

STREET/HIGHWAY   CITY   STATE

ROOM NUMBER _____ ARRIVAL TIME _____ ARRIVAL DATE _____

	EXCELLENT	SATISFACTORY	UNSATISFACTORY
(Courtesy on Arrival)			
Motor Lodge Employees (Courtesy on Departure)			
(Courtesy During Stay)			
Attractiveness of Guest Room			
Cleanliness of Guest Room			
Bedding			
Lighting in Guest Room			
Television			
Cleanliness & Condition/Bath Facilities			
Adequacy of Bath Supplies			
Heat/Air-Conditioning			
Appearance of Grounds/Landscaping			

	YES	NO
Did You Enjoy Your Stay?		
Did You Enjoy Our Pool?		
Would You Recommend This Lodge?		

It is only through concerned guests that we may learn if we have served with warm hospitality. Your additional comments would be appreciated:

_____

_____

_____

_____

_____

NAME _____

STREET ADDRESS _____

CITY _____ STATE _____ ZIP _____

Printed in U.S.A.

(To seal card – moisten this strip)

This questionnaire, and the one on the preceding page, are ways of getting information on customers' opinions.

First Class
Permit No.
41578
Boston, Mass.

BUSINESS REPLY MAIL / NO POSTAGE NECESSARY WHEN MAILED IN USA

POSTAGE WILL BE PAID BY:

Mr. Howard B. Johnson, President
HOWARD JOHNSON COMPANY
Box 654
Braintree MA 02184

   TOLL-FREE ROOM RESERVATIONS 800-654-2000

Courtesy Howard Johnson Company

in that hotel or eaten in that restaurant. However, these questionnaires do go a long way toward helping an establishment to correct problems and continue successful endeavors.

Surveys and questionnaires can be very meaningful tools when gathering specialized information. However, it is important to create a valid questionnaire. If the questions are asked in a way that *biases* the answers, meaningful information will not be obtained. (Questions are said to be *biased* if they are likely to evoke a specific response, rather than the respondent's true feelings.) Therefore, a questionnaire should either be written professionally or should be tested on a small sample before being sent to a large sample.

TRAVEL RESEARCH SOURCES

Organizations such as the Louis Harris agency run periodic research efforts to determine the habits of the traveling public. Once every two years, they run such a survey for *Travel Weekly,* an industry newspaper. Another organization that has done some very important research in the field of travel is Travel Pulse. This organization is part of Opinion Research Corporation, and provides a great deal of meaningful information to travel organizations. Most of this information is available only to subscribers; however, some of it appears in publications such as the *Travel Market Yearbook.*

HISTORICAL RESEARCH

Another type of research is historical. This is research done by looking over the history of the organization and determining future trends from past practices. The one danger in using historical information is that the situation may have changed and, therefore, the historical facts may not hold true for the future. However, it is always a good idea to know where a company has been before it can decide where it should go. One example would be the case of an airline deciding whether to add another flight to a given destination. If history shows that they have had to turn away passengers on a regular basis, the time has probably come to add an additional flight for that route.

The same thing is true for a hotel. If a hotel has consistently been full and had to turn away guests, then the time has come to add a new wing. A hotel can also obtain meaningful information for market planning by analyzing where its guests have come from for the past year. Registration forms in the hotel's own files provide this information. This information can then be used to determine where to concentrate advertising dollars for the best results.

DEMOGRAPHIC VS. PSYCHOGRAPHIC INFORMATION

Demographics is statistical, objective information about a person, such as age, income, educational level, occupation, religion, or place of residence. This is the type of information usually requested at the beginning or the end of most survey questionnaires. Demographic information allows the researcher to analyze whether the results vary with such factors as different ages, incomes, or educational levels.

Psychographic information is more subjective information about the respondent. It includes three types of information—activities, interests, and opinions (AIO). Psychographic questions try to determine what activities respondents enjoy, what their interests are, and what their opinions are. Questions that request a respondent to rate an opinion of something on a scale of 1-5 are obtaining psychographic information.

This information is becoming more and more important as the public is given a wider variety of products from which to choose. The danger is that impartial questions are very hard to create, and very often respondents answer as they think the surveyer expects them to, rather than as they really feel. For example, when people are asked what television shows they watch, answers to these questions on surveys differ quite markedly from results that are obtained from a recorder attached to their TVs. People very often want the interviewer to believe that they are watching a "higher level" show than the situation comedy they are really enjoying. The same thing holds true in travel. People's attitudes toward what they really want to do may be different from what they think they should say. Therefore, psychographic questionnaires or interviews must be very carefully developed in order to gather accurate, meaningful, useful information.

In order to save money and increase accuracy, it is a good practice to test a small sample (perhaps up to 10%) before going into a large-scale effort. Thus, you can determine whether the questions are understandable, whether the answers have any meaning, and whether the questionnaire is achieving reasonable results. After surveying the small sample, make any necessary changes in the survey instrument and go forward to a large, full-scale sample. However, it is important to realize that effective research has been done with fairly small samples and results have been found to be predictable for a larger group. Again, if you are looking for statistically meaningful results, these need professional personnel expert in statistics. If, however, you are just looking for some trends in a given market, it may be sufficient to ask people informally in that area. If research is being conducted in preparation for a large, expensive new marketing effort, it is, of course, advisable to spend more money for more accurate information.

Although market research is helpful and necessary, it is not infallible. We all know the stories of polls that showed the wrong political candidate to be the winner. Good market research, however, is correct most of the time.

MARKET SEGMENTATION With market research it is possible to analyze a market and divide it into separate parts. The consuming public is made up of many different parts, or *segments*. Young, single persons comprise quite a different segment from senior citizens or young families. In order to avoid wasting valuable resources, it is important for a marketing manager to segment this market so that products can be developed that are "right" for each target market, and so that promotional resources can be allocated to each specific market.

EXTERNAL MARKET SEGMENTATION

Travel has a universal appeal, but few travel products themselves are universally appealing. This is because travel is so varied that almost all of the public can find some type of travel that satisfies their needs. However, a specific travel product may have a very limited appeal. For example, a singles' tour will obviously not appeal to a family market. The singles' tour market can be segmented even further—into various age brackets. The singles' tour that appeals to the young bachelor will be quite different from the one that appeals to the seventy-year-old widow. When researching a potential market, it is necessary to segment it as much as possible so that products can be developed to appeal to each specific target market.

Once the target market is identified, it is then possible to tailor the product itself. Members of this market may be surveyed concerning their desires and needs for travel, and a product created that answers these needs.

Once these needs have been identified, it becomes important to find a way to inform the members of this target market that the product exists and will meet their needs. This is done by researching what media serves this segment of the public. If, for example, the product is one that will appeal to golfers or tennis players, the marketing manager may advertise in golfing or tennis magazines. Ads for these products would be wasted on another type of publication (an arts and crafts magazine for example). This does not mean that some readers of an arts and crafts magazine might not also be golfers or tennis players, but the majority of readers will not be in the target market.

Another type of external market segmentation is that of geography. Certain products appeal to people from particular geographic areas. For example, Bermuda finds that a majority of its visitors comes from the northeast section of the United States. For this reason, it advertises and promotes heavily in this geographic area. Thus, the value of promotional expenditures is maximized. Finding a new market and promoting it is extremely expensive, and not always successful. The risks are frequently not worth the potential gain.

INTERNAL MARKET SEGMENTATION

Within any business several products are usually marketed. These are known as the *product lines* of the company. For a hotel, there is the business travel market, the family vacation market, and, perhaps, the business meeting or convention market. An airline may have the same type of segmentation. In addition, however, an airline must look at its different destinations and routes as separate market segments. A restaurant might segment its product line into family diners, young singles, and older couples. They also might segment their product into

"This vacation was made to order for a travel agent—a cruise to nowhere with Tom Selleck!"

the food segment and the liquor segment. A travel agency might be marketing products such as domestic air, international air, tours, commercial travel, groups, cruises, rail, or bus tours. Different marketing techniques must be used for different segments, since the motivations and needs of users vary for each segment.

For effective management of the marketing effort, it is important to analyze internal market segments and determine the profitability of each one. While a business may be making a profit, certain product lines may be losing money. A marketing manager must determine the profitability of each product line so that unproductive ones may be changed or eliminated. When a hotel finds a particular segment of the market to be more profitable, it should try to increase that segment of its market. The same is true for other parts of the industry. When an airline finds a particular route unprofitable, it will reduce its service or eliminate that route and replace it with one that it hopes will be more profitable. Any business has a limited amount of resources. These resources should be focused on profitable product segments.

Las Vegas is a good example of this concept. Before the days of Howard Hughes, most Las Vegas hotels lost money on the room and food segments and made all their profit on the gambling segment. When Howard Hughes bought the Dunes, he analyzed this situation and determined that each segment of the operation should be profitable on its own. This resulted in the elimination of extremely inexpensive rooms and food for the small gambler. Room rates went up to the normal rates for luxury hotels. The restaurants in the hotel also began to show a profit. Only the "high roller" gamblers continued to get the benefits of cheap (often free) rooms and food. These rooms were then charged against the operating expenses of the casinos. Each segment of the hotel showed its own profit, and the overall profit of the operations increased.

CONCLUSION

Market research does not have to be expensive or sophisticated. It is, however, a necessary part of marketing management. When the company is considering starting a new product or greatly changing an existing one, money spent on research will be very well spent and should result in an ultimate financial savings.

In order to effectively market any product, it is necessary to segment the market, both externally and internally. Without knowledge of the needs of the potential consumer, much time, effort, and money will be wasted. Only through ability to determine the profitability of each product line can a business be sure of maximizing its profits.

SUMMARY   Market research is the systematic gathering and analysis of information about potential customers. It can be formal or informal, and cost a great deal or very little.

Information may be obtained from two sources:

1. primary research, done yourself through phone surveys, or questionnaires;

2. secondary research, in which information is derived from such things as censuses or United States Travel Data Center studies.

Sophisticated primary data is expensive to gather and analyze, and is usually used only by large segments of the travel industry, such as airlines or hotel chains. A small company may gather some primary data inexpensively, however, by observing the lifestyle of the surrounding community. In addition, historical research may provide useful information.

Demographic data is statistical and objective. Psychographic data is more subjective in nature, dealing with people's attitudes. This second kind of information has become increasingly important as the number of choices consumers face rises. Psychological questionnaires must be carefully formulated and tested to produce valid results.

Information derived from market research allows a company to segment, or divide, the market into different parts, to decide what portion of it will be most responsive to a specific product. External market segmentation refers to such divisions as age, interests, or geography. Internal market segmentation refers to such divisions as, for a hotel, the business travel, family vacation, and convention markets.

QUESTIONS FOR THOUGHT AND DISCUSSION

1. *Compare primary and secondary research. What are the advantages and disadvantages of each?*

2. *How can historical research help in marketing decisions within travel? Give three examples of travel businesses that could benefit from this type of research.*

3. *Define demographics and discuss how this information can be used meaningfully.*

4. *Define psychographics and describe how this research can help in marketing.*

5. *Discuss market segmentation—both internal and external—and discuss how a business should use this information.*

6. a. *If you are in a restaurant, a hotel, or any place where a questionnaire is provided, bring the form in for discussion. Note where you received it and what your own comments would be in completing this form. How can this information help the business?*
   b. *Design a short questionnaire for a hotel, restaurant, or airline to use to determine customer satisfaction.*

5
IMAGE

image
logo
product differentiation
public perception
value judgment

In marketing, image is everything. When the truth differs from the public's perception of a product, it is the public perception—the image—that will determine that product's success or failure. It is critical for any business, in the travel industry or any other, to maintain a positive image with the public it is trying to serve. Unfortunately, it takes constant work to maintain a positive image. Negative images, on the other hand, can arise very quickly and are very difficult to change.

What is *image*? Image is nothing more than the mental picture the public has of the company or product. There have been many times in the history of the travel industry when an image has hurt a hotel, airline, sightseeing attraction, restaurant, travel agency, or destination.

IMAGE PROBLEMS

Safety

In the 1970s, Jamaica and the Virgin Islands suffered greatly from the American public's perception of those areas as ones of danger and political hostility. Local events outside the tourist areas occurred and were featured in United States newspapers. Articles appeared about shootings among the local people, and about political unrest. These events were reported in a way that convinced the public that it would be physically dangerous to travel to these destinations. The fact that the tourist areas were still quite safe was unimportant. The public, when confronted with potential danger, does not take chances. Occupancy of hotels plummeted. As occupancy levels fell, money was not available for necessary improvements to the hotels, and reports of inadequate facilities came back from those willing to chance the destination. The cycle resulted in a downward spiral, and many hotels in both destinations were forced to close. Only in the early 1980s have these destinations begun to make a comeback. The cost of these image problems to the area was immeasurable. Similar problems exist in many parts of the world where there is political turmoil.

Cost

Another type of image problem can be one of incorrect perception of costs. Some destinations have an image of great cost. Many people on the East Coast of the United States perceive Hawaii as a very expensive destination. In fact, it is one of the best values for resort hotels and restaurants. The primary reason for this incorrect image is the relatively high air fare from the East to Hawaii. Most inexperienced travelers assume that the hotels will cost as much as those in the Caribbean and that the overall trip will therefore be too expensive. Hotels in Hawaii must work constantly to correct this image.

Product Differentiation

Airlines, which sell basically identical products, work to sell the public on their image. Both Eastern Airlines and American Airlines have used advertising promotions emphasizing the care that their employees give to their customers. Studies of the traveling public show that there is actually little difference among major carriers in their service levels, but the advertisements try to promote these slight image differences as much as possible. In 1979, after an accident involving the DC-10 airplane and the subsequent fear of much of the traveling public about flying on this particular aircraft, airlines that did not fly DC-10s promoted the fact. There was a perceived image in the public's mind of greater safety, when, in reality, the carriers promoting the lack of the DC-10 in their fleet had virtually identical safety records to those that flew the aircraft.

If a hotel has an image as a commercial or convention property, it might find that vacation guests do not visit. On the other hand, if the hotel has a reputation as a vacation hotel for individuals, it will find that business meetings pass it by. It generally takes a great expenditure of both time and promotional funds to change an image. However, some companies have been successful in so doing. Holiday Inns have successfully attracted business and convention visitors, after many years of an image as a family motel.

FOSTERING AN IMAGE

It is also important to remember that many images are neither positive or negative. The value judgment differs with the attitudes of differing segments of the public. What is quaint to one may be simply old to another. What one sees as modern and streamlined may seem, to another, cold and "plastic." To one traveler, a nude beach is exciting and modern; to another it is immoral and decadent. The important message here is that few places can promote an image that will appeal to all potential travelers. It is necessary for a hotel, airline, destination or such to decide what type of clientele it wishes to attract and then to be sure that all of its promotional efforts help foster the image that will appeal to that market segment.

EMPLOYEES AND IMAGE

In all too many cases, the image promoted with a very expensive advertising budget is rendered ineffective by employees who do not conform to the intended image. The hotel trying to convince the public that its employees will pamper guests and cater to their every desire will not keep that image for long when guests come home complaining about sullen and uncaring front desk personnel. It is critical for any company to train its personnel to reflect its desired image, and to control the quality of its employees. A pleasant, helpful employee adds greatly to the positive image a business is trying to convey. The front desk person at the hotel, the flight attendant serving the passenger, the guide at the amusement park, the counselor in a travel agency, and all other travel industry front-line people are the final determinants of the image the

"This hotel aims for a homey image."

guest will take home. All the advertising in the world will not make up for inadequacies of personnel.

NAMES, LOGOS, AND SIGNS

The name a company chooses and the logo or design symbol it uses is very important to the image conveyed and sometimes to the very success or failure of the company. Names can convey the very activity that the company provides (the amusement park, "Wet 'N Wild"). The name can help to give an image of security and quality, such as "Quality Inns." On the other hand, a name can be misleading, such as a vacation travel agency named "Sun and Fun Tours" that now decides to market to commercial business. A corporation will not feel too comfortable having its business travel handled by "Sun and Fun Tours."

Some companies have been able to overcome an image that their name would be expected to convey and have made their names almost generic. Again, the Holiday Inn chain offers a good example. The name "Holiday Inn" would seem to convey an image of a person or family on a vacation or holiday. Although vacation travelers were the original intended customers for Holiday Inns, it has now entered very successfully into the business and commercial market. Since the name has become so well known, it would not be worthwhile to try to change it to one that would describe the broader image. Most people today think of Holiday

"What we have here is an image problem. We need more advertising!"

Holiday Inn's "great sign," a familiar sight near many of the nation's highways for the last thirty years, was necessary when the chain depended on walk-in tourist trade for most of its business. Marketing personnel at Holiday Inns had suggested changing the sign to suit market conditions, but at first the proposal was resisted, even though the "great sign" turned off certain market segments.

The new Holiday Inns sign responds to both changing market conditions and increased costs. The familiar Holiday Inn green color as well as the script lettering and a new version of the familiar starburst are retained but in a subdued way suited to the business traveler, now a major part of the chain's market. The sign will cost about 34% less to construct; about 50% less to maintain; and be 69% more energy efficient.

Courtesy of American Airlines.

The evolution of American Airlines' eagle logo is shown above, in versions dating from 1933 to the present.

Courtesy of United Airlines.

*United Airlines' logo has changed
significantly over the years since 1934.*

Inns as a broad type of accommodation facility, good for both vacation and business clientele, and recent advertising has concentrated on making the name "Holiday Inn" synonymous with reliability and consistency (the "no surprises" campaign).

Naming a small company for its geographic area might be perfectly logical. However, this type of name does not allow for future growth. The name loses meaning as soon as the company expands beyond its original geographic market area. A very good example is USAir. Originally known as Allegheny Airlines, it operated primarily in the region of the Allegheny mountains and was a small regional carrier with all the image problems of a carrier of that size. In the late 1970s, with deregulation of the airline industry, Allegheny Airlines decided to expand considerably. The decision was made to change the name of the airline in order to lose the image of a small regional carrier.

Much research was done, and the name USAir was chosen. A name change is an important and expensive undertaking. When a name is changed, very large promotional expenditures are necessary to let the public know that this is not a brand new business but an experienced, larger one. USAir's name change has been an outstanding success story.

"George, is this what 'Homey Highlands' meant to you?"

It was able to lose the negative parts of the image of Allegheny Airlines—the impression of a regional carrier with limited resources—yet keep the positive images it had earned as an old, established line.

The logos and signs used by businesses also convey an image to the viewer. As styles change, it is sometimes necessary to change and modernize these identifiers. What was perfectly good ten years ago might be out of date today and make a company appear old fashioned. However, the design choices will be influenced by the specific image the business wishes to convey. A hotel located in a historical area might intentionally use an old-fashioned style logo to blend in with the atmosphere of the destination. An airline, however, which wants the public to see it as modern and forward-looking, will usually choose styles that convey that impression. Most of the major airline carriers have modified their logos during the past ten years. Hotel designs also change as time goes by. When a logo is effective, the public can recognize the company by its logo and does not need to see the name.

COLOR AND STYLE

In addition to logos and signs, the image of a business—whether travel agency, hotel, or airline—is also conveyed to its customers by means of the colors and styles (the decoration) chosen for lobbies, offices, aircraft, and even employees' clothing. One of the most striking examples of an attempt to create image by means of decoration was Braniff's aircraft of some years ago, painted in designs created by a famous artist. The decorated aircraft did attract a great deal of attention; it is unclear whether or not they contributed to the right kind of image for the airline. Other airlines' use of famous designers to create uniforms for their flight attendants has a similar purpose. (Of course, choice of a *famous* artist or designer to create image in this way is also an attempt to use the artist's status to create an image of expensiveness.)

Color is probably more immediate in its effect on viewers than is style. Colors can be quite effective in conveying emotional images. Blues are generally considered soothing, cool, calm, and secure. Yellows are looked upon as cheerful and active colors. Reds, on the other hand, evoke strong emotional feelings in most people. Travel offices, hotel lobbies, and other public areas frequently use blue/green combinations or yellow/orange/brown combinations for their decor. The blue/green colors seem to give a feeling of visiting tropical paradises and portray colors of the sea, the land, and the sky which increase the desire for travel. The yellow/orange/brown tones are reminiscent of sunsets and warmth on the beach. Bright colors such as reds are best used for occa-

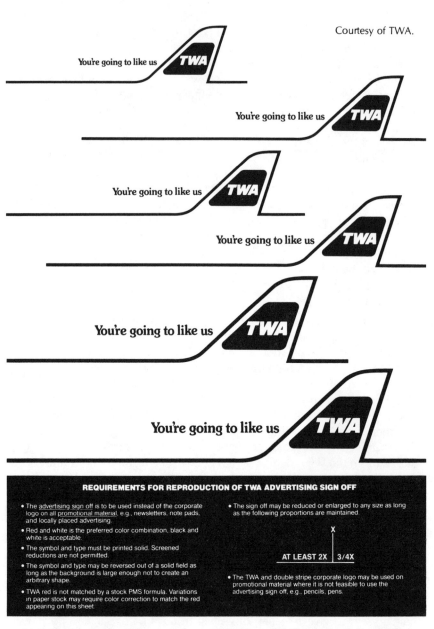

Courtesy of TWA.

Use of a corporate logo or other symbol is carefully controlled to produce the desired impression. Notice the detailed instructions (above) for use of the TWA advertising sign off.

sional accents rather than as major parts of a color scheme.

Other colors, such as pink, purple, or gray, are not as defined in terms of the images they evoke in the "average" person. A business trying to appeal to a mass public will usually stay with the muted, neutral colors. When a company wants to promote a vivid, different image, it might try an unusual color scheme, but there is potential danger in that attempt.

Something that must also be kept in mind is that different colors have different meanings for various cultures. White may mean either "hospital" or "ultramodern" to a Western viewer (like the white-on-white decorating schemes in decorating magazines). White means death and mourning to some Eastern cultures, however. Similarly, pink has a very different connotation for American and for Japanese viewers.

CONCLUSION

When an image is positive, part of the job of selling has already been done and marketing becomes much easier. The image that is portrayed should be intentional; it should not be allowed to just happen. Salespeople who must meet with potential customers and defend a business whose previous image has been poor start with two strikes against them, and the chances of a successful sale are greatly reduced. The salesperson coming into a sales situation for a business with a good image, on the other hand, starts with the sale partly made.

SUMMARY Image—the public perception of a thing, as distinguished from its actuality—is very important to any marketing plan. A good image must be constantly monitored—once lost it is very difficult to regain. Image problems may arise in the travel product over such considerations as safety, cost, and product differentiation.

It must be remembered that many images will be either positive or negative depending on the perceiver, and his or her attitudes. For this reason, no one image will appeal to an entire market.

No matter how well promoted, a good image can be destroyed by employees who do not conform to it. Images also depend for their effectiveness on appropriate business names, signs, and logos. Color and design in such things as uniforms, aircraft, and interior appointments can be very important, because they also contribute to the image the public perceives. A good image, well-supported by well-trained and motivated employees, makes the salesperson's job much easier.

QUESTIONS FOR THOUGHT AND DISCUSSION

1. *Obtain business cards from several companies (both travel and others) and discuss the image the card gives you of the business it represents. If you are familiar with the business, discuss if this is the image the business wants to portray.*

2. *As you shop in different stores (at least three), make notes on the decor, color, and general appearance of the store or business. Write or give a report on your findings.*

3. *Choose three different destinations and survey five people who have not been to these places (do not use students or employees in travel) on their opinion of the destination. Get information on their view of the cost, the people, the sights and activities, the weather, and any other images they hold. Then try to find three or more people who have visited each destination, and ask the same questions. Compare the results.*

4. *Bring in samples (from newspapers, magazines, direct mail pieces or other sources) of company logos or signs. Do these logos or signs accurately represent the business? What image is conveyed by these designs?*

6
THE MARKETING MIX IN TRAVEL AND TOURISM

communications mix
credit
direct operator
distribution mix
four Ps
marketing mix
marketing plan
multilevel distribution system
product/service mix
rates of exchange
retailer
terms-of-sale mix
wholesaler

Marketing is, essentially, a planning process. Once you have a target market in mind, you need to develop a strategy to meet the perceived needs of this market. Knowledge and application of the concept of the marketing mix—the elements involved in the marketing process—can be very helpful in developing a needed strategy.

Figure 6-1 is a model of the marketing mix. The central focus of all the parts of the marketing mix is a target market segment. The use of the mix is only effective when the buying power and other demographic characteristics of the target market are known.

COMPOSITION OF THE MARKETING MIX

The marketing mix consists of four separate submixes. Each of these submixes interacts continuously with the other three. In a sense, creating the mix is a juggling act, in which you balance elements of the four submixes to meet the needs of the target market. These four submixes are product and service; distribution; communications; and terms of sale.

The product and service mix is the inventory of products or repertoire of services that the organization is engaged in marketing. The distribution mix is the methods or channels by which the products and services are distributed to the consumer. The communications mix is the tools or methods used to inform potential customers of the existence of products and services and the ways in which such products and services will benefit the consumer. The terms of sale mix consists of the alternative methods of payment that are available to consumers to pay for the organization's products and services.

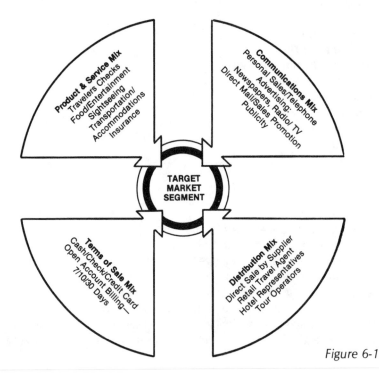

Figure 6-1

PRODUCT AND SERVICE MIX

In the travel and tourism industry, the product and service mix is essentially the varied components of tourism. Transportation, accommodations, food service and entertainment, and sightseeing activities can all be considered part of the product and service mix. The retail travel agent, the member of the industry who markets the broadest variety of products and services, would have to consider almost all of these things in the market planning process.

Airlines Product and Service Mix

In contrast, organizations that market within a single component need only consider the various possibilities within that component. However, that does not always mean that their product and service submix will be simpler. For example, an airline really markets many different services; from one point of view, the various routes served by the airline represent different services. Decisions to expand or contract route structure are based on analyses of how potential travelers will accept new routes, as well as on analyses of how existing routes are doing. Decisions on classes of service (such as first class, coach, or business class) also represent the provision of alternate services to meet differing consumer needs. Not all airlines offer the same classes of service.

Furthermore, many carriers do not offer the same selection from the class of service (product) mix on all routes. Most carriers offer first class and coach service on their domestic routes. However, the Eastern Shuttle between Washington and New York and New York and Boston is an all-coach service. United Airlines now offers an all-coach service called "Friendship Express" on many of its short-haul routes. From time to time, some carriers expand their first-class service while others decrease it. There have even been proposals for all-first-class service, although at the time of this writing none have been successful.

Within the airline industry, basic safety and types of aircraft equipment are the same among all airlines of a similar type (long distance, medium distance, and commuter). As a result, other less important items, such as food service, drinks, and other amenities become part of the service mix. While Eastern Airlines provides a no-reservation, no-frills, no-food shuttle between New York and Washington, New York Air requires reservations and offers free snacks and drinks. It then emphasizes this difference in its advertising (see next two pages).

What you get your clients on Eastern's shuttle.

1. A trip between New York and Washington.

This two-part advertisement appeared on facing pages.

What you get your clients on New York Air's shuttle.

1. A trip between New York and Washington.

2. A confirmed reservation.

3. Flight attendants who attend.

4. Extra legroom.

5. An assigned seat.

6. Free New York-style food.

7. Free drinks, including a featured red and white wine of the month.

8. A $45 Better Business fare, available on selected flights.

DEPARTURES	
LaGuardia to Washington	Washington to LaGuardia
7:00a exSA/SU	7:30a exSA/SU
8:00a exSU	8:30a exSU
9:00a	9:30a
10:00a	**10:30a**
11:00a	**11:30a**
12:00p	**12:30p**
1:00p	**1:30p**
2:00p exSA	**2:30p**
3:00p	3:30p exSA
4:00p exSA	4:30p
5:00p	5:30p exSA
6:00p	6:30p
7:00p exSA	7:30p exSA
8:00p exSA	**8:30p exSA**
9:00p exSA	**9:30p exSA**

Bold type indicates $45 Better Business Fare (Q-fare) flights, available weekdays. Other weekday flights are $65 (Y-fare). Most weekend flights are $40 (K-fare), food and drink service excluded.

New York Air

For reservations, call the Apple Desk:
Nationwide: 800-221-9710. New York State: 800-522-5166. New York City: 565-1327.
New York Air also serves Boston, Cleveland, Detroit, Newark, Orlando and Raleigh/Durham.

Advertisement courtesy of NY Air.

Hotel Product and Service Mix

In the hotel industry, the product and service mix is far broader than just the differences in room and bath. Location, availability of meeting space, convention services, types of suites, a variety of restaurants and entertainment, recreational facilities, and room amenities such as nightly turndown service, refrigerators, and candy, are all part of the variety of services available at hotels and resorts. The hotel marketer uses the appropriate mix to meet the needs of the target market.

The differing needs of various classes of travelers will affect the choice of products and services offered by both hotels and airlines. The business traveler looks for convenience, frequency, and flexibility of schedule, all within a certain expense level, from the airlines. This traveler looks for location, availability, and price when deciding on a hotel. Vacationers, who are more flexible in time and destination, will often change destinations or location within a destination based upon budget. Groups also have needs that differ from those of individual travelers.

THE DISTRIBUTION MIX

Establishing a distribution mix for a product or service involves decisions on how to transmit or transport the product from producer to consumer. In general the travel and tourism industry features a multilevel distribution system. Direct distribution from producer to ultimate consumer is a major method of distribution. Hotels, food service facilities,

"Hey, Martha! Some dummy put mirrors on the ceiling!"

and car rental firms use direct distribution as their predominant method. Airlines also use direct distribution, although it is not their major means of servicing travelers.

Wholesalers

The wholesale level of distribution, by definition, purchases from the producer and sells to the ultimate consumer through a retail level of distribution. This level does exist in the travel industry, primarily in the category called *tour operator*. A tour operator secures a variety of travel services (such as hotel rooms, sightseeing, tour services) and promotes them by means of brochures and other travel literature through the travel agent to the actual traveler. Retail travel agents look to the wholesaler for a variety of packages or services of interest to clients.

The wholesaler or tour operator can keep costs under control through volume purchasing. The convenience of communications with wholesalers and tour operators is very attractive to the retail agent. Otherwise, the retailer would have to participate in extensive and expensive communications with a variety of travel service producers. Through the purchasing and packaging of hotels, transportation, meals, and tours, tour operators create unique travel services (such as hosted and escorted tours) that add to the overall travel and tourism product and service mix. However, since the tour operator secures the travel services from direct operators, such as hotels, and bus companies, the tour operator can be considered a distributor as well as a direct supplier.

Retailers

The retail travel agent sells a variety of products and services directly to the traveler. Some of the services (airline reservations, car rental reservations) are secured from service producers while others (tours and hotel packages) are secured from wholesale sources. With more than 20,000 locations throughout the United States, travel agents are the most accessible suppliers from which a traveler may secure travel services.

Mixing of Distribution Channels

Distribution of the travel and tourism product is further confused by a mixing of distribution channels. While airlines are direct suppliers of their own product as well as suppliers to tour operators and retail travel agents, the airlines are also a source of securing reservations for other services. Hotel, car rental, and often tour programs can be secured through an airline reservations office. A traveler can do this directly; a travel agent can also use an airline to make hotel and car rental reservations for a traveler.

The multilevel roles played by other organizations add to the confusion in the travel and tourism distribution system. For example, the American Express Company is heavily involved in financial services. Its major programs include international banking, the world-famous credit card ("Don't leave home without it") and the travelers check. However, American Express is also a major wholesaler and tour operator, with hosted and escorted tours throughout the world, as well as operator of the second largest chain of retail travel agencies in the United States (the largest is Ask Mr. Foster). Furthermore, American Express has appointed several hundred retail travel agencies throughout the country as "representative agents." These representative agencies sell American Express travelers checks and provide travel assistance as do other American Express offices, but they are independently owned and operated travel agencies. They do receive additional commission for the sale of American Express tour products.

Establishing a Distribution Mix

The major consideration in establishing a distribution system is to determine the most effective method of profitably providing tourism services to potential travelers. Does a company have the resources to do all its distribution on its own? Will the use of a representation service help a hotel or chain of hotels promote its product and secure bookings? Will the commissions paid to travel agencies be a fair return for the bookings they are providing? Will low group rates fill space that will otherwise be empty? Will cooperation with wholesalers and tour operators help fill seats or rooms? Is a balanced use of the multiple levels of distribution an effective method to use? Each travel marketer must answer these questions to help determine the best distribution mix for the product or service offered.

THE COMMUNICATIONS MIX

The communications mix is a marketer's tool kit, providing a variety of ideas and means of informing prospects about various products and services, the benefits of these products and services to the prospects, and the call to action for purchasing.

The most critical form of communications is personal sales. Whether handled over the telephone or in person, in response to inquiries or as outside sales calls, the personal sales effort is the major method for securing commitments from prospective customers. Chapters nine and ten in this book provide more detailed information on the sales function in the travel and tourism industry and on specific sales techniques.

Advertising

Advertising is a major communications tool in the tourism industry. Designed to inform, remind, and persuade, advertising is paid one-way communication. The major advertising forms used in the industry are print media (newspapers, magazines, and direct mail) and broadcast media (radio and television). Advertising is a major expenditure for large tourism supplier organizations, such as airlines, hotels, tourist boards, and steamship companies. While expenditures for advertising decrease at the wholesale and retail levels, advertising does remain a major method of attracting business. Chapter 8 discusses advertising in the travel and tourism industry in detail.

Sales promotion is another important communications tool. Contests, window displays, and point of purchase displays, posters, slides, and films are all used to support the marketing effort.

Public Relations

Publicity is unpaid or free coverage in the media or other free promotional activities. Much money is spent on public relations efforts designed to influence the media and generate favorable stories, articles, pictures, and presentations on behalf of travel and tourism organizations. The advantage of publicity over advertising is that a news article or picture is usually perceived by the general public as being impartial and therefore more credible than a paid advertisement. This is true even though many articles and pictures were developed by the organizations they describe. Publicity articles and photographs are often used by media hungry to fill space. Speeches and presentations before civic organizations represent another way of gaining publicity in a positive and impartial manner.

THE TERMS OF SALE MIX

Basic pricing is critical to any marketing effort. Generally speaking, pricing should relate to costs of production and produce some degree of profit. However, varying degrees of competition in the transportation industry often result in fares unrelated to actual costs, with travel to some far-away destinations available at a lower cost to the traveler than fares to nearer destinations. While the overall amount of discretionary travel may not be affected by specific prices, the choice of destinations by vacation travelers is often directly related to pricing. The volume of travel to many destinations (for instance, Hawaii or the Caribbean) has often risen and fallen as a result of pricing cycles. When more distant destinations become available at a lower price or at a price as low as closer destinations, the more distant destinations are perceived as a better value. Tourism to those farther destinations will generally grow. The development of special promotional airfares to many destinations has had great impact on the growth of tourism to those places.

Credit

The availability of credit has had a positive influence on the growth of the tourism industry. Beginning with the travel and entertainment (T & E) credit cards, such as American Express and Diners Club, through the development of airline credit cards designed to encourage flying on a given airline, through the recent growth of local bank-supported credit cards such as Visa and Master Card, credit is now available to almost all levels of the working population.

The credit card makes it possible to buy a high cost item and pay over time without getting a specific bank loan. Even when used on a thirty-day paying basis, the credit card has made the ability to purchase without cash a reality. In addition to credit cards, tourism services are often provided by one company to another on a billing, or open ac-

count, basis. For example, the availability of an open account is often a requirement when a company decides to give its travel business to a travel agent. On the other hand, the limited availability of credit from the airline to the travel agent (approximately two weeks on the average from the writing of an air ticket to the requirement to pay the airline) requires travel agents to be exceedingly careful in granting open accounts to business clients.

Rates of Exchange

The rate of exchange (the fluctuation of currency rates on the international scene) is another terms of sale factor that must be considered when dealing in international travel. Foreign destinations rise and fall in popularity as the relationship between their currency and the United States dollar changes. Obviously, each party to a transaction seeks the terms most favorable to itself. For example, the recent drastic drop in the value of the Mexican peso against the United States dollar has led to turmoil in the Mexican tourism industry, as hotels there attempt to recoup some of their losses and travelers appear in record numbers at overbooked facilities. *Travel Weekly* reported recently that one tour operator who offered Mexican packages withdrew from the market because of this confusion.

USING THE MIX

The factors in the marketing mix can be used as the basis for the development of an operational marketing program. Once information about the lifestyle of the target market (information gained by market research, see Chapter 4) is obtained, the tourism products and services most needed by the segment can be selected. The tourism organization can design the most effective distribution system for the target market and determine the proper mix of communications through sales representatives, advertising, and promotion to meet the needs of the market segment. Pricing and credit arrangements must also be developed to meet the needs of the market segment, provide a profit to the company, and be competitive in the field.

The marketing mix should be considered only a framework and general model. Real world activities will require substantial flexibility, with the need to make continuing adjustments as competitive factors change. The philosophy of the marketing mix should not be slavishly followed as the only methodology. Rather, it should be a guide for planning marketing activities.

THE FOUR Ps OF MARKETING

Many writers on the subject of marketing recommend that marketing programs be developed focusing on the Four Ps—product, price, place, and promotion. All planning and action should take these factors into consideration.

There are great similarities between this approach and the marketing mix model. All four Ps can be found in specific parts of the marketing mix. *Product*, obviously, is covered in depth in the product and service mix. *Price* is a major factor in the terms of sale mix. *Place* refers to the relative position of the company and its marketing program within a given industry and to its geographical location. This parallels the overall marketing mix with respect to the choice of products and services, communications tools, and terms of sale determined to be appropriate for a target market segment.

THE MARKETING PLAN

As noted earlier, the marketing mix can be used as a decision-making guide when developing a marketing plan. The marketing plan is a blueprint for action. The development of a simple but logical marketing plan provides a road map that can direct activities with a minimum of wasted effort. Use the following six steps when developing and operating a marketing plan:

1. *Analyze* the present situation.

2. *Establish* measurable goals and objectives.

3. *Determine* strategies to achieve the objectives.

4. *Allocate* resources to achieve the strategies.

5. *Implement* the plan.

6. *Evaluate* results and adjust goals, strategies, and budgets.

The starting point of any plan is to determine where you are now. What are the current business climate, competition, potential client needs? What are the existing resources of the company?

Establishing Goals

Establishing goals and objectives answers the question, "Where do you want the company to be, and by when?" Based on the present situation, a determination is made of the business to be accomplished: specific objectives are established for each phase of the business; and, most importantly, a time frame is established for achievement of the goals and objectives. Without the time frame and without specific objectives, there are no criteria or standards that can be evaluated to determine success or failure.

Deciding on Strategy

The marketing mix can be applied most successfully to the strategy section of the marketing plan. In establishing strategy to achieve an objective, it is necessary to consider the target market segment and choose the proper mix of products and services, distribution methods, communications tools, and terms of sale to best achieve the objectives. As a marketer, you are tailoring your recipe of ingredients to meet the needs of both your company and your target market.

Allocating Resources

The allocation and budgeting of resources to achieve strategies is the final phase that must be accomplished before implementing the plan. The current status of resources (manpower, money, and material—the three Ms) was evaluated when determining the present situation. These resources (especially time and money) must be allocated reasonably to reach desired results. The balanced use of time and money will go a long way toward a successful final product.

Implementing and Evaluating the Plan

After reviewing the previous processes and determining that together they form a reasonable, workable marketing plan, it is time to implement the plan.

Earlier, when developing objectives and strategies, specific time frames were established to measure results. Proper management of the marketing process requires that evaluations be made of progress at the times specified. The evaluation will allow necessary midcourse adjustments because plans rarely go exactly as designed.

If results are not being achieved as planned, try to determine why. Is the advertising and promotion not effective? Have economic conditions changed so that projected results are no longer achievable? Were you not realistic in determining objectives? The goals, objectives, strategies, and budgets should be adjusted as needed. If sales are not as strong as expected, some budget cuts can be made. It is also possible to reallocate resources to other, more profitable activities. Evaluation is also necessary if results are better than planned. Perhaps assigning additional personnel or doing promotion will increase sales and profits even more.

Proper evaluation and feedback is often the most neglected phase of the marketing plan. It is an ongoing process that should be conducted regularly through the implementation of the plan. Adjustments of goals, objectives, and strategies based upon the evaluation results in a marketing plan managed by the company—not a company managed by a marketing plan.

CONCLUSION

Knowledge of the submixes that make up the total marketing mix is necessary before a successful marketing effort can be planned. Once the submixes are identified and marketing goals and strategies are established, an effective marketing plan can be put into operation.

SUMMARY   The marketing mix is composed of four submixes:

- Product and service—in tourism, such components as transportation, accommodations, food service, entertainment, and sightseeing. A retail travel agent would probably need to consider all these components, while an airline would be concerned with only one. However, one component may have many aspects—classes of service and various routes might each need to be considered separately by an airline.

- Distribution—in tourism, a multilevel system. Some organizations, such as hotels and car rental firms, use direct distribution. Wholesalers, while not common, also exist as in the form of tour packagers. Retail travel agents form the third part of the distribution mix. In addition, some organizations may act as distributors at more than one level. Airlines, for example, act as direct suppliers, wholesalers, and also secure reservations for such other services as hotels and car rentals.

- Communications, which includes personal sales, advertising, sales promotion, and public relations.

- Terms of sale—including pricing, credit, and rates of exchange.

The components of the marketing mix identified above are similar to the "Four Ps" of marketing: product, price, place and promotion. These factors must all be considered in developing a marketing plan. The plan is developed in the following steps:

1. analyze the situation
2. establish measurable goals
3. determine strategies
4. allocate resources
5. implement the plan
6. evaluate results and adjust the plan as necessary.

QUESTIONS FOR THOUGHT AND DISCUSSION

1. *List the four parts of the marketing mix, describe them, and give examples of each part.*

2. *List and describe the "Four Ps" of marketing.*

3. *What are the six steps in the marketing planning process? List and explain.*

4. *Discuss the differences between a retailer and a wholesaler in the travel industry.*

7
COMMUNICATIONS

communications
customer relations
jargon
nonverbal communication
one-way communication
two-way communication
verbal communication

Communications is at the heart of all of marketing. All marketing efforts are aimed at bringing supplier and consumer together, and without some form of communication, this would not be possible.

COMPONENTS OF COMMUNICATIONS

Communication has three parts—a message, a sender, and a receiver. All three are equally important to the act of communicating. The *message* is what is being communicated. This can be something as simple as "Hello" or as complex as a lengthy report. The *sender* is the individual from whom the message originates. The *receiver* is the one to whom the message is directed.

VERBAL AND NONVERBAL

Communications can be either verbal or nonverbal. Both forms are equally important. Verbal communications are those using spoken or written words. Nonverbal communications are those depending on such unspoken forms as a nod, shrug, or a tone of voice. Even facial expressions can send a message, and qualify as nonverbal communications.

Frequently, nonverbal communications may contradict the verbal message the sender is trying to transmit. When this happens, the receiver will get a confused message, and may take either signal as the "true" one. For this reason, tone of voice is a particularly important nonverbal means of communication. As an example, sarcasm depends on this contradiction between verbal and nonverbal messages. In sarcasm, the words say one thing while the tone makes it clear that the message really means quite the opposite. Similarly, a friendly smile and a warm tone of voice make a hotel clerk's "Welcome" mean one thing. A cold stare and an icy tone of voice can change that meaning drastically, even when the word—"Welcome"—is identical.

It is extremely important to remember that you are sending nonverbal as well as verbal messages. Be sure that the total message (verbal and nonverbal) is the one really intended for the receiver.

ONE-WAY AND TWO-WAY COMMUNICATIONS

Communications can be either one way or two way. Examples of one-way communications are advertising by newspaper, radio, or TV. In one-way communication, a message is transmitted but the sender cannot get an immediate response from the receiver. The sender hopes that the message is received and understood, but it is not possible to discuss what is in the message at the time it is given.

Advertising communication—one-way communication—will be discussed fully in the next chapter. Here, we are considering only two-way forms of communication. A sales conversation is a good example of two-way communication. In these situations, a receiver as well as a sender is immediately involved. Sometimes the salesperson is the sender, with the customer acting as a receiver, and sometimes it is the reverse, but there is always one in each function. Of course, there is

"What do you mean, the seasons are reversed down here?"

always also a message. In this example of two-way communication the salesperson has the opportunity to study the buyer and to adapt what is being said to the buyer's reactions. The salesperson should be alert and look for nonverbal signs of agreement, disagreement, or even confusion, so that the presentation can be altered as necessary. This is true in a face-to-face sales conversation as well as a telephone conversation. In telephone communication, nonverbal signs are greatly diminished, but they are still there. Tone of voice is the primary nonverbal communication on the telephone conversation. The tone of voice says a great deal, if one is listening carefully. Pauses can also be most significant.

Failures in Communications

Most problems in marketing, if not in much of life, are due to miscommunication. Misunderstandings usually arise from differences between what the sender meant to communicate and what the receiver understood. In business situations, especially those relating to sales efforts, the ethical professional knows that it is important to be sure that sender and receiver are getting the same message.

Making Things Clear

In business communications, it is wise to use basic expressions that are clear in meaning. Current fad or slang expressions may be easily misunderstood. The use of simple words is also advisable. It is more important to convey a meaning clearly than to impress your customer with the extent of your vocabulary. Your receiver may be too embarrassed to admit that he or she does not understand the meaning of a word, and fail to ask for clarification. As a result, your client may make an incorrect assumption of meaning.

Jargon

Another dangerous form of communication is the use of jargon. Every industry has its own jargon—words that have a particular meaning for a given group of people, but that are not in common use elsewhere. For example, it would be better to tell a potential consumer that the price of the hotel includes breakfast and dinner rather than to say that the price includes MAP. When it is necessary to use jargon in talking with a customer, it is important to define the jargon as it is being used. For example, a salesperson could say, "This price is MAP—modified American plan. Breakfast and dinner are included." The consumer is then introduced to a term used in the industry, but because it is defined, there is no chance for misunderstanding. Always assume that special words are not understood and define them. It is better to define unnecessarily than to assume understanding that may not exist.

Listening

A good communicator is a good listener. Remember, listening is part of communicating. Many people talk without listening. All too often, each member of the communications effort concentrates on sending. Then, instead of listening carefully so as to respond correctly, the other party spends time that should be receiving time on planning his own response. Neither participant is really sure just what the other said, and each is answering based on the message that he or she *expected* to receive. Many arguments could be settled quickly if each party would just listen to the other; many misunderstandings would be avoided if people learned to listen. The technique of listening—of really receiving—is a very important technique for a salesperson. Look at the other person and concentrate on what *that* person is saying.

Effective listening is hard work. We can hear and assimilate verbal communications at a rate two to four times that of normal speech. This discrepancy leaves gaps when our minds can become distracted, or wander, losing track of what the speaker has said. Thus, it is easy to become distracted. Most salespeople believe they are better listeners than they really are. You will do well to underestimate your own listening ability, and to work hard on sharpening this critical skill.

Confirming Messages

It is advisable to confirm important items in writing to avoid misunderstandings later. Much of the communications in the travel in-

"Well, I've checked JAX FAX and the OAG—your best bet would be to go shoulder season on an APEX fare, or maybe open jaw. . . . On the other hand, we could arrange a fly/drive with MAP, leaving from LAX. . . ."

dustry is oral only. In most cases this is sufficient, but where a misunderstanding could result in a serious problem, put all agreements in writing. Thus, there will be no argument later about whether baggage handling expenses were included in the price or whether the meeting room was complimentary in the price for the group at the hotel. Where arrangements are complex, written itineraries should be provided, with all prices and features spelled out.

When sending complex and lengthy written communications, it is also advisable to have someone else in the company read them before they go out. In this way, you can be sure that what you said is what you meant. Frequently, a person who *knows* what is meant may say something ambiguously without realizing it. Another person, who reads the communication without knowing what was meant, will be more likely to question what was said. Then the planned meaning can be clarified before it is too late.

Misleading Advertising

Misleading advertising deliberately sends an inherently false message with the hope that the receiver will believe the false message, while nothing provably false has actually been said. This type of intentional miscommunication can be dangerous, and it is eventually unprofitable. The first sale may be made, but the customer will not return, nor will referral business be created.

CUSTOMER RELATIONS Customer relations, of course, *is* communications, and any business that hopes to grow through repeat and referral business must be concerned with communicating its concern for its clients' wellbeing and satisfaction. Advertising, low prices, or unique products may get the first-time customer, but unless this customer is satisfied, the repeat sale will not be made. Since there is a limit to the number of first-time customers in an area, it is important to keep the customers you get. Customers are kept by strict attention to effective communication.

Importance to Repeat Sales

It is much easier to make a sale to a repeat customer than to a new one. When selling to the new customer, part of the sales process is first selling the customer on using this company's service—that is, communicating the desirability of the service. The customer must be convinced that the business is reputable and knowledgeable and that it is safe to use. When a customer comes back as a repeat sale, this part of the sale is already made. Then the salesperson can concentrate on selling the particular product that will meet the customer's needs. This is also true of the referral customer. When a buyer has been referred to a business by someone he or she knows, the sale is partially made.

Since repeat business is so important, all business people must be concerned with customer relations. Customer relations is that part of the marketing process that helps to ensure satisfied customers. When everything goes as expected, customer relations should be an easy process. Pleasant personnel, good communications, efficient service, and products that are as advertised will help with the greater part of the task of maintaining good customer relations.

Ways of Handling Problems

The true measure of a business's ability to promote good customer relations comes when there is a problem. Unfortunately, problems do arise in some transactions. If complaints are too frequent, the underlying reasons for the problems needs to be discovered. Perhaps personnel need more training. Or perhaps more up-to-date reference materials are needed. In a properly managed business problems will be infrequent, but they are important when they do occur. The way in which these problems are handled will determine the business's success or failure in gaining repeat clientele.

Compensating for Errors

First and foremost, it is important to remember to remain pleasant and sympathetic when a complaining customer confronts you. Even if the problem was completely of the customer's own making, you must offer sympathy and friendliness—you must communicate your concern. When the problem resulted from your company's mistake, it is necessary to admit the error and compensate the customer as needed. Of course, this is difficult to do in the travel business. One cannot give back the lost time from a ruined vacation. However, out-of-pocket expenses can be reimbursed.

For this reason, airlines have traditionally been quite generous about compensating travelers for meal or accommodation expenses due to missed connections even where the fault was not of the the airline's own making, as with weather problems. The cost of such reimbursement will be more than recovered by the promotional value of this instance of positive customer relations. The traveler taken care of in this manner will tell friends, and encourage them to use the carrier's service. On the other hand, a traveler on an airline that did not take such care may very well return, telling friends of horrendous experiences where no one cared and suggesting that friends avoid that carrier. The same is true when a hotel overbooks and must move a guest to another hotel. The manner in which the customer is cared for will determine how that person feels about the supplier. Most people are reasonable (even when they are angry) and a smile goes a long way to diffuse the anger. It is hard to stay angry with someone who is sympathizing with you and saying "I'm sorry," with a reasonable offer of help.

Helping with Other Problems

In some cases, the client is angry because something happened that is not the fault of the company receiving the complaint. Retail travel agents must often handle complaints of this type. Once the agency sells the product, it cannot control the delivery of the product. The agent may have done everything possible to assure the client of a happy experience and then an airline, hotel, car rental company, sightseeing company, or even Mother Nature (in the form of poor weather), spoils part of the plan. In such cases, a sure way to guarantee an unhappy customer is to refuse involvement and refer the complainant to the supplier that was truly responsible for the problem. It is important, again, to

"So it's my fault it rained on his vacation?"

sympathize and listen to the customer and to offer to help in any reasonable way.

Frequently, just listening as the customer verbalizes the complaint is enough, and nothing further is needed. In other cases it is advisable to ask the customer to put the complaint in writing. Offer to send that copy of the complaint along with a cover letter of your own to the supplier. Even if you know that nothing can be done, the interest you show by spending a little of your own time to help the customer goes a long way toward making you a friend. This feeling of care and friendship can often help avoid a potential lawsuit. Where the customer is due compensation, it is important to use the resources of the agency to help the customer obtain it.

Unfortunately, a service as complex as travel cannot always be provided without problems. The mark of a good salesperson and a good business is handling problems without losing potential repeat business—so important to a business's growth.

CONCLUSION

The travel professional must be aware of the importance of both verbal and nonverbal communications in marketing the travel product. He or she needs good listening skills as well as the ability to communicate clearly and accurately, so that misunderstandings do not arise, and so that problems can be handled effectively.

SUMMARY Communications involves a message, a sender, and a receiver. It may be either verbal (spoken or written words) or nonverbal (tone of voice, facial expressions, or movements). It can also be either one-way (newspapers, TV commercials) or two-way, as in a face-to-face or telephone sales conversation.

Communications failures are usually not planned, and result from poor choice of words (use of slang or jargon) or failure to listen carefully. At times, however, a false message may be sent deliberately, as in misleading advertising.

Customer relations is an extension of communications that is vital to developing repeat sales. Handling problems and compensating for errors pleasantly and efficiently communicates concern and professionalism.

QUESTIONS FOR THOUGHT AND DISCUSSION

1. *List and describe the functions of the three components of any communication.*

2. *Give examples of nonverbal communication.*

3. *Describe and give examples of one-way and two-way communications.*

4. *Define jargon and give three examples.*

5. *Discuss the importance of customer relations. How is this part of a company's marketing efforts?*

8
ADVERTISING, PUBLICITY, AND PROMOTION

advertising
area of dominant influence (ADI)
broadcast media
brochure
direct mail
directional advertising
ethics
intrusive advertising
legality
media
print media
promotion
public relations
publicity
shell

Advertising, publicity, and promotion are the major communication activities designed to attract potential customers. This chapter will discuss these activities in broad terms; the next chapter will give specific information on the use of print and broadcast media in advertising.

ADVERTISING

By definition, advertising is paid communications. It has three primary uses: to *inform,* to *remind,* and to *persuade.* The main limitation of advertising is the one-way nature of the communications. While effective advertising may direct prospective customers to action, the give and take of personal communications is lacking. Unless and until the prospective customer comes into an office or makes a telephone call, there is no opportunity for in-depth discussion.

There are two primary types of advertising—directional and intrusive. Directional advertising emphasizes where to buy a product or service while intrusive advertising emphasizes what to buy. In general, the prospective customer seeks out directional advertising, while intrusive advertising, on the other hand, seeks out the customer.

The yellow pages of the telephone book are the prime example of directional advertising. Prospects responding to directional advertising are already interested in a product or service. Advertising in a specific section of a newspaper (for example, the travel section) is also basically directional, even though products and services are featured. People with no interest in travel rarely look through the travel section of a newspaper.

The broadcast media—radio and television—are the best examples of intrusive advertising. TV commercials and radio spot announcements literally intrude on the viewer or listener during regular programming. To be effective, intrusive advertising must be heavily repetitive. Since prospects are not looking for the information conveyed by intrusive advertising, frequent repetition is needed to create a lasting impression. For example, United Airlines' "Friendly Skies" slogan has earned lasting identity.

PRINT MEDIA

Newspapers, magazines, and direct mail are the major types of print media advertising. All are used extensively in the travel industry and each has its own characteristics. An analysis of the characteristics of print media will help you to understand proper usage, which will be discussed in more detail in the next chapter.

NEWSPAPERS

Newspapers can be categorized into two types: the large circulation city or metropolitan area daily newspaper, and smaller local newspapers usually issued on a weekly or twice-weekly basis. The daily newspaper is a very transient medium—it has a very short use life. Readers get it delivered to their door or buy it on a daily basis. It is generally discarded with the same regularity.

Only the largest organizations tend to use the daily newspaper effectively. For example, airlines often announce new fares and schedules through large, expensive newspaper advertisements. However, many large city dailies have Sunday editions that include special feature sections, such as a travel section. Smaller travel and tourism organizations can use this medium effectively. A smaller advertisement will be noticed in a travel section more easily than elsewhere in the paper because the reader of that section has travel in mind and is often looking for destination ideas, comparative prices, or other information.

Small-town and suburban semiweekly and weekly newspapers are rarely used by national or international travel organizations. However, these newspapers are not as transient as the daily paper. Often they are kept for several days or even a full week. These newspapers are often leafed through several times before being discarded. An advertisement in such a newspaper does not have to be huge in size to be noticed. Local travel organizations such as retail travel agencies find the local newspaper an important means of telling prospective clients about their services, as well as reminding regular clients that the agency is still in business.

MAGAZINES

Magazines represent a most interesting advertising potential for the travel and tourism industry. The magazine is a more lasting publication than the newspaper. Because it is smaller and printed on better paper, people tend to save magazines for varying periods of time. The vast majority of magazines are published on a monthly basis, although a substantial number of weekly and quarterly publications are available for advertising.

The major feature of a magazine for the potential advertiser is the degree of specialization available. Magazines are available for almost every special interest imaginable. Most organizations and special interest groups publish monthly or quarterly magazines. While the general circulation type of magazine (for example, *McCalls* and *Sports Illustrated*) is an attractive marketplace for large national advertisers, including airline and hotel chains, travel-oriented magazines (for example, *Holiday* and *Travel and Leisure*) offer advertising opportunities to a broad range of travel interests, including tour operators and steamship lines as well as airlines and hotel chains. Special interest magazines are excellent, also, for the promotion of special interest tours. For example, tours to the Galapagos Islands (noted for wildlife) are often advertised in Audubon Society publications.

BROADCAST MEDIA   The broadcast media are the most transient and intrusive of all. Both television and radio rely on the ability to produce images in the mind of the listener that will be retained and remembered. *Repetition*—using the same commercial or message again and again and again—is required for effectiveness in these media, because in broadcast advertising there is no hard copy that can be kept by the hearer for minutes, let alone days, weeks, or months.

TELEVISION

Television is the leading form of advertising in America. It is also the most costly. A one-minute commercial during prime time on a national network can cost hundreds of thousands of dollars. Thus, a full television campaign can be quite an expensive proposition. Television does combine video and audio in a moving format so that it is possible to see and hear activity. A travel destination or organization can show a destination's beautiful beaches. Airlines can show deluxe meal service and smiling cabin attendants. Properly used, television can make far deeper impressions on the viewer than any other form of advertising medium. Because of cost, however, only the larger components of the travel industry, such as airlines, destinations, and hotel/motel chains, can afford network time.

RADIO

While television often holds the complete attention of the viewer, radio is generally a background medium. As a result, it is easier to ignore or not even notice commercial material. It is possible, however, to make a commercial impact using radio at relatively reasonable costs. For this reason, radio is preferred by some large and many smaller advertisers. While most radio commercials tend to be quite straightforward, and some commercials are actually the sound tracks of television commercials, radio does provide the opportunity for creativity. With radio there

American Airlines

"We're Giving You Our Best" :60

SINGERS: We try a little harder every night and every day.

We work a little longer 'til we find a better way.

We're givin' you our best.

Yes, we're American and we're givin' our best.

AIRCRAFT MECHANIC: Every single one of us.

TICKET AGENT: In the airport...

FLIGHT ATTENDANT: And in the air...

PILOT: From take-off to landing.

SINGERS: We're givin' you...
RESERVATIONS AGENT: Low fares on every flight.

SINGERS: We're givin' our best.
FLIGHT ATTENDANT: And something more.
SINGERS: We're givin' you...
2ND FLIGHT ATTENDANT: High standards all the way.

SINGERS: We're givin' our best.
SKYCAP: Just what you'd expect from American.
SINGERS: We're givin' our best.

SINGERS: We're givin' you our best.

Yes, we're American and we're givin' our best.

No matter where we fly, we're out to lead the rest.

Yes, we're American, and we're givin' our best.

We're American Airlines. Doing what we do best.

TV story boards, or plans for commercials, are shown here and on the next two pages.

Courtesy of American Airlines.

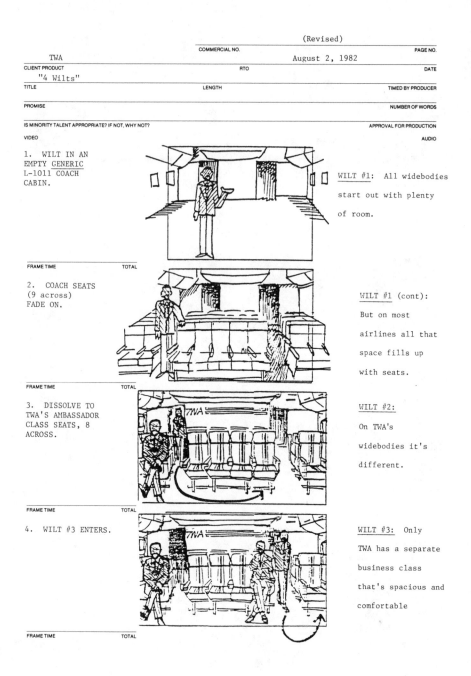

(Revised)

	COMMERCIAL NO.		PAGE NO.
TWA		August 2, 1982	

CLIENT PRODUCT   RTO   DATE

"4 Wilts"

TITLE   LENGTH   TIMED BY PRODUCER

PROMISE   NUMBER OF WORDS

IS MINORITY TALENT APPROPRIATE? IF NOT, WHY NOT?   APPROVAL FOR PRODUCTION

VIDEO   AUDIO

1. WILT IN AN
EMPTY GENERIC
L-1011 COACH
CABIN.

WILT #1: All widebodies
start out with plenty
of room.

FRAME TIME   TOTAL

2. COACH SEATS
(9 across)
FADE ON.

WILT #1 (cont):
But on most
airlines all that
space fills up
with seats.

FRAME TIME   TOTAL

3. DISSOLVE TO
TWA'S AMBASSADOR
CLASS SEATS, 8
ACROSS.

WILT #2:
On TWA's
widebodies it's
different.

FRAME TIME   TOTAL

4. WILT #3 ENTERS.

WILT #3: Only
TWA has a separate
business class
that's spacious and
comfortable

FRAME TIME   TOTAL

	COMMERCIAL NO.		PAGE NO.
TWA			
CLIENT PRODUCT	RTO		DATE
"4 Wilts"			
TITLE	LENGTH		TIMED BY PRODUCER
PROMISE			NUMBER OF WORDS
IS MINORITY TALENT APPROPRIATE? IF NOT, WHY NOT?			APPROVAL FOR PRODUCTION
VIDEO			AUDIO

5.

WILT #3:

on every

widebody flight.

FRAME TIME   TOTAL

6.

WILT #4:
TWA's Ambassador
Class has
bigger, wider
seats, and
fewer of them,
so you have
plenty of room.

FRAME TIME   TOTAL

7.

WILT #2: Couldn't have

said it better myself.

WILT #4: That's right,

you couldn't.

FRAME TIME   TOTAL

8.

You're going to like us.
TWA

SINGERS:

You're going to like

us... TWA...

FRAME TIME   TOTAL

Courtesy of TWA.

is the opportunity to play on the mind and the imagination of the listener.

Like the magazine compared to the newspaper, radio presents an opportunity for concentrating an advertising message to specialized markets. In addition to the existence of generally-oriented radio stations, many specialized programming stations can be found. Specialized formats include all news, contemporary music, top 100 record sellers, hard rock, classical music, and country and western. Each station has listening audiences with separate demographic characteristics. It is thus possible to use radio in a highly targeted fashion.

DIRECT MAIL

Newspapers, magazines, television, and radio are media that have primary purposes other than providing advertising. Most people read newspapers and magazines for the information contained in them. People view television and listen to radio primarily for the program content. Advertising, to the reader, viewer, or listener, is secondary. Direct mail, on the other hand, is a totally advertising medium. The only purpose of a direct mail piece is to inform a reader of a product or service and, hopefully, persuade the reader to take some action.

Advantages and Disadvantages

One of the greatest advantages of direct mail advertising is its ability to pinpoint audiences to an exact target market. It is possible to compile a mailing list to meet any need. A second important advantage of direct mail is the wide latitude of control in both the content and amount of information that can be sent. On the disadvantage side, direct mail is the most expensive form of advertising on a per-potential-reader basis. In addition, direct mail pieces compete with other pieces of mail received at the same time.

The question is often asked: Will a given direct mail advertisement even be opened? Surveys, however, have shown relatively positive results. Contrary to popular belief, the vast majority of so-called "junk" mail is opened. As a general rule of thumb, it can be said that the more specialized the product or service being offered, the more chance a mail advertisement will be read and acted upon if the advertisement is sent to truly potential users. Thus, a properly matched direct mail campaign and mailing list can produce very positive results.

THE TRAVEL BROCHURE

Because of the intangible nature of the travel product, some relatively inexpensive mechanism had to be developed to capture, even for a fleeting moment, some of the features and benefits of travel products and services. The mechanism that has evolved is the travel brochure. Travel brochures are issued by almost all types of tourism enterprises. Government tourist offices spend vast sums of money to develop full-color brochures and booklets describing the features and advantages of tourism in the host country. Almost every hotel in the world has issued a brochure of some sort describing its facilities. Most are in full color. Tour operators and cruise companies depend upon travel brochures as the primary means of describing their services. Even airlines have issued a variety of brochures describing equipment and service. Travel brochures are thus both an advertising medium as well as important support material for those selling travel.

Many airlines, hotels, and tourist offices can provide "shell" brochures to tour operators, travel agencies, or groups to help promote a tour. These shells are brochures containing full-color pictures of the destination, but not copy. They may then be customized to the needs of the user, and printed by the tour operator. This allows a personalized, full-color brochure to be offered by a small group at a reasonable cost.

To those considering the purchase of travel, the travel brochure is a means of analyzing the alternatives in the choice of such products as tours, cruises, or hotels. To the travel agent selling the travel service, the tour brochure is a way to show prospects what they will be getting for their money. To the people who have purchased a tour or cruise but have not yet departed, the travel brochure is a promise of what is to come. To the traveler who has returned from a trip, the tour brochure is a souvenir and record of the travel experience.

"Little Markie had such fun with your brochures!"

CHOOSING THE RIGHT
ADVERTISING MEDIUM

No single advertising medium can ever meet the total communications needs of any part of the travel industry. The combined use of two or more media usually has a multiplier effect over the use of one medium alone. Thus, we often see the same travel producer using a variety of print and broadcast media for different purposes.

For example, when an airline is introducing a new destination or a new fare, it will use newspaper advertising for several purposes. Newspaper advertising can be done on short notice, which is very important for a new fare proposal, and can present more information on rules and restrictions than other forms of advertising. This campaign will then be followed by radio and TV advertising to encourage public awareness. This combination of media takes advantage of the best features of each. If well done, it leads to the highest possible level of public awareness of and desire for the new product.

The object of any advertising campaign is to get a message to as many truly potential users as is possible with lowest possible cost. Critical to this is choosing the media that are read, viewed, or listened to by those who are truly potential users, while avoiding paying for advertising that is in media read, viewed or listened to by nonusers. This is the critical factor of media choice.

AREA OF DOMINANT INFLUENCE

One concept that is often useful in choosing media— especially on a regional or local basis—is the area of dominant influence (ADI). Every newspaper, magazine, television, and radio station as well as every mailing list broker publishes demographic information on readers, viewers, and listeners. The primary areas of service, readership, and reception in terms of geographic location, as well as population characteristics including age, sex, education, and income can be described for the area of dominant influence of each of the advertising media.

Proper marketing requires that the demographic characteristics of the target market segment must also be defined. It should be possible to make media decisions by matching the ADI characteristics of potential advertising media with the demographic characteristics of the target market. The closer the ADI matches the demographic characteristics of the target market segment, the more effective the media should be. The advertising message in these cases will be read, viewed, or listened to by more real potential purchasers than media whose ADI do not match the target market segment as well.

For example, if a target market segment is comprised of people in a limited geographic area, the best media buys would probably be those print and broadcast media whose ADI characteristics cover the geographic area desired and no more. If the ADI of a newspaper, magazine, television, or radio station covers an area much broader than that identified with the target market segment, the extended coverage would, of course, be included in the cost of the medium but would not benefit the travel-producing organization.

Thus, it makes little sense for a travel agency in a suburb on the edge of a metropolitan area to use the large metropolitan daily newspaper. While the target market segment would be included in the coverage of the newspaper, the agency would be paying for coverage of a wide area not likely to be potential clients. Greater value would be achieved by using the suburban area weekly newspaper. It is important to note that many national magazines, such as *Time, TV Guide*, and others have regional issues that make advertising for regional suppliers effective.

LEGAL AND ETHICAL ISSUES

As well as choosing the correct medium for the marketing message, those involved in marketing travel must be concerned with the content of the message. Although, from the point of view of legality, only the most blatantly improper types of advertising are truly illegal, many others may be considered unethical. It is *illegal*, for example, to advertise a product that does not exist or a price which is truly not available. Federal Trade Commission regulations can be invoked when advertising is completely misleading. United States Postal Service regulations govern illegal activities conducted through the mails. Thus, direct mail advertising of a tour that does not exist would subject the advertiser to charges of mail fraud.

The *ethics* of travel service advertising is a much broader area. One of the main functions of advertising is to persuade. Persuasion requires that travel be shown in its most positive light. Good travel advertising describes a dream that can come true. Problems arise, however, at least in the mind of the traveler or potential traveler, when what is presented is somewhat tricky or when the dream is one that can only almost come true.

For example, a cruise is advertised with rates beginning at a certain level. Out of several hundred cabins on the ship only one or two percent are priced at that rate and the next rate is substantially higher. There is nothing truly misleading or deceptive in this advertising, at least from a legal point of view, but does price advertising of this type truly represent the product for what it is? Resort hotels with very small numbers of minimum rate rooms can fall into the same category if they feature that minimum rate in their advertising.

Overzealous promotional efforts in travel brochures are another source of potential ethical problems. Are the rooms pictured in the hotel brochure characteristic of the hotel, or are they just the large suites? Does the picture of the hotel make it appear to be on the beach when really it is not? Is the swimming pool shown at an angle that makes it look much larger and more inviting than it really is?

Satisfied travelers will return again and again to their favorite spots. However, if travelers are led to believe that a resort or a ship is something that it is not, dissatisfaction will be rampant. Abe Lincoln's adage: ''You may fool all of the people some of the time; you can even fool some of the people all the time; but you can't fool all of the people

''Alice, let me see that air-sea brochure again!''

all the time," will certainly apply. Those responsible for travel and tourism advertising should consider long-range implications as well as short-term needs when they are deciding how to present products and services.

PUBLICITY AND PUBLIC RELATIONS

The real distinction between publicity and advertising is cost. Advertising, as defined earlier, involves payment for printed space or broadcast time. Publicity, on the other hand, involves the securing of free space in print media and free time in broadcast media. This space and time is usually found within the program content of the particular medium.

While it may sound contradictory, many organizations in the tourism industry spend considerable amounts of money to generate free publicity. Public relations departments and consultants specialize in securing coverage in print and broadcast media for their employers or clients.

Publicity appears in print media as part of the news or feature sections of the newspaper or magazine. In broadcast media, publicity is generated through guest appearances on talk shows as well as the reading of releases on news and feature programs.

Most readers and listeners do not view publicity content with the same skepticism as they do advertising. Advertising is seen by consumers as paid content, showing only the point of view of the advertiser. Publicity, on the other hand, is usually viewed as "truth." Few realize the efforts of a company and its public relations personnel to place such information in the media.

Favorable publicity and public relations can be generated by positive relationships with three primary groups—the media themselves, the business community, and the entire public community served by the organization. Special events and activities, such as travel shows, inaugural flights, and the opening of new facilities will often generate press coverage. The more spectacular the event or the more localized the medium, the greater the opportunity for free publicity.

On the positive side, the placement of a press release or photograph can greatly enhance a company's image and therefore its business opportunities. However, publicity is not always positive. When a problem occurs (for example, an airplane crash, political unrest at a tourism destination, or a hotel fire), the negative publicity that is generated can take a long time to overcome. An example of this point appeared in a recent issue of *Travel Weekly*. It was reported that the president of Lounge Car Tours, Al Mintz, had sent a letter to performer Johnny Carson, asking him to stop his joking references to the bad weather California experienced in early 1983. These references, Mintz claimed, were adversely affecting tourist reactions to California as a destination. He said that April 1983 had been ''totally destroyed'' for his company because of the bad weather and publicity about it, and that some May cancellations had already come in.

As with all marketing efforts, a planned campaign for publicity and public relations will achieve better results than a hit-or-miss approach. A publicity campaign should be planned as carefully and precisely as all the other phases of marketing.

SALES PROMOTION

The Committee on Definitions of the American Marketing Association states that sales promotion includes ''those marketing activities other than personal selling and advertising and publicity that stimulate consumer purchasing and dealer effectiveness, such as displays, shows and exhibitions, demonstrations, and various non-recurrent selling efforts not in the ordinary routine.'' These promotion efforts are generally one-time activities that attempt to encourage communication between the selling organization and prospective buyers.

Sales promotion may be directed toward the ultimate consumer, the trade, or the salesman. Activities such as special displays, contests, and product demonstrations characterize the promotion process. Successful sales promotion is part of the overall marketing plan and promotion efforts are highly integrated with advertising.

A successful hotel does not limit its marketing efforts to out-of-town visitors. Today, hotel profitability depends on getting local business as well, especially for restaurant and banquet facilities. The next three pages show a coordinated promotional campaign developed for Iceland's largest hotel, Hotel Loftleidir, Reykjavik.

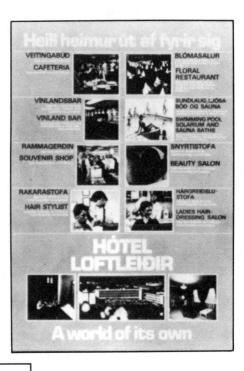

Above: a house poster used to position the hotel as "a world of its own." The poster is also displayed in bus stations, airline terminals, and certain airline offices. Left: a poster displayed on the property and in local travel agencies and airline offices. It is intended to promote the country's "nationality" dining experiences to residents.

The illustrations are reproduced courtesy of *HSMA Marketing Review* from an article by Emil Gudmundsson, CHSE, General Manager of the Hotel Loftleidir (Autumn 1982).

Left: a poster promoting nationality theme parties, in this case a Hungarian Weekend. Displayed in stores and shops, the basic copy of this poster is also used in local newspaper advertising.

Right: a promotional folder distributed to local organizations and businesses. It promotes a health-oriented program that includes jogging, swimming, sauna, and special breakfast in the hotel's cafeteria.

Left: fashion shows are promoted to local residents with posters, flyers, and other material in department stores and other retail shops.

Right: the "Gourmet of the Month"—in this case a former mayor—is a promotion featuring local community leaders who also attract local food and beverage business through their own personal contacts.

In the airline industry, sales contests represent a type of promotion activity. Pan Am's new "World Club" is designed to reward travel agents who sell a certain number of tickets on Pan Am. Airlines also participate heavily in trade shows and provide display material to support advertising efforts.

Hotels are major participants in trade shows, especially those involving travel agents and associations. These promotional activities enable hotel sales representatives to make many contacts and "sales calls" in a short period of time.

Tour wholesalers engage in a variety of promotional activities to attract the attention of retail travel agents. One example is that of a company offering escorted motorcoach tours, which sent coupons for free ice cream cones to 30,000 travel agents because they wanted agents "to get to know us better."

Travel agents often volunteer to provide programs about destinations and travel services at meetings of local clubs and service groups. Contests and free gifts with purchase are other promotional activities often found in travel agencies.

Destinations, of course, also engage in promotion. The New York Convention and Visitors Bureau recently produced a 19-minute film highlighting the attractions of New York City. The color film uses theater and movie personalities, and is available for rental or sale to retail travel agents, tour operators, and incentive travel planners.

No matter what segment of the industry uses it, sales promotion must be controlled if it is to build sales without cutting profits. It is easy to fall into the trap of using low-profit promotional activities as the normal way of doing business. Managers must recognize the dangers as well as the opportunities involved in the sales promotion process. Once again, proper planning is essential.

CONCLUSION

Advertising, publicity, and promotion together constitute one of the most important components in the communications mix. They are a primary way of bringing a potential customer to the point where personal selling efforts may close a sale. For this reason it is important to understand the various choices available and to make use of a combination that will be effective. To do this, the marketing manager must plan the advertising and promotion campaign carefully. Planning must be done with full understanding of the needs of the target market and the resources of the business.

SUMMARY   Advertising—paid communications—is designed to inform, remind, and persuade. It is a one-way method of communications that may be divided into directional and intrusive. *Directional* advertising, as seen in the yellow pages, emphasizes where to buy something; *intrusive* advertising, such as in TV or radio commercials, emphasizes what to buy by means of repetition. Publicity is, essentially, unpaid advertising, placed by public relations specialists to enhance an image and promote awareness of a product or service. Sales promotion involves a variety of one-time activities, excluding advertising, that stimulate interest in a product.

The media used in advertising include print (newspapers, magazines, direct mail, brochures) and broadcast (radio, TV). Each of these has its own advantages and disadvantages, as well as a specific range of costs and a series of techniques for effective use. A medium must be chosen that will reach the target market as effectively and inexpensively as possible. One useful concept in selecting a medium is to determine the area of dominant influence, which can be done by studying the demographic information on readers, viewers, and listeners that the various media provide. In developing any advertising campaign, ethical and legal standards must be maintained for the ultimate good of the company.

QUESTIONS FOR THOUGHT AND DISCUSSION

1. *Define advertising, promotion, and publicity. How are they similar and how are they different?*

2. *Discuss and give examples of directional and intrusive advertising.*

3. *What are the three primary purposes of advertising?*

4. *Discuss the advantages and disadvantages of different advertising media.*

5. *Discuss some of the legal and ethical issues of advertising. Bring in examples of ads that you feel violate these principles.*

9
USING ADVERTISING EFFECTIVELY

circulation
copy
cost per thousand
headline
institutional advertising
layout
mailing list
prime time
spot announcements
teaser copy
white space

DESIGNING EFFECTIVE ADVERTISING

Two questions are often asked about advertising. First, what is good advertising? Second, what is effective advertising? The second question is the most important. What is good and what is effective are often not the same. *Good* advertising is aesthetically pleasing and pleasant. *Effective* advertising brings results. The best advertising, perhaps, should be pleasant and bring results. But results—sales—is what is required from effective advertising.

According to a *Wall Street Journal* source, one of the most effective advertisements in the detergent industry is the "ring around the collar" ad for Wisk liquid detergent. According to some Madison Avenue professionals, it is one of the most obnoxious advertising campaigns on television. Critics say it is irritating, insults women and even damages the credibility of advertising in general. But it can also be argued that "ring around the collar" is one of the greatest advertising campaigns ever. It has lasted fifteen years (far longer than most) and has outscored dozens of alternatives in terms of results at the supermarket. (You may be wondering why we have not used an example of travel advertising. However, by the nature of the product travel advertising sells—dreams—it is difficult to find truly obnoxious travel ads.)

PRINT MEDIA   In using print media, whether newspaper or magazine, effectively, it is essential to know specifics about the media. It is also essential to be aware of the tricks of the trade—the techniques of handling the verbal and visual aspects of the advertisement. These techniques are the same for both kinds of print media. Before discussing technique, however, here are some specifics about circulation costs and about advertisement size.

CIRCULATION

An important factor affecting both newspaper and magazine advertising rates is circulation, or the number of readers that will probably see the newspaper. The circulation of the large city daily newspaper may range from 50,000 to more than 200,000 copies per issue. The circulation of a

"He promised good circulation for our ad, but this isn't what I had in mind."

suburban or small-town weekly is usually only a small fraction of that (from two or three thousand to twenty thousand). Obviously, the higher the circulation, the more expensive the advertisement.

However, one must also consider the concept of cost per thousand, or CPT. *Cost per thousand* refers to the cost of an ad appearing in 1,000 copies of the publication. Normally, the larger the overall circulation of a newspaper, the lower the cost per thousand copies from an advertising standpoint. For example, a large city daily newspaper issuing, on the average, 100,000 copies per day may have an advertising cost of $50.00 per column inch. On a cost per thousand basis, this translates into fifty cents per thousand issues. On the other hand, a suburban weekly may have a circulation of 10,000 and an advertising cost of $8.00 per column inch. This translates to eighty cents per thousand copies. The cost of advertising in the daily newspaper has a higher dollar amount but a lower cost per thousand copies.

Ad Size

Two important measures of newspaper ad size are the *agate line* and the *column inch*. Advertising rates are based upon these measures. A *column inch* is a unit of newspaper space one inch high (from top to bottom) and one column wide (from left to right). One column inch contains fourteen agate lines. Space contracts with newspapers offer lower unit rates for larger users. The lowest unit rate goes to the advertiser using the most space on a daily or weekly basis over a full year. The rates are designed to encourage the use of more space.

Magazine advertising is generally sold by the portion of a page (for example, 1/16 to a full page). Because of the lower frequency of issue of magazines as compared to newspapers, more advance planning is needed when considering magazine advertising. While the deadline for advertising for newspapers is as short as a day or two before publication, many magazines have advertising deadlines one month or even two months before publication.

PRINT MEDIA TECHNIQUES

A number of basic techniques can be used when developing effective print media advertising. Newspaper specialists believe the following elements of advertising setup or "layout" will increase the effectiveness and readership of the ads:

Above: This ad shows effective use of a dominant headline. The heavy type works effectively in a reverse—white lettering on a black background. Type faces for reverses must be carefully chosen. Right: Another ad example, with good use of white space as well as a border and clip art (illustrations that are sold, ready to use, by the sheet or in books of various subjects).

1. Make the advertisement distinctive and consistent. Newspaper advertising, especially in a travel section, puts competing organizations face to face with each other. Each ad vies for the reader's attention with other travel advertisements. When used outside the travel section, the ad competes with ads that are not travel related

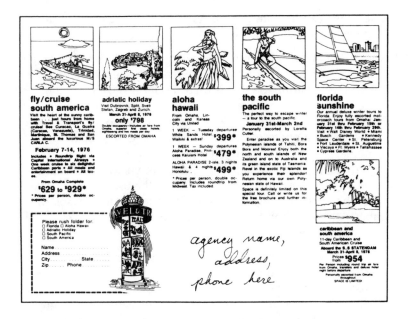

This single ad effectively advertises several products. Each is clearly identified by its accompanying, eye-catching illustration. The elements of the ad are arranged so that it does not seem crowded despite the number of items being promoted.

at all. The primary objective should be to make an advertisement stand out from the others. Use distinctive artwork, borders, or typefaces. Stay consistent with the image of your organization and keep promoting this image.

2. Keep the layout—the arrangement of the type, white space, and illustrations—simple. The advertisement should be well organized and uncluttered. It should be easy for the reader to understand. Keep the demands on the reader simple. If more than one service is advertised, divide the total space into segments and separate the items with lines, boxes, or white space. The reader's eye should flow through the message easily and in sequence. The headline or illustration should make the first impression, followed by explanatory detail. Avoid the use of too many different typefaces and sizes. Overly fancy borders tend to confuse readers. Reverses (white type on a black background) should be used only for head-

lines; they can be hard to read. When distracting elements are eliminated, readership will be increased.

3. Use a dominant element in the advertisement. A large headline or a photo or drawing will capture the reader's attention and arouse interest. Any illustration that is used should be clean, simple, and large enough for the reader to understand. Photographs of people, action, and destinations are very successful—although somewhat expensive. If a photo of people is used, a release should be obtained for permission to use their picture. When an illustration is not available, make the headline dominant enough to attract attention. When pictures are not available, the use of clip art (black and white line drawings ready for reproduction, usually sold by subject category) can be very effective. Several companies specialize in the sale of clip art.

4. Use white space and borders effectively. Use white space to make illustrations and headlines stand out, and also to separate different items in the ad. White space can also separate the advertisement from others on the page. Simple black borders around an advertisement (especially a small one under 1/8 of a page) increase readership. Don't crowd the advertisement.

In addition to the general layout, certain elements make the content or "copy" of an advertisement more effective. There are three primary elements that should be considered.

First, a major benefit headline should be used. Put the number one product or service benefit in the headline. And remember, factual benefits are important but emotional benefits are equally significant. For example, a major benefit of a trip to the islands in January is to get away from cold weather. Saying "The Caribbean—$250.00" in a headline is not as effective as saying "Give your cold away in the sunny Caribbean—$250.00." The headline must answer the first question of any reader—"What's in it for me?"

When the advertisement promotes more than one item, use an overall headline for focus and to hold the ad together. For special interest groups use selective headlines. For example, say "For the SCUBA diver . . ." or "Golf away today." A headline that asks a question or announces a new program attracts attention.

A second major point in copywriting is to be direct, simple, and complete. Amplify the headline in the rest of the advertisement. Give all relevant information including prices in simple, clear language. Do not generalize and do not make excessive claims. Also, do not forget the name of your organization and its address and telephone number so that a reader can take action.

Taking action should be the result of the third element. Urge action! Tell readers what they should do—call, write or complete and return a coupon. If a coupon is included, it should be large enough to be filled out. It should be next to one of the ad borders where it can be clipped without destroying the rest of the ad. If choice of location in the newspaper is available, place an ad with a coupon near the border of the page so that the page is not totally destroyed and the coupon can be clipped easily.

An advertising agency can be of great help in developing layout and copy for print advertising. However, many small organizations in the travel and tourism industry do not have a substantial enough advertising budget to make use of an advertising agency worthwhile. In these situations assistance can be sought from the advertising medium itself.

A good working relationship with the newspaper's advertising representative can be a great benefit. The representative can assist with almost every aspect of advertising. The newspaper's advertising department will often be able to do the layout of the actual advertisement. Most newspapers use offset printing, and "camera-ready" copy is what is used to make the printing plate. It can often put the ad together from your design. The newspaper can also suggest freelance artists who, for a reasonable fee, can help you. They may even have an artist on staff. However, working with an artist for a short time may be worth the cost and establish a direction so that an organization can produce its own effective layouts in the future.

PREPARING EFFECTIVE DIRECT MAIL PIECES

The guidelines provided above for preparing effective newspaper advertisements are just as important when preparing direct mail presentations. Since more space is available for direct mail, the guidelines should be easier to apply. However, it is easy to get carried away in direct mail and provide too much information. Care must be used to choose the proper information to print and to assure an even flow for the reader. Keep direct mail presentations simple and eyecatching.

While direct mail advertising allows for the preparation of brochures and flyers that should be developed in accordance with the above guidelines, there are two other types of presentation pieces that differ from other print media. First is the letter and the second is the newsletter.

LETTERS

Letters are the most widely used of all direct mail forms. Often, they are used alone as sales letters or thank you letters. They can also be used to transmit flyers, brochures, invoices, or other material. Letters can be either individualized or printed form letters. The individually-typed letter is the most effective because the reader will consider it more personal than a printed form letter. Today, the use of word processors, along with computerized mailing lists, make it possible to produce an individually-prepared letter at a fraction of the cost of individually handtyped letters.

With direct mail, the sender can control the amount of copy and the space it takes to say what it is necessary to say. The benefits of a travel service should be described in glowing (but not repetitive) detail. A balance is needed without making the mistake of saying too little or being too repetitive. The content of the letter should be direct and basically simple.

Ample margins should be used on the letter to make it more attractive and readable. A personally-signed letter is quite impressive. This, of course, is not possible in mass mailings. Hand-addressed or hand-typed envelopes will help to personalize direct mail—but they, too, have a very high cost.

The use of good quality paper stock for letters and envelopes will make them more attractive. The organization's name, logo, or symbol, as well as its complete address and telephone number, should appear on the letter.

Teaser copy on the envelope (for example, "Important Information Enclosed") or other information can increase the chance of letters being opened. Postage stamps rather than metered or printed postage make a letter more likely to be opened. The use of commemorative stamps attracts even more attention.

Postal Cards

Postal cards are another form of direct mail "letter" that should not be forgotten. They are well suited to short, direct messages and they are less costly to mail and print than letters. A 1974 postal service study found that 83% of people who received postcards actually read them.

NEWSLETTERS

All kinds of newsletters are mailed by almost all elements of the travel and tourism industry. They range from multipage, professionally prepared, typeset and slick printed publications that are almost like magazines to one-sheet typed and mimeographed pieces. Airline clubs and frequent flyer programs (for example, Pan Am's Clipper Club, Eastern's Ionosphere Club, and United's Mileage Plus Program) send regular newsletters to their members, as do steamship lines to their past passengers, hotels to their frequent visitors and club members (for example, Intercontinental's Six Continents Club), and travel agencies to present prospective clients.

The newsletter is an excellent way to provide both sales promotion and institutional messages. (Institutional advertising is designed to convey the overall image of an organization and create an awareness in the consumer's mind, rather than selling a particular product or service.) Providing "nonselling" articles that directly benefit the audience demonstrates the company's concern for the traveler's needs. Examples of such articles are those giving information on customs regulations, how to pack a suitcase, or what to do when certain problems arise during travel.

Product messages should be handled as in a letter. Give all the pertinent information and elaborate on it, including details that emphasize the emotional benefits to the traveler. Details that might not fit into newspaper advertising or would be too expensive to include in the broadcast media can be added. Flyers or brochures can also be inserted with the newsletter.

The audience of a newsletter should be invited to take action on at least one item within the newsletter. Coupons to return can also be effective.

As for newspapers and letters, copy for newsletters should be simple, informal, and briefly convey information to the readers. Clear and interesting communication of the main idea of each item should appear near its beginning. Gain the reader's attention and keep it. After conveying the main idea, build it up in future paragraphs and sentences. Again, avoid using overly pompous words or superlatives. Show benefits, but make them accurate and believable.

The format of a newsletter should be designed for easy reading. The print and type should be large, dark, and clear so that even older readers who may be a bit farsighted can read it. The same rule applies to illustrations and photographs. White space aids in clarity and readability. Ample margins on all sides and ample space between paragraphs and articles adds to readability. Don't crowd copy. It is better to leave out an item or shorten it than to crowd the material.

Clean simple lines or borders around special items draw attention to the items and make the page look clean and orderly. Borders should not be fancy and ornate. Colored paper or colored ink can often be used to attract attention. Black ink and white paper, however, are the least expensive.

FLYERS, BROCHURES, AND OTHER PRINTED MATERIAL

The guidelines provided for newspaper and direct mail advertising copy and layout apply as well to flyers and brochures. Keep the copy content simple and clear so that the reader will be attracted and will understand.

Costs of Direct Mail—Mailing Lists

Several costs must be considered when planning direct mail advertising. First among these is the cost of a mailing list. Many retail travel agencies maintain lists of their clients and of people who have requested information. Cruise lines and tour operators also maintain lists of previous customers. For the solicitation of new business, mailing list brokers offer lists of categories of people of all types. The lists may be subscribers to certain magazines, members of certain types of organizations, or specific businesses. The general cost of a list varies from $30.00 to $70.00 per thousand names, with some highly-specialized lists costing even more. When using a broker's list, the advertiser is actually renting a one-time use only. Mailing lists are generally sold on labels that can be affixed directly to an envelope or self-mailer.

Other Costs

Postage is one of the highest costs of direct mail. Current costs vary from nearly $80.00 per thousand pieces for bulk mail up to $200.00 per thousand for first-class (based upon a one-ounce mailing). To these costs must be added the costs of creating the advertising piece, plus printing, folding, and often stuffing and sealing costs if envelopes are used. Thus, the cost of a one-ounce mailing can vary from a minimum of about $.15 per piece to $.30 or $.50 or more per piece. On a cost-per-thousand basis this translates to $150 to $500 per thousand pieces mailed. Some complex mailing items cost even more.

YELLOW PAGES

Advertising in the yellow pages or in other private local telephone directories is a major method of effective directional advertising. Reuben Donnelley representatives (or other publishers' sales representatives) can help in developing effective copy.

Several basic elements should be kept in mind when developing telephone directory advertising. Along with the organization name, complete address and phone number, include the organization's logo and office hours. As in other print media, use a headline or illustration to attract the reader's attention. Line illustrations reproduce far better than photographs in the yellow pages.

Since this type of advertising lasts for an extended period, it is not wise to try to advertise timely products. This form of advertising is best suited to institutional advertising—informing the reader of what services you offer and where to locate you.

Because your yellow pages will be competing with ads for other similar organizations, any special feature of your product or service should be included in the body of the copy. Conveniences such as delivery service, ability to take appointments during off times, credit cards accepted or other features should be included to give you a competitive edge. Don't forget to urge the reader to action. "Call for fast friendly service..." or "Come in and visit..." can be effective.

BROADCAST MEDIA

As with the print media, cost and placement (timing) of broadcast media advertising are important factors that must be considered when planning an advertisement. The techniques used in creating advertisements for broadcast media are specialized. In most cases, the travel professional will be wise to turn to other professionals in these fields for help in planning effective use of the media.

TELEVISION

Television time is sold on the basis of length of commercial and time of airing. *Prime time* is the time of highest viewing and also highest advertising cost—8:00 pm to 11:00 pm in the East and West and 7:00 pm to 10:00 pm in the Midwest. Weekend special events such as professional football games also carry a prime rate. The lowest cost television time is after the late night news and on non-network stations. In addition to air time, the production of television commercials can be an expensive proposition. It is necessary to consider both the cost of creation as well as actors, camera, crew, and film or tape production and editing. For these reasons, television advertising will not be cost-effective for many components of the travel industry.

RADIO

Radio, unlike television, can be used effectively even by smaller components of the travel industry, if timing and station selection are done carefully. The prime time of radio listenership is the morning rush hour (approximately 6:00 to 9:00 am). This is the most productive radio time because people are freshest and most alert at the beginning of the day. Thus, they are least likely to ignore commercial announcements. The next most popular and most expensive time is the afternoon rush hour (4:00 to 7:00 pm). Evening time (television prime time) is relatively inexpensive.

Radio commercials, usually called spot announcements, are generally sold on a per spot announcement basis. While it is possible to sponsor short programs (for example, newscasts) and segments of programs such as traffic reports, most advertising is on a run-of-the-show basis. Substantial cost savings can be obtained for a long-term contract and for contracts using some of the less popular times.

Most radio programs run from one to four hours with the same host or disk jockey. As a result, regular audiences develop varying degrees of identity with radio personalities. Since the radio personalities have personal followings, a successful travel advertising technique has been to offer tour programs led by the radio personality. This often means that the travel agency, airline, tour operator, or hotel involved buys commercial time on the radio station, and provides free travel and often fees to the radio personalities as well.

EFFECTIVE BROADCAST ADVERTISEMENTS

Preparation of material for radio advertising can be done in two ways. First, radio ads can be taped or written in advance. Second, fact sheets about the service can be given to a station announcer or personality (for example, a disc jockey) who uses them as the basis for informal discussion. The only real advantage of the latter form lies in the selling ability of the personality. The same selling ability can be used if the voice of a well-known personality is used on tape.

A radio station sales department will be quite helpful in advertising development. An advertising agency can also be used. However, a number of points should be kept in mind when developing or helping to develop radio advertising.

First, the number of facts in a radio ad should be kept to a minimum. Give only the essentials. Radio is a background medium and radio listeners are only half listeners. They do not absorb a lot of detail. Second, important words should be repeated. The name of the service, the price, and where to go to take action should be emphasized.

Third, a radio ad should attract attention immediately. If listeners are caught at the very beginning, they'll probably listen to the whole message. Sound effects, music, or other special techniques should not be saved for the middle or end of the advertisement. Capture attention as early as possible and try to hold it throughout the ad.

As for print media, copy should be simple, informal, and believable. Superlatives and generalizations usually miss the mark. A radio ad should be written as if it were part of an informal conversation.

The ad should end with a call for action. Do not leave the listener wondering what to do. Give a phone number, a location, or some other way that the listener can order the product or service or at least get more information.

Guidelines for Television Advertising

It is not advisable for an inexperienced person to try to develop television advertising without professional help. Organizations wishing to use television advertising, even on a local level, should consider working with people who are knowledgeable about TV commercial production. This may be someone from an advertising agency, an employee of a TV station, or a public relations professional who has worked in the medium.

Just as with radio and with the print media, it is important to work closely with the sales department of the television station. The TV advertising account executive can give valuable information about production as well as placement of the commercial.

The preparation of television advertising copy should follow similar guidelines to that of radio. Because a broadcast medium is used and there is no hard copy for the viewer to retain, the number of facts must be kept to a minimum. The viewer's attention must be attracted immediately and the copy must be simple, informal and believable. Like all advertising, the ad should end with a call for action.

CONCLUSION

A knowledge of the costs, vocabulary, and techniques in both print and broadcast media is necessary to make the right decisions in using them for effective advertising.

SUMMARY   *Good* and *effective* are not always synonymous in advertising, because what is effective may not always be pleasant. However, the nature of the travel product makes it easy to produce advertising that is both good and effective.

Circulation and *ad size*, as well as the nature of the publication, will govern the cost of advertising in newspapers and magazines. In direct mail, important costs include the price of renting a mailing list and the cost of postage. Timing, frequency, and production costs are important factors in the advertising budget for broadcast media. In both print and broadcast media, the advice and help of professionals can increase advertising effectiveness. In advertising in any one of these media, however, clarity, simplicity, and concern for communicating a message and suggesting action are essential.

QUESTIONS FOR THOUGHT AND DISCUSSION

1. a. *Collect samples of advertisements (particularly in travel) from newspapers or magazines. Discuss the good and bad points of each.*
   b. *Discuss good and bad points of some travel ads from radio or TV.*

2. *Create an advertisement for a hotel, airline, or travel agency. Use whatever features you wish to create for this company.*

3. *Write a thirty- or sixty-second radio spot for a travel business (hotel, airline, destination, etc.).*

4. *You are the advertising manager of a business. A salesman has come to you with two proposals. One involves buying ads in several local newspapers each having a circulation of approximately 15,000 readers. Each of these ads costs $45. The other involves buying an ad for $375 in a city newspaper with a circulation of 130,000. All of these newspapers are in your market area. From a point of view of the cost per thousand, which proposal is most economical?*

10
THE SALES FUNCTION IN THE TRAVEL INDUSTRY

dual distribution
inside sales
order taking
outside sales
sales presentation
supplier

The question is often asked: "How do you differentiate sales from marketing?" Earlier, we defined marketing as the total process of bringing buyer and product or service together. Later, in the discussion of the marketing mix in travel, personal sales was described as a major part of the overall marketing process. A complete marketing plan will include sales, and effective sales are part of any successful marketing effort. While the sales function might be able to exist apart from other marketing functions, using the sales function as part of the marketing definitely multiplies its effectiveness.

DUAL DISTRIBUTION   As we noted earlier, most components of the travel and tourism industry are characterized by a dual distribution system. To recapitulate, travel services generally have three distribution levels—producer, wholesaler, and retailer. In other industries, the producer sells to wholesalers (and often directly to retailers); wholesalers sell to retailers; and the retail establishment is the prime distributor to the general market of individual purchasers. For example, in the food industry, Dole grows and cans pineapples. Its place in the distribution system is that of producer. Dole sells canned pineapple to food jobbers (wholesalers) and also directly to large supermarket chains (retailers). Food jobbers sell to smaller retail food markets, which also sell to the general public.

In travel and tourism both the producer and the retailer sell to the general public. Airlines, hotels, car rental companies, railroads, and most other service producers sell directly to the general public. However, these producers also sell their services through wholesalers and through retail travel agents. Most cruise lines and some tour operators are the only suppliers that have chosen a purely unitary system—through the retail travel agent.

TRAVEL AGENT VS SUPPLIER

Under the dual distribution system, consumers have a choice. They can purchase travel services directly from the producer or through a travel agent. More than 20,000 travel agency offices are currently open in the United States. Are they engaged in sales competition with their own suppliers (such as airlines) who are also selling the same service to the public? Actually, true competition only exists in a small segment of the overall market where both airline and agent are seeking the same customer.

Most airline marketing efforts (advertising campaigns) support both direct sales and sales through agents. Since travel agent sales ultimately benefit the supplier of the travel service, suppliers recognize the need to keep direct competition to a minimum. The 20,000 agency offices eliminate the need for a multiplicity of airline, hotel, and other supplier offices throughout the country. The use of travel agents as the prime distribution network for sales to consumers makes economic sense as well. The operation of a ticket office is a fixed expense to the carrier, no matter how small the sales volume. Since travel agent commissions are based on a percentage of sales, suppliers incur costs only when actual sales are made. Further, no money is spent by the supplier until sales are made. The travel agency assumes all operations expenses, collection costs, and business risks.

The sales function, essentially, is the culmination of the marketing process. Through personal communications techniques the transfer of services (or at least the promise of services) from seller to buyer is accomplished. Through the efforts of sales personnel, the traveler receives an airline ticket, hotel confirmation, cruise ticket, or other benefit. The marketing process has been completed—almost. The services must now be provided as promised for the buyer to be satisfied and want to buy again. As emphasized earlier, successful travel and tourism marketing depends heavily on repeat business for profitability.

BUYING AS A LEARNING EXPERIENCE

Anyone in sales has a continuing opportunity to improve his or her ability to sell effectively. Salespersons are also consumers, constantly experiencing both good and bad selling efforts. As they experience these selling efforts, true professionals will analyze them, and use the examples, both good and bad, to improve their own sales abilities. As John Zeeman, Senior Vice President, Marketing of United Airlines, has stated:

> One of the most valuable sales experiences is as a 'buyer.' In my career with United, I started in advertising where, obviously, it is important to make significant media purchases...both because of the importance of media to carry messages as well as the magnitude of dollars involved. When one is in a buying environment one has the opportunity to clinically evaluate sales presentations. How well did the salesperson understand my needs? How well did the salesperson fit the product or services to those needs? How persuasively did the salesperson present and explain this fit?
> I think travel counselors could learn a lot about selling if they would evaluate the mistakes suppliers make in their presentations and to extract the strong selling points that are likewise made. In addition, they should give some thought as to how they, as consumers, react to sales people. How do they choose both merchandise and services? How do they quantify among differing values of importance to them in making purchases?

Tourism professionals will use personal experience as an aid to on-the-job effectiveness if they are in either of the two categories of sales positions found in the industry.

INSIDE AND OUTSIDE SALES

Travel industry sales includes two different types of positions—*inside* and *outside* sales assignments. While some jobs include both functions, most are either one or the other.

INSIDE SALES

Inside sales is the most basic of the positions. The inside salesperson answers telephone calls and responds to inquiries from potential customers coming into the office. Other marketing functions including advertising, sales promotion, and outside sales efforts generate inquiries. The inside salesperson takes over at the time of the call or visit.

Inside positions may deal with travel agents, tour wholesalers, the general public, or any combination of these. Airline reservation offices as well as city ticket offices and airport ticket counters are staffed by inside salespersons. Hotel reservation offices and car rental reservation facilities and rental offices require inside sales skills as well.

Most travel agency positions are of the inside sales type. The primary characteristic of the position is the fact that the potential purchaser made a decision to take action before the contact with the inside salesperson was made. The action decision may be to actually purchase or just to seek information, but a decision was made before the sales contact. The contact was initiated by the potential purchaser. Thus, the inside salesperson is dealing with an interested, motivated party.

Selling vs Taking Orders

Does the person performing inside sales truly sell—or just take orders? Unfortunately, too many are really ordertakers, not salespeople. Their activities are limited to that of a fulfillment clerk who provides what is asked for—no more and no less. There is, however, ample opportunity for the use of professional sales skills in the inside position. It is essential that the inside salesperson understand customer needs and how to meet them. The sales techniques described in the next chapter should be understood and mastered by both inside and outside personnel. The

"Would you like the sunrise special fare. . . the early morning fare. . . the midafternoon fare. . . the midmorning fare. . . the early afternoon fare. . . the high-noon fare. . . the late afternoon fare. . . the early supper fare. . . the supper super fare. . . the dinner fare. . . the deluxe dessert fare. . . the late night fare. . . the late late night fare. . . the midnight fare. . . the super-duper excursion fare. . . the dawn fare. . . the. . . ?"

challenge of helping a potential customer identify and meet needs is just as strong in both types of positions. Unfortunately, it is easier for the inside person to become lazy and not truly try to identify customers' needs.

OUTSIDE SALES

An outside sales job involves public contact work outside the employer's office. Rather than waiting for a prospect to make contact, the outside salesperson seeks prospects by telephone and personal visits. A full knowledge of selling skills and techniques is required for outside sales, as well as the ability to identify potentially interested parties. Some outside sales positions follow up "qualified leads"—potentially interested parties attracted by advertising and other marketing processes. Other positions require "cold calling," where the salesperson canvasses all offices in a given area, or all people on a certain list.

Outside sales people with travel and tourism suppliers generally deal with wholesalers and retail travel agents. Only the largest potential users within the general public (business accounts, government agencies, and associations) receive the attention of an outside representative. The position title "sales representative" or "account executive" is often associated with such positions in the airline industry. Hotel chains, car rental companies, and cruise lines, all of which have substantially fewer sales positions, often give the title "sales manager" or "district sales manager" to such positions. Airlines use the title "sales manager" to signify personnel responsible for managing sales representatives. These sales managers do little if any selling, but usually have come from the sales background.

THE MARKETING PLAN AND THE SALES PRESENTATION

The effectiveness of a sales effort can be heavily influenced by the placement of sales within the overall marketing plan of an organization. While it might be said that if you do not know where you are going, any road will get you there, this philosophy has no place in marketing and sales.

The marketing plan should be a road map leading the way to a final goal of bringing service and buyer together. Target markets should be identified and the mix of products and services, distribution methods, communications techniques, and alternative terms of sale should be planned. Assuming that outside sales contact is part of the overall plan, attention should be given to a planned presentation. Whether oral, written, or both, an organized presentation helps ensure the success of an outside sales call.

Specific Objectives

Every contact initiated by a sales representative should have a specific objective and a plan to achieve that objective. Depending upon the situation, the objective may be to complete a sale based upon previously identified needs or merely to identify potential needs—but the objective must be determined in advance. The sales representative should prepare a logical, step-by-step action plan to achieve the objective. A simple yet effective strategy is the following:

- Introduction (A brief overview describing what you are going to develop in detail).
- Presentation (Provide the detail to support your objective using appropriate sales techniques).
- Summary (Restate what you have said in a concise manner and summarize points of agreement and difference).

Written Sales Presentations

When the sales objective includes a complex program or set of services, a written sales presentation should be prepared. Often, when two or more organizations are competing for the business, the written sales presentation is a requirement. The proposal clarifies the concepts being covered orally, and also serves as a basis for comparison of services. A sales proposal should be clear and concise and follow the basic presentation strategy. The ability of the organization to meet the needs of the prospect and the benefits to the prospect of accepting the proposal should be emphasized. The proposal should be neatly typed (or word processed) and the original (not a photocopy) should be given to the decision maker at the time of the sales presentation. A professionally prepared proposal is especially important when several people, such as a board of directors or a selection committee, are involved in the decision making process or when much time will elapse between sales presentation and decision making.

CONCLUSION

The sales function is a vital part of the broader process of marketing, and sales efforts will be most effective when they are planned and executed as part of a total marketing plan.

SUMMARY

The sales function in travel and tourism marketing is most effective when understood as part of an overall marketing plan that takes into account the dual distribution system present in the travel and tourism industry.

Dual distribution means, for example, that an airline ticket may be purchased directly from the airline or through a travel agent. However, the costs of operating ticket offices make it more efficient for retail travel agents to serve as the prime distribution network for the travel product.

Travel industry sales is handled by two positions—inside and outside sales. The inside salesperson responds to telephone calls or visits from prospective clients, while the outside salesperson seeks out prospects by phone or personal visit. Selling should not be confused with simple order taking, and whether in an inside or outside sales position, the travel professional will use personal experience as a consumer to enhance selling skills.

The marketing plan gives direction to the sales function, and ultimately to a sales presentation, which may be oral or written. In either case, the sales presentation must have an objective, and a strategy to achieve that objective. The strategy may be as simple as deciding on an introduction, a presentation, and a summary. Written sales presentations, usually employed to present a complex proposal, should always be carefully and neatly prepared.

QUESTIONS FOR THOUGHT AND DISCUSSION

1. *Define dual distribution and explain its existence in the travel industry.*

2. *What is the difference between inside sales and outside sales positions?*

3. *Create a written sales presentation relating to travel. Describe who your client is and what you are trying to sell.*

11
SALES TECHNIQUES

benefits
closing
commitment
features
follow-up
identifying needs
objection
probing
qualifying
sales interview
solving problems
telemarketing

As a lawyer logically develops a case...as an engineer plans a project...as a doctor diagnoses sickness...similarly, a sales representative in the travel and tourism industry is a skilled professional who diagnoses client needs and shows how specific travel services will meet those needs.

When you sell a service to a first-time client, you are really selling two services. First, you must sell your own and your company's ability to provide the required service. Then, you must convince the client that the service you are recommending will meet the requisite needs.

Before you can sell anything, you must sell yourself. Because a client's first impression of you will probably be of your physical appearance, you may be judged on such points as:

- Clothes clean and pressed?

- Hair combed and neatly cut?

- Cosmetics appropriately used?

Chewing gum or dangling a cigarette gives a negative impression. (In fact, smoking at all during the sales process is probably not acceptable.) The successful sales representative conforms to accepted standards of dress and behavior. Overdressing is almost as bad as underdressing.

Neither the dandy nor the unkempt person starts on the right foot. Your general appearance must be pleasing, but not striking. Practice good posture and display a warm, friendly smile.

That smile can be your greatest sales tool. It has tremendous positive value. Friendliness and a warm smile perform miracles. Your smile radiates warmth to your prospect—and that warmth is reflected back to you. A friendly smile sets the perfect sales climate. If you are moody or unhappy, it will reflect on your prospect and the opportunity for a successful sale will be lessened. When dealing with complaints or the difficult client, don't forget the smile. You may want to scream or argue—but don't. Finish your conversation with a warm, friendly smile. You will get startling results.

THE SALES PROCESS   To many people the word "selling" means a glib-talking peddler with his foot in the door, hypnotically inducing people to buy products they don't want with money they can't afford to spend. That kind of selling has no place in the travel profession. Professional salespeople do not operate in that way. Ethics aside, in the long run, it would do more harm than good.

The sales activity does not exist in a vacuum. It is an integral part of the overall marketing process. It is part of the communications mix—the submix within the overall marketing mix that contains the tools used to bring prospective buyer and product together. To many people, sales is the most important part of the communications mix.

THE IMPORTANCE OF COMMUNICATING

Communication skills are critical to the sales process. Personal selling, where buyer and seller engage in face-to-face or telephone discussions, is the only part of the communications mix that is not one-way in nature, like an advertisement in a newspaper or a direct mail letter. Two-way communications, where salesperson and client can provide direct feedback to each other through verbal and nonverbal techniques, is, indeed, the most effective method of imparting information and securing commitment.

As part of the overall consumer-oriented philosophy of marketing, professional selling should also be consumer oriented. The entire process is devoted to identifying customers' needs and providing the right service to meet a specific need. In a nutshell, a professional salesperson is one who finds a need and fills it.

Identifying and Filling Needs

In many situations in the travel industry, helping clients identify their needs and providing services to meet them is the core of the process. A travel agent helps a client find the right vacation at the right place, the right time and at the right price for the client's need. An airline cargo sales representative shows how the additional speed of air freight offsets the extra cost of the service. A hotel sales representative shows how one hotel is good for business meetings while another is best for rest and relaxation. The needs orientation is clearly the basis of operations.

Identifying and Solving Problems

In more complex situations, needs orientation is not enough. In these cases the salesperson must act virtually as a member of the prospective client's executive staff to help identify and solve the client's problems. A hotel salesperson must help a group determine their meeting room needs and banquet requirements. A sales representative for an airline manufacturer must help an airline identify the future needs of travelers on its routes and the type of craft that will meet those needs.

Only after identifying the problem in detail, can the sales representative show how a company's product will best meet that need. Similarly, a travel agency sales representative approaching a large corporation or organization must first help identify the basic problems of the organization or company before showing how his or her agency can meet those needs. The basic needs of a corporation may be to save money or it may be to control traveling within the company. An organization's main problem may be to communicate with its members,

"All right! Who suggested Club Med to Sister Mary Agnes?"

and travel products such as a convention or series of regional meetings can only be recommended after identifying that basic communications problem. In these cases, the sales representatives must immerse themselves in the prospective client's companies and become, in effect, consultants.

THE SALES INTERVIEW

The personal sales process, where buyer and seller are in direct communication, is essentially an interview process. The salesperson is the interviewer and the client, the interviewee. In the most successful situations, the salesperson controls the interview. It should be noted that control is not domination but rather direction. The salesperson has one or more objectives clearly in mind at all times.

The interview should be structured. Overall, the general goal is to find out what the customer needs, recommend products or services to fill those needs, and persuade the customer to accept the recommendations and buy the travel product.

Obviously no two sales persons are exactly alike and no two prospective clients are exactly alike. That means that no two sales conversations will be exactly alike. Yet, there is a pattern that will work to generate sales. Certain elements should be found in all successful sales conversations. Keeping the elements in mind as a guide during the conversation will help to decide where you've been, where you are now, and what ground you must cover to complete the process.

It is somewhat misleading to pull apart a sales conversation into separate pieces, because the actual conversation is a flow rather than separate steps. However, knowledge of the elements is necessary to be sure you cover everything which must be covered. The steps in this process were identified by Porter Henry in 1970 for the American Society of Travel Agents. These steps are as valid today as when they were originally identified. The major elements in the sales process are:

1. *Getting the Initial Information*
   There are certain basic pieces of information that a sales representative needs in the beginning. When planning a sales call, this information is gathered ahead of time. However, when a prospective client comes to you, it is necessary to get this information right away. This information is the basic who, when, where, and how many.

2. *Finding Out What the Customer Really Wants*

After the initial who, when, and where, it is necessary to dig deeper to identify the real needs of clients. Will the traveler's destination request really meet needs? Is the budget realistic? Can this hotel handle these needs?

Getting the initial information and finding out what the customer really wants are, together, the "qualification" phase of the sales conversation. It is essential to qualify a customer in order to determine service recommendations and to decide on the amount of time you can afford to devote to the prospective sale. A professional sales representative will devote substantial amounts of time only to substantial prospects.

3. *Selling Your Recommendation*

Once you have qualified the client and know what is really needed, you should recommend the product or service that will provide the maximum satisfaction within the client's allotted budget. You sell your recommendation by convincing clients that you understand their wants and needs and that the product or service you recommend is the best way to meet those needs.

4. *Handling Objections*

Often the customer will accept your recommendation right away. However, many times the customer will not accept your recommendation immediately. If you really believe your recommendation will meet the needs, you must analyze the objections and overcome them.

5. *Getting the Commitment*

Traditionally this is called "closing the sale." Essentially, it is asking for the business. The salesperson who hands a purchaser a set of brochures or other sales aids and says "Call me when you've decided what you want," has not closed the sale. A professional salesperson will gain as much of a commitment as is possible during each sales conversation. If it is not possible to close the sale, the representative will at least get the commitment to talk again. It is better for the salesperson to say "I'll call you next week to check on what you need," rather than "Call me when you decide." The latter leaves no chance for a follow-up without intruding, whereas the former approach leaves the way open without offense to continue the sales process with a follow-up effort. Of course, if there is no reasonable possibility of closing the sale in the future, no further commitment should be requested and the sales conversation should be terminated as quickly and graciously as possible.

QUALIFYING THE CLIENT

In the description of the sales process above, steps one and two were described as being part of the qualification process. Every professional sales representative develops a system for qualifying the prospect. You need to know if the person inquiring about travel service is truly serious. If you are calling on a prospect, you need to determine whether that prospect has any real potential to use your services.

Getting the initial information should be accomplished in the first minute or so of the session with a prospect. In a travel agency setting for example, where a traveler has come in for the first time, a good set of basic questions to ask if the destination is given initially is as follows:

When do you plan to go?

How long will you stay?

How many people will be traveling?

Have you ever been there before?

Do you prefer to travel independently or in a group?

Possibly ask about basic budgetary considerations at this point.

A hotel sales representative might ask the first two questions above and then add:

How many rooms do you estimate?

How many nights?

Do you need meeting rooms, exhibit space, or meal functions?

An air cargo representative might ask:

What kind of material do you ship?

How frequently?

Is special handling required?

These questions will give the basic parameters from which to work. If the prospective traveler is hedging about answering the above questions, the agent can't be sure the prospect is "real."

If the prospective traveler is not sure about destination, the agent needs to get the rest of the initial information and then start qualifying the person to find out likes and dislikes. Questions such as the following might be asked:

What do you like to do?

When did you take your last vacation?

Where did you go?

What hotel did you stay in?

Did you like it?

What activities don't you like?

Prospects' answers will show preferences for types of activities such as beaches, pools, sightseeing, or nightlife. If a family stayed at deluxe hotels before, they won't be happy with first class this time. Questions about a previous vacation give a good indication of a client's available budget. The more the agent knows about a client the more intelligent the recommendations will be.

PROBING FOR INFORMATION

The agent must probe deeply (almost like a psychologist) when advising a first-time client about a trip. Before making recommendations the agent must be sure what the client really wants. When a couple comes to the office and says "We want to go to Puerto Rico," the salesperson

"How much breathless, exotic living on a romantic South Sea island can I swing for $39.50?"

needs to probe further to see if this is the destination that will meet their needs. While the easiest thing to do would be to pull out a brochure on Puerto Rico, quote the air fare and discuss hotels, this could be a mistake. Do the clients like gambling and nightlife? Do they like the hustle and bustle of a large city? Upon probing, it may be found that the client really prefers a quiet hotel with a good beach and nothing more than a combo in the evening. This couple's reason for asking about Puerto Rico (or any other destination) could be because a relative or friend recommended it. Further questioning could show that the likes and dislikes of the person recommending the destination were totally different from the likes and dislikes of the prospective travelers. A salesperson performs a major service to clients by helping them identify their real needs.

The travel professional must also be careful not to take the easy way out, even if that is what the client seems to want. For instance, extensive advertising and promotion has given the general public the impression that tour packages generally are bargains providing more for the travel dollar. Many vacationers often ask their travel agent: "Do you have a package to . . .?" Package tours are not automatically bargains or even the best value. Many are priced at exactly the sum of the individual parts if purchased separately. Thus, if a couple bought a Caribbean Island package with hotel, ground transportation, and sightseeing tour, priced at the sum of the individual components, and they did not really want the sightseeing tour, they would not be getting the best value for their money or needs.

Often, packages represent good values because of the volume pur-

"You and your bargain tours!
Anything to save a buck!"

chasing power of the tour operator. Sometimes, however, packages cost more than the sum of the parts. Special event packages such as the Super Bowl or the Rose Bowl or Mardi Gras have large profit mark-ups but sell well due to the demand to attend. Other programs include 'development' or 'operations' costs. The existence of such costs is usually noted in the small print in the package brochure—but few customers ever read the small print.

Travel marketers should be aware of the tour package and its potential usefulness. However, those dealing with the traveler directly should be careful to select those packages that meet traveler needs and are good values—not just the easiest to sell with the highest profit.

In another example, a hotel sales manager, talking to the leader of a prospective meeting group might ask:

How many people will be coming?

Will you need single or double rooms?

What meal functions would you like to include?

What audiovisual equipment will you need?

How would you like to have the meeting room set up?

The same process continues, to make the sale, as that described above for the travel agent. The sales process is the same regardless of which segment of travel is being sold.

Qualifying prospects is rarely an automatic procedure. Simple questions and direct answers are not always the case. People are often indefinite concerning dates, destinations, lengths of stay and other key information. They may, for instance, be unwilling to let the salesperson know their true financial situation.

A serious mistake that travel sales people make, in contrast, is giving too much information at one time. The client says "Thank you," and leaves in confusion. It is easy to let the client control the conversation. When this happens, the salesperson is rarely qualifying and much time is wasted.

For example, a prospect may call and ask what the round trip fare to London is. If you automatically decide that the client wants the lowest fare and answer the question by saying, "The lowest fare is $450.00," the prospect could easily just say "Thank you," and leave or hang up the telephone. There is a better way to do it. Give some information, by stating that there are a number of fares that depend upon such things as time of travel, or length of stay. Then add, "When do you want to go?" This brings your client right into the qualification process. By doing this, you differentiate the real traveler from the student completing a school project. You can continue to pin down the prospect and find out what is really wanted with minimum time wasted.

CONTROLLING THE CONVERSATION

In the qualification process, it is better to ask broad, open-ended questions that allow customers to give full information about their desires than to ask simple direct "yes or no" type questions. Instead of asking "Do you like Las Vegas type review shows?" ask "What type of entertainment do you like?" or "What type of evening activities do you enjoy?" With the open-ended question, the salesperson has a future avenue of discussion regardless of the answer given. With a "yes/no" answer, the discussion can effectively be ended if the response is not the one expected. When that happens, the salesperson must back up and virtually start over. The flow of the conversation is stopped and the salesperson has lost control of the conversation. An open-ended response allows the salesperson to continue controlling the conversation and to lead the customer down the path toward a recommendation that will satisfy the needs and result in a sale.

LISTENING EFFECTIVELY

The chapter on communications showed how important listening is in the communication process. Effective listening is also essential in the sales process—especially during the qualification phase. Every person wears an invisible sign. The sign says, "I want to be important!" The best way to make someone feel important is to listen attentively and show that you care.

Several years ago the Minneapolis *Star* did a survey that shows dramatically the results of ineffective listening in a business situation. The objective of the survey was to find out why people did not return to retail department stores after shopping there at least once. The survey

"I'm sorry, but none of these brochures has exactly the trip I've been looking for."

revealed the following information:

1% died

3% moved

9% shopped elsewhere for convenience or because of friends' recommendations

9% shopped elsewhere because of cheaper prices

10% were chronic complainers

68% said "sales persons were indifferent...they didn't seem to listen"

The customer-oriented sales strategy is totally nullified when a salesperson forgets that the customer is the center of activity. Keep your eyes and ears on the prospect. The more effective you are in analyzing the real needs of clients, the more successful your sales will be.

Industry sales trainer Porter Henry provides the following hints for the needs analysis phase:

- Do *not* do all the talking—allow the client time to voice needs and wishes.
- Helping clients discuss their travel plans is the primary purpose of counseling.
- Let the clients know you respect them and that you sincerely care.
- Give clients some positive feedback that relates to their comments.
- Frequently paraphrase what the clients have said—to let them know whether you understand correctly what is being said.

As well as listening to your client, you must know what you are selling. In travel and tourism this means that you must know both the product or service you are providing and the methods by which your company will provide the service. Since tourism is such an intangible, the prospective customer is buying you and your company as much as the product or service you are providing. For example, if you are representing a hotel or chain of hotels, you should thoroughly understand the facilities of your properties (rooms, banquet facilities, recreation activities, amenities) and the way your company does business (credit terms, promotional support activities, type and quality of staffing for the projected event).

When making recommendations, refer to your prospect's needs and show that your recommendation will fit the needs. One very effective technique is to refer to your prospect's statements or preferences. Stating "as you said a moment ago" automatically puts you in the client's frame of reference. Stating "You will like this hotel because you said you like small, intimate places with luxurious facilities" proves you have been listening to your prospect's request. Paint word pictures using colorful language to conjure images to put the prospect in your hotel...on your tour...or on your airline. Do not be dishonest and describe something that doesn't exist; rather emphasize the comforts and amenities that are really there.

Sell the Benefits, Not the Features

Since your job is to fill a need, a most important technique is to sell the *benefits* of a travel product, not the *feature* itself. You must convey to your prospect the real value of your product or service in a way that will appeal to the prospect's emotions. For example, if you are a travel agent or a tour operator selling an escorted tour, one important feature is that the tour is fully escorted. However, you must talk about more than "a fully escorted tour." You must stress the benefits of the escort—being advised of places to eat and sites worth seeing, as well as being provided with direct transportation and baggage handling (no worry about tips, for example).

A major feature of a cruise is that the price is all inclusive. What is the benefit? Budgeting is easier and your prospect need not carry as much cash or travelers checks. There is no right side of the menu with prices, and the choice of food can be made without considering individual item cost. The list goes on and on.

As the previous examples show, the *feature* is a noun, a name for something. The *benefit* is its personalized value to the buyer. Communicating benefits must be more than the transmission of words or facts—it is the transmission of ideas that are understood by the listener,

"Let me give you an idea of what your tour to Britain will include..."

who interprets them according to experiences and purpose. Knowing the benefit will help the prospect feel that wants are being met. In contrast, features have no direct emotional value.

Using Your Own Experience

Porter Henry suggests three other techniques for selling your recommendations. First, refer to your own experience when you have had an experience and your client has not. Referring to your own experience can often be reassuring. This is particularly useful if the prospective client is slightly worried about something. Your personal experience can often allay the fear. Be careful, however. Some clients are know-it-alls. They are experts in everything. Personal experiences will not help with this small percentage of prospects.

Using a Third Party

Referring to a third party is another helpful technique. A satisfied client's reference can be helpful in selling a new client. If the XYZ Company has problems similar to the ABC Company, showing how your service helps XYZ can help sell ABC. Two words of caution are necessary with respect to using references to a third party, however. First, the "third party" should know and approve of you using them as a reference. Secondly, don't overdo it. Some prospects, especially those with well developed marketing plans, resent sales personnel who stress how their product or service helped another company and do not seem to give enough evidence on how the product or service can help the present prospect.

Reassurance

Reassuring your prospect can also help in the sales process. For example, travel agents should recognize that prospective travelers are often unsure about a prospective trip. Rather than salesmanship, they need

"Madame Zenobia, can you tell me if I'll enjoy my tour?"

just plain reassurance. Stating "You're going to have a wonderful time," can be helpful. Reassurance about how details are handled as benefits rather than features is also helpful. One warning at this point, however—Don't oversell! No travel experience can be absolute perfection. Be realistic in your promises.

OVERCOMING OBJECTIONS

You have qualified your client and recommended travel services. Now the client says "No." What do you do?

The above situation is certainly not typical. Rarely will a client say "No" without further comments. Normally, a response would be:

"No, it costs too much."
"I want to think it over."
"I want to go at a different time."

Objections are a normal part of the sales cycle. Some sales people live in fear of the "no." Professional sales representatives, on the other hand, expect objections and are prepared for them. Many see the challenge of salesmanship as overcoming customer objections.

For the most part, objections are actually requests for more information. Many objections indicate that the client has not been totally qualified, and you need to obtain more information on the client's real needs. Then you can determine whether to modify your recommendation or provide additional explanations on why your recommendation is best for the client's needs.

It is essential to prepare for objections. You must anticipate them. A prospect will not generally accept everything you propose. Modifications are a way of life. The give and take during discussions of objections really helps point out what the client is looking for. Listen effectively and be prepared with alternatives. Most important, isolate the objection, discuss it fully with your client, and don't let that objection negatively affect agreements already made. When handling a client's objection, you must make an important decision. Almost on split-second notice you need to determine whether to accept the client's objection and modify your proposal, or to bring the client around to your way of thinking. If the client's objection is valid, obviously, you must have an alternative. If you really believe the client would be better off by accepting your recommendation, take that split-second of thought and then make a polite, diplomatic, low-pressure effort to resell your recommendation.

Porter Henry describes a well-known one-two-three method for convincing your clients to accept a suggestion they have just objected to:

- If you're not sure what's behind the customer's objection, ask about it. If the customer just says "That doesn't sound too good to me," you need to know more about why the client feels that way before you can respond adequately. Don't hesitate if the objection is vague. Ask the client to explain it.

- Meet the customer part way. Never say "No, you're wrong." Avoid arguing—you want the sale. Empathize with the client and agree that he is reasonable. For example, say:
  "Yes, some people do feel that way, but. . ."
  "Yes, that is an important point, however. . ."
  "Yes, it may appear that way at first, but. . ."

- Having met your prospect halfway, explain the reason for your recommendation. You're really going back to the phase of selling your recommendation to the client's interest. Another technique is to admit that an objection is valid, but offset it with other benefits. For example you could say "Yes, the hotel is a very large one, but it has more recreation facilities and a greater choice of restaurants than any other." Sometimes a disadvantage can even be turned into an advantage. When a client objects to a high deposit, you can say "Yes, the deposit is high, but it should be easier to pay the balance when it's due."

It is very dangerous to discredit your competitors when selling your service. Few people like to hear one person discredit another. This particularly applies with regard to one's competitor. You do not prove your own worth by degrading someone else.

When a prospect brings up your competitor's name, you are on safe ground by not being critical of that company. Instead explain the advantages of the services you provide. Knocking the competition can weaken your own company and yourself.

TELEPHONE SALES

The modern term is "telemarketing," but the techniques are not greatly different from the face-to-face sales situation. When planning or participating in telephone sales situations, the basic sales process is the same. It is still necessary to qualify the client (get the initial information and determine what the client really wants). Having determined the client's real needs, it is still necessary to sell your recommendations, overcome objections (if there are any) and most importantly, close the sale. Sound familiar? It should. It's the same basic process.

However, the communications process for telephone sales is somewhat different from face-to-face sales. Some critical factors are missing. Telephone communications is purely verbal. You cannot see the face at the other end of the phone line. There is no body language and little nonverbal communication.

Just as the physically blind have developed heightened senses of hearing, the "blind" telephone salesperson must listen very carefully. Tone and inflection replace body language as signs of the client's true mental state. An experienced telephone salesperson can determine if the customer is truly receptive to recommendations or if there are any hidden objections.

Beyond the lack of visual clues, there is an additional complication in the telephone sales situation. It is much easier to terminate communications than in the in-person situation. A prospect can call and ask "What is the group rate at your hotel?" A simple, direct answer to that question could easily result in the customer saying "Thank you," and hanging up. Any opportunity for developing and closing a sale is lost forever. It is your responsibility as a professional sales representative to gain control of the conversation, find out the details of what the prospect really wants, make recommendations, and close the sale.

IMPORTANCE OF TELEPHONE SALES

The total sales process for many types of travel services can be completed on the telephone without the necessity of personal visits. The sale of hotel reservations and airline reservations and tickets is normally completed over the telephone. The traveler may call the airline or hotel directly or make arrangements through a travel agency. An experienced travel agent can handle even complex, multisegment travel arrangements on the telephone without ever seeing the client. Many long-lasting client-agent relationships continue without either person ever seeing the other.

Very often, however, the telephone is only part of the sales process. The sales representative receives a request for information about the strong potential use of a travel product. The conversation becomes the basis for qualifying the client and setting up an appointment to continue the sales process on a face-to-face basis. The telephone is also a time and money saving method for the sales representative to make direct contacts with potential buyers to determine if there is the potential for a meeting or sales presentation.

Whether receiving calls or making outbound calls to determine client potential, your objective is to sell travel. You want to close the sale with prospects who telephone just as you would with those who you meet face-to-face. Their money is just as good, and their potential may be as great or greater than that of those who contact you in person. If you are receiving an incoming call, once you determine that there is any potential sale, be sure to get contact information (name, address, and telephone number) so that you can follow up. If a client requests literature on your service, send it quickly. If you believe there is potential for a sale, make sure that you always follow up the mailing with a letter or telephone call.

Using Your Voice

Generally speaking your voice is 50% of your personality as judged on first contact in face-to-face situations. On the telephone, it is 100% of your personality—the only means of practicing salesmanship. Not many of us have the trained voices of singers and speakers, but there are some effective methods of improving speech abilities. All too often, our lips don't move, our jaws are stiff and our tongues just hang. We have no expression in our voices. We have what are known as "lazy articulators." Here are a few suggestions which may help:

- Use your articulators (facial muscles) and make a conscious effort to improve your diction.

- Speak with enthusiasm. Put expression into your voice so that you sound warm and friendly.

- Your voice should be heard as a smile is seen. Put a smile on your face while you are on the telephone and the smile will be heard by your client.

- Avoid a monotone. Attempt to vary the pitch of your voice.

- Relieve the strain from your voice by speaking at the normal pitch. The lower pitched tones carry best over the telephone. You will sound more relaxed.

- Speak slowly. Don't run on like a slow record at a fast speed. Don't let your words be lost.

It is even more important to pace your conversation on the telephone than it is when selling face-to-face. After you've made your recommendations and asked for the business, pause. Say nothing. Let the prospect say the next word, no matter how long it takes. Don't lose the sale by talking too much or too soon and giving the prospect an opportunity to back out.

Enthusiasm for the product and the challenge of serving the prospect is an essential ingredient for an effective sales representative. Most travel and tourism products are quite exciting and interesting, and therefore enthusiasm is easy to generate. Enthusiasm is contagious. Your prospect will be enthusiastic about your recommendation if you show your own enthusiasm through friendliness: a personal interest in the prospect and in providing service, and a thorough knowledge of what you are selling. Again a word of caution, however—do not overdo your enthusiasm to the point of appearing insincere or ridiculous. Your prospect may never return.

Don't confuse enthusiasm with doing all the talking. Let your prospect talk. Unless customers have the opportunity to let you know the many things they have on their mind, you will never really know what is wanted. You can easily jump to the wrong conclusion and waste time on an irrelevant detail. Do not dominate and overpower your prospect with conversation. Ask questions and control the conversation at all times.

CLOSING THE SALE

Getting the client's commitment to purchase goods or services should be the goal of every professional sales representative. Without the commitment, all the time and effort invested in qualifying the client, selling your recommendations and overcoming objections was for nothing. No commitment—no sale—no money—no job—no company!

Closing the sale refers to specific techniques that the professional sales-person uses to get the client's commitment. All efforts from the initial stages of the sales conversation must be directed toward the close. The initiative for closing the sale is clearly the responsibility of the salesperson. Too often salespeople avoid or evade this responsibility. Research indicates that

- the salesperson closes only 20% of the time;
- the customer closes 20% of the time;
- and no one closes 60% of the time.

When no one closes, there is no sale.

ASKING FOR THE BUSINESS

Closing the sale is asking for the business. Salespeople ask for the business only 20% of the time because they fear rejection—they fear the client will say "No." The time when you ask for the business is important. The method by which you ask for the business is even more important.

When do you ask for the business? It is effective to ask for the business whenever the prospects have given you a clue that they are ready to buy. Normally the initial close begins when you have qualified the prospects and know what their needs are. If they are not ready, they will raise an objection—by asking a question or indicating a lack of certainty. At this point you overcome the objection (to their satisfaction, of course). It is time to close again. Objections are often stated when the salesperson attempts to close the sale and the customer is not ready. More qualifying or recommending is needed before the close can be effective. Another good time to begin closing techniques is when you have described a benefit of your service and you have seen that the client reacts favorably.

While the anatomy of the sale process separates the closing phase of sales from overcoming objections, the two phases are totally intertwined. It is through understanding a client's objections and responding to them that the professional salesperson identifies those clues which lead to a successful close.

Closing represents the natural end of the flow of the sales conversation. Closing techniques can be soft and subtle, applied on almost a trial basis to determine if the client is ready to buy. Closing the sale does not require high pressure. Rather, it requires sensitivity to each one of the client's reactions.

Kinds of Closes

"Let's see if there is space available." This is the lowest pressure close of all. You are not asking the client for anything—not for money, not even for formal concurrence. If the clients are not ready, they will let you know—with an objection. You must then overcome the objection and try again.

There is another way to move into this type of assumptive close. That method is to say "That seems to cover everything. I'll go ahead and start looking. . ."

A slightly stronger form of close, requiring at least an acknowledgement from the client is to offer to make a reservation. In this kind of close, a travel agent might say "That's the height of the season and I know that space will be hard to get. Let me make the reservation for you now." A hotel sales representative might say "Group space is tight in October. Let me make a tentative reservation." There's always a reason you can use—"The best rooms are reserved early;" "The ship cabins in the price range you are looking for are in the biggest demand;" and so on.

Even when a deposit is required, the assumptive close technique can be effective. You can state "Fine, I'm glad you like that idea. We'll go ahead with the reservations—we'll need a deposit of . . . ;" or "We want to be sure that these (hotel rooms, staterooms, charter seats, etc.) are held for you so we will need a deposit of $_____." If the clients are not ready, they will let you know.

Another soft, low-pressure method of closing is to offer alternate choices. Does the client want A or B? Note that there is an assumption that the client wants something. The following examples of alternate choices can apply to almost any travel service:

"Will this be cash or on a credit card?"

"Do you wish to depart from JFK or LaGuardia?"

"Do you want to leave in the morning or the afternoon?"

"Do you want a sit down banquet or a buffet?"

"It's your wife. Shall I go ahead and tell her that you've decided against taking her to Hawaii?"

"We've narrowed it down to plan A and plan B. Which do you prefer?"

"If space is not available on these dates, will those dates be okay?"

Again, if you have misjudged the timing and the clients are not ready, they will let you know.

Another type of close is based on your knowledge of the travel product you are selling as well as your understanding of client needs. You can make a statement such as "From what you have told me, I know you will be happier with. . ." And move into the reservation phase. You can also say "The XYZ organization had a similar convention in our hotel, very successfully. They really enjoyed the Caribbean dinner. Which day shall we set it up for. . .?" The client's reactions will tell you where to go from there.

When Not to Talk

Too many sales are lost because the salesperson talks too much. This is especially true during the closing phase of the sale. There is one very critical procedure which must be mastered by the professional salesperson—after you have asked a closing question, wait for the client to respond. This powerful pause may be difficult. When you ask a closing question ("Shall I make the reservations?"), you have thrown the ball to your client. Wait for an answer; do not add more information. Do not confuse the client. If the client has a problem, you'll know about it soon enough.

There are many times when you try to get a "Yes" with the above techniques and the client, for some reason, doesn't want to make a decision. If you still believe that your results from qualifying the client are correct and there is a reasonable chance for a sale, you do not have to give up at this point. Offer to do something that will be of interest to the prospect—develop an estimate, get a specific piece of information, or do something else of importance for the client. At least get the client's agreement for a follow-up contact. Then you can try again. Remember, the more complex the situation, the greater number of contacts are necessary to develop the sale.

Many sales can be concluded or saved with proper follow-up techniques. If the only commitment you get from a client is an agreement to let you call back in several days, you must call back. Do not delay and do not forget. Make a note in your calendar or appointment book. Get the information you promised and call back. A good percentage of call backs will convert to sales.

CONCLUSION

If you follow the tested pattern of the sales process; if you use the proper selling tools, including yourself and your belief in what you are selling; and if you understand your client's needs, selling can be pleasant and profitable for both you and your client.

SUMMARY   In the travel and tourism industry a sales representative shows his or her professionalism in appearance, actions, and the way the sales process is handled. A sincere smile and interest in understanding the customer's needs are essential tools for a successful salesperson.

During the sales interview, the salesperson must control the conversation and listen carefully so that the necessary information can be developed. The sales process progresses in these states:

- Qualify the client

- Probing for information to discover what the client really wants

- Selling a recommendation based on the information

- Handling any objections

- Closing the sale

In the selling portion of the interview, the professional will attempt to sell benefits—what the product will do for the client—rather than features of the product. He or she will use such tools as personal experience, third-party references, and reassurance. The professional will also be prepared to meet objections by understanding them, acknowledging them, and then explaining the recommendation once again. Telephone sales interviews will follow the same pattern, but the professional will be aware of the importance of tone of voice and timing.

Closing the sale—asking for the business—is essential to the selling process. It should be done as soon as the salesperson has a clue that the prospect is willing to buy. Closing need not be high-pressure to be effective. Techniques can vary from the very soft-sell assumptive close to stronger approaches. Even if the client does not respond to attempts to close the sale, the professional will offer to provide other services, such as getting an estimate or providing more information. And if no definite response can be evoked, the professional will plan on a follow-up call, knowing that such calls often result in sales.

QUESTIONS FOR THOUGHT AND DISCUSSION

1. *What are the five steps in the sales process? List and describe.*

2. *What is meant by "effective listening"?*

3. *Give three examples of possible closing statements or questions.*

4. *Explain the advice, "Sell the benefits, not the features."*

5. *Give three examples of possible objections a customer might give to a proposal, and how you might overcome them.*

6. *Discuss the similarities and differences between telephone sales and in-person selling.*

12
MARKETING IN TRAVEL AND TOURISM— PRESENT AND FUTURE

As we have seen throughout this study of marketing in the travel and tourism industry, every action taken by a business affects the marketing effort. It is hard to say which part of the marketing process is most important, but it is easy to point out that all parts must work together. Cooperation and integration of all aspects of the process are necessary to obtain the final objectives of any marketing effort—the successful sale of the product or service, and the creation of a repeat clientele. Since all these parts are so important, they will be reviewed here.

The first step in the process is determining just what product is being sold. Management must look at the potential product mix and pull from it the products and services it wishes to sell. Then the manager must examine the potential market and determine what the needs are and how the company can meet these needs. The product must be tailored, if necessary, to meet these needs. Proper research must be done and a determination made of what will motivate the market to actually buy the product. The marketing mix concept should be employed to guarantee a planned approach to the overall market plan.

After these decisions have been made, management must make sure that the proper image is set for this particular market segment. Personnel must be trained to promote this image on the front line. Advertising is usually necessary to inform the potential consumers of the existence of the product and to persuade them to consider purchase. Advertising will develop leads for the business. The sales techniques discussed in Chapter 11 must then be used to actually close the sale. After the sale is made, management must make sure that what was sold is actually delivered. This will ensure satisfied customers and a continuation of the marketing cycle. Satisfied customers will help maintain a positive image for the company, and ensure the long life of the business.

LOOKING TO THE FUTURE

A discussion of marketing would not be complete without a look into the future. Many things happening now may have a considerable impact on the marketing of the travel product in the future. Some of these happenings are in the province of government and regulation; others are in the field of technology; still others are sociological in nature.

AFTER-EFFECTS OF DEREGULATION

When the United States Congress passed the Airline Deregulation Act of 1978, it laid down the framework for deregulating the airline industry by the end of 1984. Since its passage, this law, as it has been phased in, has resulted in the creation and operation of many new, small airlines. These airlines operate with lower costs (newer personnel, no unions, and fewer services) and are marketing primarily on the basis of price differences. The influx of these new carriers has made the public much more price conscious in regard to travel, particularly air travel.

The introduction of new carriers, both the successful and the unsuccessful ones, will continue to influence the future of the air travel market. Established carriers will have to meet this marketing challenge. One of the methods they are using at present is the various frequent flyer programs, which reward travelers who fly regularly on the particular carrier.

These programs are attempts to develop brand loyalty, a customer characteristic that has eluded the airlines in the past. Hotels and car rental companies have imitated the airlines with various gift and incentive programs for the frequent customer. This is a marketing policy that will continue in the future.

TECHNOLOGICAL CHANGES

The advance of technology is another feature of modern life that promises to influence the travel industry. Several hotel properties in major cities have been equipped for teleconferencing. Teleconferencing allows a group of people to see and speak through a TV hookup with others located in another place. Many forecasters feel that teleconferencing will reduce the need for travel. Others feel that rather than reducing the need for travel, teleconferencing will just change some of the methods currently used. All the members of a conference might not be brought to the same place, but instead will gather in four or five different cities. Each location would give the members a regional conference, and each region would be in contact with the other regions through teleconferencing. This would reduce the cost of air travel, since members could travel shorter distances.

The disadvantage of this form of meeting is, of course, the lack of the personal meetings and discussions that take place (and the business that is often done) when all members are physically together. A TV or movie screen can only do so much. For this reason, many disagree on the degree to which this technology will change the nature of travel.

Another technological advance that might affect the marketing of the travel product is the development and advance of the home computer system. Many forecasters feel that this will radically change the manner in which the public buys its airline tickets and makes its hotel reservations. They believe that purchasing will be done from the comfort of the living room over a two-way TV or computer system. Others feel that although a certain amount of travel will be sold in this manner, most travelers will continue to need the personal service they have come to expect.

Confusion over air fares and schedules, questions about the location of hotels, sightseeing opportunities, and the need for help with travel decisions should make the travel agent distribution method necessary into the future.

SOCIOLOGICAL CHANGES

Other trends that have occurred over recent history and that should continue to occur are sociological in nature. Travel to distant places for pleasure used to be the privilege of the wealthy who took long, expensive trips. Today, travel is available to the mass public, and vacations have become shorter in length. The two-week or three-week or longer cruise has become less popular than the one-week cruise. Even vacations to Europe, which used to be at least two weeks long, can now be found for one week or less. In the winter of 1983, Pan American/World had a popular program of long weekend trips to Europe at reduced air fares.

This does not mean, however, that vacations from work are still the automatic two weeks of the past. Workers with seniority frequently earn vacation time of twenty or more days a year. They frequently choose to spread these days through the year, thereby enjoying more than one vacation period. This trend to several shorter trips a year will probably continue into the future.

Travel by the middle class will also continue to grow as more young people become more sophisticated about the world outside their own community. In contrast to the class trip to the state capital, or perhaps all the way to Washington, DC, that was common in the past, high school students today take class trips to exotic places. Often, their parents may not yet have visited these destinations. Once they have tasted travel, these young people will usually continue to make travel a priority item in their budgets as they get older.

CONCLUSION

It is, of course, impossible to predict with certainty what the future holds. All we can say is that as with all things, there will be changes. However, it is highly probable that travel will continue to grow in the future. As it grows and changes, thorough knowledge of marketing techniques will be even more necessary to meet the challenge of tomorrow's travel and tourism industry.

READINGS IN
SALES AND MARKETING
FOR TRAVEL AND TOURISM

Good marketing decisions should be directed by newly identified customer needs. The needs of business travel, as identified by TWA, resulted in the airline's "Airport Express," and "Ambassador Class" services. The rationale and the marketing process based upon this rationale provide good insight into the planning process that goes on within marketing.

TWA'S AMBASSADOR CLASS CAN MAKE MORE PROFITABLE USE OF SELLING TIME

By Jeff L. Warner
Staff Vice President, Passenger Sales, Trans World Airlines

TWA will shortly mount a major campaign to convince America's leading corporations to upgrade their business travel bookings from coach to Ambassador Class. The campaign will be launched with a letter from president C. E. Meyer Jr. to the chief executive officers and chief financial officers of the Fortune 1000 companies.

The mid-section business class service has now been installed on every widebodied aircraft throughout the TWA fleet. TWA's widebodied aircraft—the 747, L-1011 and 767—make up over 70% of our system capacity. Ambassador Class offers substantial advantages that argue for a shift from coach-only travel restrictions to TWA's Ambassador alternative.

The policy of mandating the lowest possible fare for some staff travel was adopted by many cost-conscious companies at a time when the choice was between first and economy class. But there has been a growing realization among company executives that the economy class mandate has not always been of benefit to their business travelers and therefore to their companies.

As travel agents, you have expended enormous effort and time to sift through the available options in search of the lowest possible fares. The hunt through circuitous routings to find promotional and other discount fares takes a costly toll. We are convinced that the campaign to influence corporate policy-makers to authorize Ambassador Class ticketing should relieve agents of some of the pressure under which you now work, as well as yield you a higher commission.

TWA's Ambassador Class advertising, promotional material and president Meyer's letter will remind corporate heads of the wisdom of investing in staff productivity. When the quality of a business trip is enhanced by the spaciousness, comfort and special services provided by TWA's Ambassador Class, the performance and well-being of the employee will inevitably show it.

FIRST-CLASS PERKS, ECONOMICALLY PRICED

As business travel agents you are aware that clients flying Ambassador Class enjoy a number of first-class perks at a cost little above economy—especially on domestic flights where the ticket is priced at modest premiums over the lowest unrestricted coach fare. Special check-in areas, two-by-two seating in an uncrowded separate cabin with convenient carry-on luggage compartments, a choice of entrees, a travel kit on transatlantic flights and other features contribute to an ambience conducive to the work or rest busy business travelers need. The generous pitch, inherited from former first class, assures plenty of stretching space. And on 747 equipment there is an especially quiet zone—16 seats on the flight deck level—for those who prefer to pass up the free feature movie.

In approaching and selling our own business travel accounts, agents will be aided by the business- and consumer-oriented advertising campaign that emphasizes these and other Ambassador Class features. You will do well to ask the chiefs of the companies around you to seek the additional quality that such an upgrade gives to business travel. And to the extent that they are persuaded to see for themselves, you will see the results not only in higher commissions but in increasingly efficient use of your time.

FREQUENT FLIGHT BONUS

In another development that will affect agent sales to the business traveler, TWA is expanding our frequent flyer mileage program to all of our European and Middle Eastern routes. Considering the distances involved, and the extra mileage credits (125% when flying Ambassador and 150% when traveling first class) that passengers can earn, it will not take long for a client to accumulate mileage and collect awards.

These can be used by clients' companies for their employees' future flights. And it is important to note that TWA is the business traveler's carrier that is also the vacationer's airline, flying the Atlantic and Mediterranean as easily as across and throughout the U.S.A. This versatility makes our frequent flyer program appropriate as a motivational incentive that offers a bonus of personal travel—for one, for two or a family.

It is no news that TWA is conscious of the involvement of travel agents in all that we do. When we seek to motivate American business to upgrade its traveling staff members to Ambassador Class, we know we are making selling easier and more profitable for you, who sell some 70% of all TWA's volume. When considering what additional business travel services to offer, we refrain from providing those that clients can get just as readily and effectively from you, their travel agent.

What more should you be aware of that will help you put more satisfied business travelers in "the best seats in the house?"

You know about our one-stop check-in arrangements, at which your clients can receive the boarding passes and seat assignments for every leg of a trip. You know about our pleasant and convenient Ambassador Club, available at the nominal cost of just $45 a year. You are probably aware that you can offer your first- and Ambassador Class clients connecting in and out of New York free New York Helicopter flights between Manhattan and TWA's terminal at Kennedy.

And above all, now is the time to follow through on the major campaign TWA is launching, thereby cashing in on the Ambassador advantage for expanding numbers of satisfied business travelers and promoting a better 1983 for yourselves and your clients.

Lars-Eric Lindblad has developed one of the most successful, high quality, special interest tour organizations in the world. The key to his success is service. The tour participant must always want more. His article stresses the importance of quality, and its concepts can be applied on a broad basis.

SELLING QUALITY TOURS

by Lars-Eric Lindblad, President, Lindblad Travel, Inc.

The world of travel is changing rapidly in our time, but in many ways the fundamentals of travel have remained constant. We are all familiar with the revolution brought by the airlines—which have transported large groups of travelers across the oceans and been responsible for the flowering of tourism that has occurred since 1945.

But travel fundamentals—at least those for good, progressive forms of travel—remain constant. For travel to be truly satisfying, it has always required careful planning, smooth execution. But for tour operators catering to the discriminating, experienced market with quality tours, what is offered must do something else: we are obliged to create an appetite on the part of passengers for still more travel. Said in another way, the quality tour operator is always concerned with producing such good service that the passenger is left asking for more.

It is also important to realize fully that a basic "stripped" tour package is simply not enough for this market. Discriminating travelers want optimum value for the price they pay. They also want an experience worth remembering, a good time—and they certainly want to return with something more lasting than just a suntan.

I am a believer in this travel, the type of travel that really benefits the passenger, particularly people who travel more than once a year. It is important that the passenger is offered a tour that has no surprises and on which all arrangements are top flight. Obviously, I'm talking about a great package—one that really works.

One factor is critical in producing such a package. This is the care with which a destination is developed. Great care must be given to researching and developing a tour's potential. The thing to be avoided at all cost is to go into a country or location—particularly a new one for the tour operator—and exploit it to the fullest. If that happens, a destination is literally spoiled.

By research and development I mean attention to the local cultures and habits, care in not over-trafficking certain tour high points, and concern with creating for the visiting party a sense that perhaps no other person has ever really quite experienced the particular tour in quite the way he or she has.

In another sense, we are talking about preserving the environment and avoiding any sense of routine on a tour. This is one sure way to build excitement and anticipation in the minds and hearts of our participants.

The market for superior travel products should always be strong, where the "great package" is concerned. The upscale market, which we feel is a major growth area of the travel industry, is demanding ever more interesting itineraries. As a result, we are giving stronger emphasis to building maximum quality and interest into our expeditions to provide a continuous incentive to this market. New tours, improved older tours, new frontiers, stronger preparation, better lecturers and guides, and a series of interlocking tours keyed to adjacent regions are all part of the picture. Lindblad's programs in China, Africa, Egypt, India, Europe, and the Galapagos, and for various cruise destinations with the M.S. Lindblad Explorer, have been carefully planned with all of these features in mind in order to appeal increasingly to this discriminating segment of the marketplace. We are now offering interlocking one-week tours in the Orient and Europe as a response to the demand for more flexible and interesting itineraries.

The company considers the total travel experience as one combining social interaction, education and amusement—all arranged thoughtfully in a way that builds quality into tour planning and execution.

We have always felt that no plan can be too carefully drawn up in order to achieve a successful result. Unstinting attention to details is most important. Such things as the right meal or visit at the right time for the right group are critical for good results. This means that there has to be a close dialogue between the tour group and the operator to be sure that expectations are met. The growth of special interest tours, in which we are becoming increasingly involved, is a large reason for being sure that the group gets what it wants. Obviously research and development are important in this area.

There is no question that the special interest tour requires another dimension of research. The successful tour operator must be extremely careful about tuning in early to the special interests of the group. It is not enough to develop a tour that merely is a variation on a conventional tour theme. It is not a question of adaptation. Special interest tours must be approached and built from the ground up, carefully assessing the tastes, style and interests of the group not only in terms of what it wants to see and experience—but how it wants to do these things. In a way, the "how" can be more important than the "what," when a memorable special interest tour is being designed. This is where careful analysis of the group comes into play and is balanced against the time, locale and scope of the tour.

The end result must always be a great travel package. The industry is in serious need of such packages. It is our considered opinion that the future for such carefully researched and developed tours—whether they be for a mixed group or a special interest group—is virtually unlimited. To take advantage of these future opportunities, the tour operator concerned with selling quality tours simply has to make the effort to know as fully as he can the environment in which the tour will operate and tastes of the tour participants.

Many tour operators fail in the quality tour area because they underestimate both the destination and the expectations of the group. It is important to consider what the destination really is, what it can offer in an unspoiled way, and how it can be protected from over-exploitation. Equally important is an understanding of what people on a quality tour expect from the experience. We have found that in essence they want something memorable—as I said above, something more than a suntan.

Only by offering the best, the smoothest operations, the superior preparation and execution can the tour operator be successful in the quality tour market.

"America's Downtown Hotel Boom" describes a resurgence in hotel development. Perhaps history does repeat itself. Hotel development during the early days was city oriented—primarily near railroad stations. Most recent developments have been in suburban and resort locations. Now that downtown city areas are enjoying a renaissance, it is logical that growth in downtown hotels would follow.

AMERICA'S DOWNTOWN HOTEL BOOM

By Walter Roessing

New hotels have been erected or are being built in many of *Frontier's* major destination cities: Denver, Salt Lake, Seattle, Oakland, San Francisco, Houston, Dallas, Detroit and Atlanta. Among the developers are Westin (formerly Western International), Ramada, Hyatt, Hilton, Sheraton and Marriott.

Why are hotels suddenly returning to the "center city"?

I asked that question of Marriott Vice President Ed Fuller because his company recently opened "two new Rocky Mountain highs" in downtown Salt Lake City and Denver.

"The current proliferation of downtown hotels can be attributed to several factors," says the personable Fuller, a 10-year Marriott executive. "First, the downtown hotel boom is part of the urban renaissance. As a result of this rejuvenation, some center cities are under-roomed.

"Second, hotels have been drawn downtown by the introduction of modern, multi-use complexes. Often called urban malls, they typically consist of some combination of a hotel, office tower and retail space. They upgrade the downtown area and become a center of activity.

"Marriott recently opened a high-rise hotel in Salt Lake City that is directly across from the Salt Palace Convention Center/Sports Arena and interconnects with a shopping mall. Denver's Center City complex, which opened in February, is a combination 42-story office building and Marriott hotel."

Other hotel companies like Hyatt and Westin also have recognized these urban malls as "where the future lies." For example:

A 460-room Westin hotel will make its debut in early 1983 as an integral part of The Galleria, Dallas' first major multi-use development. Hyatt, already a participant in four such complexes, is building a hotel as part of Oakland's $88-million City Center Project.

CONVENTION BUSINESS GROWTH

Yet another reason for the downtown surge is the rather incredible growth of the convention business.

"There's a big demand for hotel rooms that are conveniently located close to the midtown convention centers," says Robert Richards of the American Hotel and Motel Association.

"Ten years ago only 15 U.S. cities could provide facilities for a trade show with 20,000 visitors. Now there are 28 cities with *new* convention centers and over 100 cities capable of handling large conventions. Every big city wants a piece of the convention business because it brings big dollars to restaurants, department stores, theaters and sports arenas. And it has created a demand for new hotels."

Moreover, this remarkable proliferation is bringing forth a new kind of competition among hoteliers.

A prime example of this competition is "specialization," according to Pat Foley, president of the Hyatt Hotels Corporation.

He explains, "A hotel totally for non-smokers has just been announced in Texas. There are hotels being built that consist entirely of suites, including kitchen facilities. There's a new hotel in Japan where rooms are simply 6 by 4 foot compartments, for lying down guests only, at a fraction of the cost of a regular accommodation.

"At Hyatt, nine of our hotels have corporate board rooms with permanent board room tables for top-level meetings away from company headquarters. We also provide a variety of physical fitness facilities for the traveler who doesn't want to interrupt his or her fitness routine while away from home.

"Hotels may some day set up class levels within a property, such as the airlines do, and sell rooms and services accordingly. In a limited way, some hotels already offer this service."

Most of the new first class and luxury downtown hostelries have VIP floors or concierge levels—a plushier, more luxurious and more expensive "hotel within a hotel."

Here's a capsule look at some of the VIP and concierge levels now in vogue:

Hyatt's *Regency Club* is the name given to the separate deluxe areas in 39 of that chain's U.S. facilities. The pampering of guests includes free continental breakfast, late afternoon complimentary hors d'oeuvres and wine, and a concierge to handle every need from transportation arrangements, theater tickets and restaurant reservations to secretarial services. A private lounge for reading or small client meetings also is available.

"HOTEL WITHIN A HOTEL"

Frequently located on the top floors of Sheraton's larger hotels, the *Sheraton Towers* concept truly is a "hotel within a hotel." Express elevators whisk you directly from the lobby to a reception area with a separate registration desk. And at a guest's beck and call is concierge service, limousines and an elegantly decorated private room for relaxing, meals and bar service. The "club room" at New York's Sheraton Centre Towers provides a butler, china service, and foreign and domestic newspapers.

Ramada's *Renaissance Clubs* are located in the new deluxe-category Renaissance Hotels, the first of which debuted in Denver last summer. Guests receive decorator-designed room accommodations, 24-hour maid and concierge service, an "honor" bar and such special amenities as terry lounging robes, complimentary newspapers and high-quality toiletries.

"Such amenities—influenced in part by the European 'style' of running a hotel—are designed for the individual traveler who wants only the very best in accommodations and service and is willing to pay for it," says James Hanlon of The Sheraton Corporation. "Recent studies have shown there is a significant demand for this kind of service."

Several other chains offer similar red carpet treatment and super-deluxe floors. Marriott has the *Concierge Level* and *Club Marquis;* Hilton the *Hilton Towers;* Westin the *Plaza Tower;* Intercontinental the *Six Continents Club;* and the four Fairmont Hotels in Denver, Dallas, New Orleans and San Francisco feature the *Fairmont Circle.*

Among the perks offered by these chains are express check-in and check-out, currency exchange and translation, room exercycles, free airport transportation, cognac and cigars for men, personalized luggage tags, and often flowers, wine, cheese and other gifts from the management.

Sometimes a concierge can perform "miracles" for the VIP or would-be VIP.

The urbane concierge in a downtown San Francisco hotel regularly provides tickets to "sold out" shows, arranges for admission to membership-only clubs and sports facilities, charters yachts and recommends restaurants outside his bailiwick. When the Rolling Stones were in San Francisco last October, they wanted to play handball where nobody would pay any attention to them; a concierge found them a private court.

JUST THE BEGINNING

John Pignataro, a Sheraton corporate vice president, says that city center hotels of the future will offer even *more* special services to their clientele. He cites several examples:

"Guests will be able to rent mini video cameras from their hotel to capture their vacation on video cassettes and play it back to unsuspecting friends back home. Other portable marvels which are either already available on a rental basis from hotels, or soon will be, are pocket pagers, briefcase telephones and pocket stenographers—voice activated units which give you an immediate print-out of your dictation."

Many hotel executives are convinced that the lodging industry also is on the verge of a new technological era. In fact, Hyatt President Foley prognosticates what businessmen can expect at the midtown hotel of the future.

"While I don't think we'll see a robot as a room service waiter in our lifetime, I do think we'll see the creation of full-scale communications centers in hotels.

"The telephone message from the secretary trying to reach the traveling boss would be extinct. Instead of a telephone call, a memo could be sent instantaneously. You could have a video conference on a very private terminal with your supervisor or your subordinates. You could conduct a meeting with employees in various parts of the country during a convention coffee break."

Other forecasts include:

- A self-cleaning bathroom.
- Hotel rooms sold on a standby basis like some airline seats.
- Hotels offering a "supermarket" of rooms. That is, one room may come with a universal gym, another with a hot tub or sauna, and others with different accessories like small computers.

Pignataro adds, "In the not too distant future, automation will enhance every trip—business and pleasure alike.

"Television sets in all guest rooms will double as computer video displays which will enable you to shop from your room, review a list of events in the city, reserve theater tickets, view a travelogue of the area, and summon up a display of telephone messages taken in your absence. And wherever you may be, a computerized sleep channel on your TV set will lull you to sleep with sights and sounds of breaking waves blocking out big city noises."

Marriott's Fuller, Hyatt's Foley and Sheraton's Pignataro all believe that automation means *more*, not less, personalized service to businessmen, tourists and vacationers registered in downtown hotels.

Pignataro insists that, "Computers will assume all the tedious record-keeping tasks while personnel will be freed to spend more time doing what they should be doing—servicing the guests."

Two classes of service (first and coach) have been the standard on most airlines for many years. However, experimentation with more than two classes of service is not new to the industry. In the mid 1960s United Airlines experimented with three classes of service, "red, white and blue." The middle class was in the middle of the plane with two seats on one side of the aisle and three seats on the other. (In the 1960s so-called wide-bodied aircraft such as the Boeing 747 and L1011 did not exist.) The middle class sold at a price that was a few dollars above coach in cost and provided wider seats and free liquor.

"TWA's Ambassador Class" and "United Coach—That's Class" represent current—but differing—thoughts on marketing to the needs of the business traveler. TWA (and American as well) have now brought back the middle class of service. The TWA article indicates how Ambassador Class initially failed in domestic service. Now it is again in use after successes in so-called "business classes" on international routes. United, on the other hand, has made an opposite move. Instead of copying Ambassador Class, a service which sells above coach but below first class fares, it is upgrading all transcontinental coach service with better meals, free champagne, and other amenities. Who will win? Only the marketplace will tell.

TWA

Two of TWA's most successful marketing campaigns in recent years began as attempts to satisfy customer needs. Business travelers—the backbone users of our product—were becoming increasingly disenchanted with the long lines and full airplanes spawned by the new deregulated era of travel. They told us that they would gladly pay a premium to make their trips more comfortable. TWA responded to what the customer was saying—initially with Airport Express, and later with Ambassador Class service.

Nobody likes to stand and wait in a line. New Yorkers "stand on line" and the English "queue-up", but no matter what they are called—lines are as unavoidable and as hated as those other two infamous certainties, death and taxes.

By early 1978, TWA had completed the process of automating all of its domestic airports. PARS, the airline's computer reservations system, had the capacity to issue boarding passes and store customer flight and personal information such as name and credit card number, and to transfer it to a ticket and boarding pass. Not coincidentally, other major airlines were only beginning to automate their airport facilities, a more extensive program for them, because of the number of domestic cities they serve.

Research indicated, and still does indicate, that the amount of time spent waiting in lines had a significant impact on the customer's satisfaction with the overall airline experience. Checking baggage, picking up tickets, getting boarding passes, boarding the airplane, de-planing, waiting for baggage—air transportation seemed to be an endless series of waitings-in-lines. TWA felt that by simplifying the customer's airport experience by eliminating one or two reasons to stand in line, the customer's travel would be less stressful and more enjoyable.

Thus was born "Airport Express." Trans World Airlines already had curbside check-in and luggage racks on most planes, greatly reducing baggage delays. Airport Express was designed to allow all other airport service functions for a passenger's entire trip to occur within one period of contact with TWA customer service personnel—by assigning seats on all TWA flights in an itinerary and by issuing boarding passes for all of those flights. At the initial check-in period, TWA saved the passenger from going through the same process upon changing planes and upon returning.

Since other airlines could not quickly match our service program, TWA's advertising of this exclusive service was direct and hard-hitting. All passengers were encouraged to pick up their boarding passes in advance, and TWA customer service people were told to offer this service whenever possible. For a time, TWA lost sight of for whom Airport Express was designed, the business traveler.

The customer solicitation program, offering advanced seat assignments and boarding passes, was so successful that soon most TWA passengers were taking advantage of Airport Express. Those knowledgeable about the airline business know these three things to be true.

1. Customers often do not cancel reservations and often book duplicate reservations, therefore,

2. Airlines oversell flights, that is, they accept more reservations than they have seats, and

3. Business travelers often make their travel plans at the last minute.

The combination of these factors left the procrastinating, fullfare business traveler without any of the benefits of the service. Leisure travelers on discount fares had their seats and boarding passes, while the business traveler waited until a few minutes before departure to find out which seats would remain after the no-shows failed to honor their reservations and seat assignments.

The solution to this marketing paradox was simple; direct advertising and solicitation of Airport Express to the target, the business flyer. Other customers' requests for advance seat assignments and boarding passes were still fulfilled, but their use of these services was no longer solicited. Advertising of Airport Express was reduced from the "major campaign" status to a more selective direct mail and advertising approach. TWA advertised Airport Express in *The Wall Street Journal* and *Business Week* rather than in *The Daily News* and *People Magazine* in order to reach this target market.

Airport Express has become one of the key determining factors for business travelers in selecting TWA over other airlines. Competitors have copied the program, and some are still developing similar services.

TWA is still fine-tuning the marketing of the Airport Express product. Current research indicates that "getting through the airport fast" is good, but consumers are more concerned with having time to do other things at home or at the airport. As a result, TWA's message to the target market may change, but the program components will not.

It is important to remember that the entire concept of Airport Express originated from a customer *need*, that manifests itself in a *desire* not to have to stand in lines. TWA took an action that has led to customer satisfaction.

NEED ⟶ DESIRE ⟶ ACTION ⟶ SATISFACTION

The above cycle repeats itself in every buying decision and a good program and marketing campaign should primarily be concerned with how the need of the customer can be fulfilled.

Another source of irritation to business travelers is sitting next to, eating the same meals, and getting the same "ride" as a passenger on vacation who has paid considerably less for his ticket, and is traveling with screaming infants or children whose tickets were obtained at even greater discounts, or for free. Frequent business travelers (FBTs) have pleaded with airlines to give them more for their full fare ticket—to get them out of the elbow-to-elbow compartment and into an area with more room and better service. They said they would even pay a premium, above their coach fare, for such a service.

Once again, TWA responded to the customer's needs with the introduction of "Three Class Service" in late 1978. The plan of three class service was arbitrarily to divide the coach compartment into two sections, one Full Fare Coach and one Economy, and to give the full fare passenger priority liquor and meal service and attend to the economy passengers as time permitted. Full fare coach passengers were seated in the front of the coach compartment, with the middle seat vacant when possible. Three Class Service lasted less than two months, but lessons were learned that are still being used today.

Among the reasons for the failure of this marketing and service program were:

- Multi-stop domestic narrowbodied aircraft flights on which through passengers would have to change their seats at intermediate stops because the percentage of full fare versus economy passengers would change.
- Full fare passengers didn't get increased service; economy passengers got less.
- There were no dividers or curtains between full fare and economy, complicating in-flight service delivery.
- Nonsmoking full fare passengers and nonsmoking economy passengers had a section of smoking full fare passengers in between them.
- Customer complaints from all passengers were overwhelming.

In mid-1979, international airlines began business-type classes on their transatlantic flights. TWA called theirs Ambassador Class. Fares were higher than full fare coach, but still considerably less than First Class. The problems TWA encountered with Three Class Service were addressed; Ambassador Class was a separate compartment, made possible by the all-widebodied international fleet; service was upgraded to include free drinks and headsets, an improved menu, a higher flight attendant-to-passenger ratio and other amenities. The seating configuration was six-abreast instead of nine or ten as in coach. The timing coincided with TWA's introduction of an improved First Class service product, Royal Ambassador Class, allowing us to integrate both into our services marketing plan.

The extensive domestic and international makeup of TWA's route structure presented a unique opportunity. Since some of the same aircraft used internationally were also used domestically, TWA was the only airline that had a Business Class compartment on flights operating within the United States. The airline accelerated the reconfiguration schedule for its aircraft and isolated the completed planes, those with Ambassador Class compartments, on transcontinental routes. Early in 1981, TWA introduced Domestic Ambassador Class on all coast-to-coast nonstop flights. The components of Ambassador Class and the experiences of our earlier, ill-fated attempt at Three Class Service helped make our product popular with frequent business travelers.

This Domestic Ambassador Class introduction put competitors at a disadvantage. Their reaction was to lower their First Class fare to Trans World's Ambassador Class level, which at times was only one dollar higher than coach. TWA held the First Class price firm and, surprisingly enough, continued to carry good loads on First Class at nearly twice the coach fare, serving normal First Class customers, while literally filling our Ambassador Class cabin as well.

TWA's major competitors are still trying to catch up. They are not expected to add Business Class to their planes because their widebodied aircraft are also used on routes to Hawaii, the Caribbean, and Florida, markets that are almost exclusively leisure and price-sensitive.

This fall, TWA has introduced Ambassador Class and Sleeper Seats on all of its widebodied fleet, including our 767s in all markets those aircraft serve. Now, whenever a passenger flies on a TWA 747, L-1011 or 767, they do have a choice. They can enjoy an opulent service in First Class, a comfortable working environment in Ambassador Class, or an economy service as good as any in the business.

TWA has also gained. We have become the preferred airline of business travelers across the Atlantic. We have improved our yield compared to competitors. And, most important to TWA's future, we have proven ourselves to be sensitive to the needs of the business traveler and those frequent business travelers have responded by choosing TWA for their business travel.

Reprinted with permission of United Airlines. Red Carpet Club newsletter, March 1983.

MARKETING HIGHLIGHTS
UNITED COACH — THAT'S CLASS

In today's economic environment, most corporations and individuals are looking for travel savings as never before. Knowing this, instead of creating another more costly class of service, United recently introduced "Class Coach" on all transcontinental flights from New York, Newark, Boston, Philadelphia, and Dulles to Los Angeles and San Francisco. We will direct our efforts at providing superior coach service at very competitive prices.

For some travelers the dollar premium for business class is as much as $150 to $200 over the fare you'd pay in the coach section. Based on this fare differential and our knowledge of the market place, we anticipate a very small demand for this product.

Our objective is to provide quality transcontinental coach service. United's transcontinental "Class Coach" includes more leg room, complimentary champagne with meals, unique dessert-cart service on afternoon departures, and fold-down center tables on most flights. We've also made sure we're fully competitive in the basics. That includes a full range of competitive low fares, meal service with a choice of three entrees, a wide selection of inflight entertainment, curbside baggage check-in and advance seat assignments with roundtrip boarding passes. As for schedules, we've retimed several flights to more convenient times as well as offering more nonstop widebody flights than any other airline.

Coast to coast — there's no value equal to United's "Class Coach." We hope we'll have the opportunity to share this Class and value with you soon.

"Airline Marketing" shows the role of marketing in the development and growth of Delta Airlines. The article was originally a speech
to the American Hospital Association. (That means that the comments
with respect to the role of travel agents in the marketing process were
not made to flatter travel agents.) The speech emphasizes the integration of service patterns and customer satisfaction with sales efforts and
advertising to form a total marketing program.

AIRLINE MARKETING

*(A speech by W.W. Hawkins, Delta Airlines' Assistant Vice-President,
Marketing, to American Hospital Association, May 5, 1980.)*

Unfortunately, for many years airline marketeers have been considered "ticket sellers" or "order takers" by many of our colleagues.
The cruel irony of this, now that many of our peers feel intimidated by a
sagging economy and the uncertainties of deregulation, is that they are
looking to us in marketing and saying: "Boy, do *you* guys have a problem. What are *you* going to do about all of the terrible things facing us?"
You will note that there's a good deal of second person thinking in
those comments. I am confident that once we weather the present
storms—and I'm positive we will—we will find that our colleagues will
be proud of the way *we* have handled it all.
The truth of the matter is that marketing has played a significant role in
the development and growth of the airline industry for many years. It
has, however, taken on some new looks in the past couple of years and
particularly in the last few months. We have, for all of our fifty year
history, been in the business of trying to influence customers. In the early going we had to convince people that they should fly in the first place.
Then we had to compete with all forms of ground transportation for
many years. After that, air transportation began to be accepted as a
viable means of travel. With the advent of the jet airplane, airlines soon
became the dominant means of intercity transportation. In fact, airlines
now account for 85% of all commercial intercity transportation.
We have been highly competitive for years. One of the great ironies of
this is that due to the nature of our business, our biggest competitors are
our biggest interline customers. You may want to think about just how
much business you can generate among yourselves. It is inevitable in
our industry that this must happen, as there are many destinations that
an originating passenger simply cannot reach by traveling entirely on

one airline. For this reason, we spend a lot of time actually calling on the reservations, ticketing and sales people of other airlines to keep them fully apprised of our schedules, connecting points, in-flight amenities, etc. Inasmuch as all airlines reservations systems are automated, it is also imperative that we make sure that our flights are favorably displayed in the computers of other airlines. It is amazing how much intelligence you can pick up from airline employees who are in constant contact with the public. We keep these people adequately supplied with information on any new service features or schedules which will make their daily selling jobs easier.

Speaking only of my company, I can tell you that over half of our total sales are made by travel agents. There are presently over 20,000 appointed travel agents in the United States who are authorized to sell our services, in return for which they receive a commission from the airlines. The customer does not pay a fee for this service. This is very big business to the airlines. For instance, in 1981, travel agents sold approximately $1.96 billion worth of travel on Delta alone. Delta's total passenger revenues were $3.5 billion.

It is imperative that we stay in close touch with the needs of our agents and keep them fully aware of any changes in our service pattern. They must be kept advised of service features which would make our service more attractive to their clients while being profitable for them.

Travel agents are so important to the airline that for the last few years we have been busily engaged in placing automated reservations systems in their offices, which would give them direct access from their offices into our central computer systems just as our own reservations offices have. It is also a matter of highest priority for us to see that service received from us keeps us competitively strong.

We expend a tremendous amount of energy providing a high level of service, which will, hopefully, influence travelers to want to do business with us and influence travel agents to want to book our flights. This is where the service delivered by our professional employees becomes a very important factor.

We enjoy the finest record in our industry in customer satisfaction. The only measure we have for this is a statistical report prepared by the CAB, which records the number of passenger complaints they receive per 100,000 passenger enplanements. Delta has consistently finished number one in fewest complaints received. We feel this must contribute significantly to our overall boarding records and consequently manifests itself on the bottom line of our financial statements, where we finished with a respectable profit in the first quarter of 1980, compared to frightening losses experienced by most other trunk carriers. No matter how great your marketing effort is and how clever your advertising is, if you aren't producing the service, you'll find both your customers and your agents avoiding you. It is absolutely imperative to build loyalties based on service. Repeat business demands it. For this reason we consider customer service and follow-up on complaints an integral part of our marketing effort. Many times we have converted an unhappy customer into a regular customer and, in many cases, an outright fan.

A marketing strategy which we pioneered is our so-called hub and spoke traffic-generating philosophy, which simply means we will fly some short-haul markets such as SAV-ATL, AGS-ATL, JAX-ATL, etc., if we can connect the traffic to our long-haul segments such as ATL-LAX, ATL-SFO, ATL-SEA, etc. This is one reason we have the largest single airline operation in the world in Atlanta. Last August, for example, we boarded over one million passengers here for a world record. However, seventy percent of those passengers originated at a point other than Atlanta. You can afford the less profitable short hauls if by properly managing them you can achieve good loads on your profitable long-haul flights.

We have found that different markets have very many peculiarities that set them apart. It gets to be a real challenge to try to fit the right service patterns to the right markets. For example, we have some markets that are for the most part vacation or pleasure oriented. A good example would be our Florida, Bahamas, and Bermuda markets. These markets by their very nature are more likely to be patronized by customers looking for discounted fares and economical vacation packages. We do not package tours ourselves, nor do we derive any income from them. Rather we work with tour operators to produce and promote tours which can be sold in conjunction with our air service. Our only revenue source is a seat sold on our airplane. Years ago we pioneered the so-called package vacation and encouraged the Miami Beach hotel operators to start keeping their properties open in the summer months. Our idea was to keep our aircraft better utilized and we felt the hotels could better maintain their staffs, their facilities, maybe make a little money and certainly enhance their area as a desirable vacation destination. It has been an overwhelming success.

We have also been very fortunate in having a route system which has been seasonal in nature. For instance, our north-south routes (Midwest and Northeast to Florida) have historically been strong winter markets. Our east-west routes (Southeast and Southwest to California) have been strong summer markets. This has enabled us to shift larger flight equipment on a seasonal basis and heavy-up our schedules to accommodate the varying demands. Our promotional and advertising activities obviously follow the same pattern.

Last year we engaged in a new promotion from the Midwest and Northeast to Florida. After taking a look at our advance bookings for May and June, we felt we had to do something to try to generate some traffic. We filed an innovative "area fare," which gave a common fare from several cities in the Northeast to Florida and from the Midwest to Florida. We went to a tour operator who worked with some Florida hotels and a rental car firm with the same low traffic problems we faced and they came up with a 4 day, 3 night package in Florida at selected quality hotels and threw in a car for $99 for four people. You can't stay at home for that! Anyway, it is generating traffic and at least salvaging something from an otherwise bleak period.

One of the strangest things to hit any industry has occurred in the airline industry recently. With fuel costs going absolutely out of sight—our increase in the last year was 83%—the managements of some carriers, confronted with quite a relaxed atmosphere in the marketplace, have decided to get into a price-cutting war. How in the world they can reconcile this position is totally incomprehensible to us. For competitive purposes we, and other carriers, have met a lot of these discount filings. Price competition is fine if economic conditions are satisfactory, but we feel that other forms of competition would better serve our industry at this time.

We are seeing some really wild promotional efforts in our marketing recently. United, American and TWA are running contests to give away free trips. We are not sure this will generate much traffic but you can bet that we will watch it very, very closely. This probably is the forerunner of many merchandising efforts which will be new to our industry such as premiums, discount coupons, trading stamps, etc.

And there may be some other twists, too. Already we have seen proposals to place ticketing devices (similar to automated tellers at banks) in supermarkets, branch banks, etc. There's no doubt about it, our industry is changing rapidly.

Marketing is going to become more and more important to airlines as some will literally be fighting for survival. Take the case of one major carrier, which has dropped service to a number of smaller cities only to announce that they will soon enter the long-haul New York to Los Angeles and New York to San Francisco markets where there are already six incumbent carriers. Somebody is going to get hurt in that one. It may turn out to be a real bloodbath, as there is just not enough traffic to support that many carriers. In the short term the public will probably benefit from the price war which was already started there. In the long term some airlines may disappear. That would hurt the economy, deprive even more cities of air service, and do damage to the world's finest air transportation system, which has put more service into more markets by more carriers with more competition with greater variety and at lower rates and fares than exists anywhere else on earth.

One last item I'd like to cover is advertising. Our advertising, which is an integral part of our marketing, is basically hard sell, what is known as retail advertising. We keep it simple. It's as simple as where, when, and how much. Said another way—destinations, schedules and fares. We want to give the consumer as much information as we can about the basic product. We don't like image or corporate advertising. If our schedules are convenient and priced right, it's left in the hands of our 36,000 employees to deliver the kind of service that makes the sale and provides the total service which will keep the customer coming back to us. We do highlight our personnel as "Delta Professionals" in some national ads but other than that we tailor our ads to each individual city we serve, as each market is indeed different based on the destinations we serve from it and the type of aircraft we fly there.

Rather than explaining one carrier's approach to the challenge of marketing effectively to the business traveler, this article summarizes strategies for a number of carriers.

CARRIERS STEP UP SERVICE FOR FREQUENT TRAVELERS

Inflation and a softening dollar may cut a sizeable chunk out of leisure travel this year, but business will go on as usual.

That's the opinion of most domestic airlines who report that businessmen, convention and incentive groups represent about half the total passengers flying between major cities on their route system. Moreover, they say, the first class business share may climb even higher in 1979 because of recent fare reductions and the narrowing gap between the cost of a coach and first class ticket. (First class fares, which cost 67 percent more than economy at the beginning of 1978, now run only 70 percent more.)

STEADY, STABLE MARKET

Unlike pleasure travel, which may go by the wayside when budgets are cut, business traffic is largely mandatory and usually frequent; they say, "It's a steady, stable market that can turn out large profits for travel agents—particularly those aware of the special services we offer both in flight and at the airports," one airline spokesman said.

Carriers questioned in a recent *Travel Agent* survey disclosed a wide variety of services geared specifically for the business traveler. Some pointed out recent reductions in first class fares, inauguration of shuttle service, special seating and meal plans especially targeted for the businessman, while others mentioned conveniences such as special baggage tags and I.D. cards, airport lounges offering conference facilities, working desks, interpreters and free soft drinks and snacks.

Several stressed newsletters or flyers sent regularly to frequent passengers, which contain information on new services, flight and route changes and current timetables. Teleticketing, the United Air Travel Plan and a computerized reservations center, were among other features ticketed off by carriers as essential for the frequent traveler, along with staff assistance on choosing convention sites and packages with built in business features.

The following is a carrier-by-carrier rundown of airline services offered to frequent travelers:

- *American*—"Fifty-three percent of our passengers are business people," according to a spokesman "and we cater to them with special meal selections, first-class check-ins at 17 airports and our Sabre computer used by 800 travel agents and a number of commercial accounts." The carrier's Admiral's Club membership (available at $35 per year) offers conference room rentals; lounges with bar and complimentary coffee at a number of airports, including a new club at LaGuardia Airport in New York. A quarterly newsletter called "Insights" contains current information on facilities, new routes and informative destination features.

DELTA: 50% BUSINESS TRAVEL

- *Delta*—About 50 percent of the carrier's total traffic is business-motivated. Although a variety of fare structures are available, the recent reduction in first-class fares may generate more sales, even if legislation is passed prohibiting their use as tax deductible, according to a spokesman. Delta offers a variety of meal plans such as low-calorie, dietary and ethnic, providing they are requested at the time of reservation. Top cities for business traffic are Atlanta, Chicago, Dallas, Boston, New Orleans and Detroit. Special convention check-in desks and procedures are offered at airports in Boston, New York (Kennedy), Atlanta, Chicago, Detroit and Miami, and many of these and other major stations have conference rooms.

- *Continental*—Business travelers account for 52 percent of its traffic, and 30 percent of these purchase their tickets through travel agents. The carrier's Statesman Reservation System contains a personal profile of frequent travelers and permits faster ticketing with a simple code number. A Coach Pub on DC-10 aircraft serves slight snacks, beer and wine, and offers video games. There is also a first-class buffet and table for four provided on a first-come, first-served basis, provided a reservation is made. Annual dues for Continental's Presidents' Club is $35, $30, based on nine members. There is no charge for spouse. The carrier assists with convention planning, business meetings and incentive programs publishes a guide series offering information on particular destinations and types of accommodations there.

- *Eastern*—The carrier has an air shuttle for business people on its New York-Boston and Washington, DC runs seven days a week. Ninety-five percent of the Monday-Friday shuttle passengers are business people, according to a spokesman. On its L-1011 flights to Washington, it provides a section behind first class where no movies are shown for businessmen who wish to work. Commercial female passengers are also catered to with Eastern's quarterly "Business Woman" brochure, mailed to frequent women travelers free of charge. It contains profiles on businesswomen and tips on what to pack, hotel accommodations and car rentals, as well as flight information. Eastern's Ionosphere Clubs have 100,000 members, at least 90 percent business people. Annual dues are $30 (free for spouse) and offer telephone facilities, seat selection, change in reservations, snacks and soft drinks, working desks and stationery at 22 airports. Some clubs have private meeting rooms, but reservations must be made in advance. First class fares will continue to do well, particularly since they have been cut, according to a spokesman. "If first class can no longer be tax deductible, we feel businessmen will simply take the deduction on the coach fare and absorb the difference," he said.

• *National*—The carrier can book hotels and arrange car rentals for conventions. It also provides mail and telephone service to remind members of convention dates and offers assistance in designing incentive travel packages. National's Sun King Clubs offer club rooms at 18 major airports, including JFK and LaGuardia in New York, Newark, Washington, DC, Jacksonville, Orlando, Tampa, Palm Beach, Ft. Lauderdale, Miami, New Orleans, Houston, Los Angeles and San Francisco. Many have a multi-lingual staff, and the Miami conference area has a blackboard. Annual dues are $40, $350 for lifetime membership. The carrier also provides special meals on advance notice and has recently developed tour packages for business travelers that include hotel and car rental along with complimentary wine and a daily copy of the *Wall Street Journal*.

• *Northwest Orient*—A VIP Travel Plan caters to the frequent traveler by providing special bag tags and I.D. cards. The carrier's Top Flight Club lounge is available to everyone with a Northwest ticket. Locations are in Chicago, Cleveland, Miami, Minneapolis, New York (JFK), Seattle, Tampa, Washington, DC (National) and at Northwest's Orient stations. The lounges have meeting facilities and a hostess who can expedite seating. "The business market is vital to us and consequently 75 percent of our national advertising is placed in business media," a spokesman said.

• *United*—The carrier flies from 50,000-70,000 business people a day and because of first class fare reductions is doubling the size of this section on its medium and long-haul routes. It has also installed a separate first class check-in counter at 22 airports. Business travel is highest at the airports in Cleveland, Chicago, New York, San Francisco and Los Angeles, a spokesman noted. Membership in the Red Carpet Club is $35 per year, $10 for spouse. There are 19 rooms available for conferences and the club distributes a bi-monthly newsletter providing special courtesies, discounts on rental cars, restaurants and hotels. United is also installing a stock quotation computer in the O'Hare lounge (Chicago) for all-day readings of market activity. Closing prices, posted in all its lounges, will be posted there as well. The carrier's Executive Air Travel Program has replaced its 100,000 Mile Club and also offers a bi-monthly newsletter to members.

• *Western*—The VIB (Very Important Business) Club offers a 20 percent discount on purchases at inflight shops for members and issues a quarterly newsletter containing information on fares and amenities. Western will also cash personal checks up to $50. It provides computerized reservations with a new IBM 370 Accu-Res system, which is tied to American's Sabre system at Western's domestic stations. The carrier has 13 Horizon Clubs, and privileges in Eastern's Miami lounges. Membership dues are $35 per year. Travel agent sales are picking up, according to a spokesman, who noted that 55-60 percent of the carrier's bookings now come through retailers.

• *TWA*—As a special service, TWA passengers can make advance seat assignments if they wish. For example, the non-smoking passenger can arrange long before flight for a seat in a non-smoking section. Another convenience, a spokesman noted, is that a passenger flying roundtrip can pick up the return boarding pass at the same time that he checks in for outbound flight.

Direct-mail flyers keep the frequent TWA traveler informed of changes in schedules, rates, and services that may affect him. Published four times a year, these mailings keep the traveler posted on major schedule changes from home cities, and provide updated flight and services changes. They also help keep him informed of general trends in the airline business which could affect the passenger.

⟶

Reprinted with permission of *Frequent Flyer* magazine, February 1983.

"Airport Chaos: The Search for Sanctuary," shows another aspect of the airlines' recognition of the needs of frequent flyers. Ground service problems have been major complaints of the frequent traveler. From a marketing standpoint, repeat business is far more profitable than new business. As a result, airlines are now emphasizing the services they provide both in the air and on the ground to the frequent business traveler. This article describes efforts to minimize airport time as well as to make time spent at the airport more relaxing and less of a hassle.

AIRPORT CHAOS: THE SEARCH FOR SANCTUARY

By Theodore Fischer and Coleman Lollar

Airline advertising copy may occasionally suggest images of carefree luxury, but carrier marketing executives indeed know what frequent flyers really think: air travel is an occupational hazard, more often endured than enjoyed. Wider seats that convert into beds, microwaved feasts and top-shelf liquors may ease the monotony of long flights, but airlines are learning the limitations of en-route cosseting. Even an airborne Valhalla begins and ends in airport purgatory.

"Airports are insulting and demeaning," says Benjamin Weiner, president of a New York consulting firm. "There are crowds, confusion, long waits and longer walks. The airport is the worst part of travel; once I'm on the plane I can cope with just about anything."

Tampa businessman T. L. Thomas agrees. "When will the airlines decide to strike a blow in favor of the frequent flyer where it really counts: on the ground?" he asks.

A growing number of airlines *are* beginning to turn their attention toward ground services that save time, money and aggravation. In their search for a competitive edge, carriers have introduced novel airport-transfer services, expedited ticketing and baggage handling, airport clubs, hotel deals and information services designed to lure passengers into the air by catering to their needs on land.

The pressure to do something on the ground is particularly intense since the carriers aren't just competing with each other: airport chaos may be part of the excitement of travel for some vacationers, but it is the kind of stimulus that can cause the full-fare passenger to stay home.

The pace of ground-service improvements has quickened within the last year. On June 1, for example, Pan American began offering free helicopter flights from midtown Manhattan to JFK for first- and Clipper-class passengers.

The helicopter option is now spreading beyond New York. In Houston, Continental first-class and all KLM full-fare passengers qualify for free Executive Air Link helicopter rides between Houston International Airport and five city heliports. In San Francisco, United, Continental and Western have similar deals with SFO Helicopter.

Free limousine transfers are also growing more common. Finnair offers the service for first- and business-class passengers from Helsinki Airport to downtown hotels, and Philippine Airlines provides the service in Manila.

In-town check-in, once a common air travel institution that went the way of complimentary cigarettes and ear-clearing chewing gum, could relieve much of the waiting. In a few places, the system is being tried once again. In Tokyo, for example, JAL will pick up luggage at offices or hotels and deliver it directly to Narita (check-in still takes place at the airport, however).

In the U.S. in-town check-in regained its first foothold recently when Pan American began checking bags at its New York headquarters ticket office.

While in-town check-in remains a rare luxury, most U.S. airports provide curbside baggage check, and at least four domestic airlines—American, United, TWA and Eastern—offer advance-roundtrip seat selection and, in some cases, deliver boarding passes with tickets.

For frequent flyers, avoiding lines at airports—with a little advance planning—is easier than avoiding the marauding masses in waiting areas and along concourses. Airport executives estimate that for every departing or arriving passenger wandering through their facilities, at least three or four others are there to send off, welcome back or just look.

Ultimately the best hope for salvation from airport turmoil lies in segregation of business travelers from tour groups and budget flyers. Such refuge is most often found at airline clubs or lounges. On international trips, a first- or business-class fare almost always includes admission to a plush—and, *quiet*—lounge. Passengers in the lounges are often boarded last, so even that final airport insult—the boarding-gate crunch—can be avoided. Unless the carrier puts full-fare economy passengers in its business-class cabin, however, those passengers have little choice but to endure the overcrowding of departure areas, where architects have planned seating with no apparent comprehension of the number of seats on a widebody jet. A lot of frequent flyers stand and wait. . . and wait.

For U.S. domestic air travel, membership clubs are still the rule ("A Guide to Airline Clubs," July 1982). The advantage to the U.S. clubs, however, is the admission is open to any card-carrying member, regardless of the class of service he has booked (or whether he is traveling at all). Much of the recent activity in ground-service improvements in the U.S. has taken place at such facilities. And within the last year, two new airline clubs have been launched: Delta's Crown Room Club (replacing formerly free first-class lounges) and the USAir Club. Throughout the industry, airlines have been expanding facilities and adding executive and VIP services over the last year.

Both in the U.S. and overseas, uniformed passenger-service representatives are increasingly seen in check-in and departure areas. In the best of cases, these airline employees can answer questions, solve minor problems, give directions and even provide boarding passes to passengers who despair at the idea of waiting in a long line of luggage-laden tourists.

Deregulation was supposed to create all sorts of new ground services for U.S. air travelers, as airlines outdid themselves to be nicer than the competition. For the most part, the reality has been quite the opposite. Hotel and meal vouchers are about as rare as Confederate bank notes at airports these days. Abroad, however, free and reduced-rate accommodations are increasingly available to the passenger who is savvy enough to seek them out. Full-fare British Airways passengers making an onward connection (even on another airline) that requires a night's stay at Heathrow qualify for free hotel, meals and even drinks. And throughout Europe, national flag carriers have turned to free-stopover packages to lure American business travelers onto their connecting services to other European cities, to Africa, the Middle East and the Pacific.

Worldwide, hotel tie-ins—usually in the form of businessmen's packages or straight room-rate discounts—are becoming a major area of carrier ground-service competition. The variety of carrier/hotel chain programs is almost unlimited. Lufthansa, for example, is issuing VIP cards to all first-class passengers, entitling them to discounted rates at Inter-Continental, Kempinski and Steigenberger hotels. The cards also guarantee early check-in and late check-out without surcharges. Singapore Airlines has launched a Premium Accommodations Plan with twenty-four hotels in the Orient, available to first- and business-class passengers. SAS offers deep discounts at first-class hotels in Copenhagen, Stockholm and Oslo to individual full-fare business travelers.

It is conceivable that a well-informed full-fare passenger could avoid almost all of the airport madness on departure: he could check his bags in town, hop a helicopter to the airport, rush to the sanctuary of a private club and then be ushered to his gate by an airline hostess just minutes before takeoff. Arrivals, however, remain a trial by fire for almost every traveler.

When the Boeing 747 was introduced in 1969, much attention was given to the jumbo's eight exit doors. Passengers would be off the plane in a flash, the public was told. In fact, almost all 747's offload through a single front exit. The process can take up to fifteen minutes, a period when anarchy often reigns in overcrowded, overheated cabins. Use of the single exit can be blamed on two developments: first, airports charge fees for each jetway used, making it cost-effective for the airlines to order just one; second, few airports have been redesigned for multiexit boarding and unboarding.

Besides, airline managements know that little is gained by getting passengers off the plane and into baggage-delivery areas sooner, when the bags generally arrive later. Few airline spokesmen will even attempt to explain why baggage delivery takes so long. Clearly, eight or ten luggage containers could be rolled off an aircraft and hauled to baggage delivery areas faster than 380 passengers can file out of a single door and make the trek to carousels. But it almost never happens. And "priority baggage handling" for premium-fare passengers usually remains an unfulfilled promise. The first-class, VIP-card-carrying passenger is as likely as the APEX-fare tourist to get his belongings last.

In some cases, delays in baggage delivery can be attributed to excessive demand at peak traffic hours (a.k.a. understaffing or poor staff scheduling). In most cases, however, the culprit seems to be years of neglect by carrier management. Baggage handlers are not an easy group to motivate.

Baggage delivery remains an area in critical need of attention by airlines in their ground-based competition for the frequent flyer. But other improvements may come first. Intense competition has led to many experiments with ground services, but expedited check-in, segregation from frolicking pleasure travelers, free transfers and free hotel rooms remain isolated glimmers of hope in an otherwise dismal story. Enhanced ground services have a long way to go before they become as common as the business-class cabin and the first-class sleeperette. The coming year should see a lot of matched offers, expansion of existing improvements to more airports and, no doubt, some new ideas.

The history, growth, and development of services of the Gray Line Sightseeing Association provides interesting insight into a relatively small but critically important component of the tourism industry. Sightseeing activities represent a relatively small part of tourism expenditures. However, sightseeing is often the primary reason for visiting a location. Professional services properly marketed are essential to meeting the needs of any traveler.

GRAY LINE—HISTORY, GROWTH, SERVICES

Gray Line was founded in 1910 by Louis Bush, who refurbished an old chassis manufactured by Mack Truck Company, painted it blue and gray, and offered his first sightseeing expedition in Washington, DC. An original tour promotional piece described the newly formed Gray Line company: "A spirit of friendship and welcome for the guest is combined with Gray Line 'Spirit of Services' that prevails throughout the entire organization. It is this spirit which is largely responsible for the pleasure of the traveler and success of the service." The earliest Gray Line tour folder suggested that the company logo was "an emblem of services, a sign of welcome."

Within months, Louis Bush and Gray Line had become the major tour service in the nation's capital. By the end of 1926 Gray Line had motorcoach sightseeing services in Asbury Park, Boston, Philadelphia, Chicago, New York, Baltimore, Chattanooga, Los Angeles, San Francisco, Salt Lake City, Toronto, New Orleans, Detroit, Havana, Portland, Spokane and Richmond. During the next two years, dozens of other Gray Line member companies were formed. When the Great Depression hit, fifty-three cities had Gray Line sightseeing services.

With the advent of the Second World War, much of the equipment owned by the company was given to the military for transport use. After the war Gray Line moved ahead in the number of markets where its products/services were available, in the range of tours offered (from half-day city sight-seeing to expanded week-long all-inclusive packages) and in the sophistication of equipment (sleeper and executive coaches, tinted-roof windows, lavatories, air conditioning, heat control, earphones for multilingual tours). The company was the dominant factor in sightseeing and related travel services by the early 1950s.

Its range of services is extensive; in addition to standard sightseeing tours, most member companies offer charters, cultural and industrial excursions, including overnight stops and hotel accommodations, group and special interest tours, foreign speaking service, transfers (from major air and rail terminals), hotel accommodations, chauffeured limousines, night tours including dinner and entertainment, air-sightseeing, ship-to-shore excursions, rental cars, and meeting/convention services.

THE EIGHTIES—TECHNOLOGY AND MODALITY

The President of Gray Line—Patrick R. Sheridan—is a travel industry veteran who feels the best is yet to come. His philosophy centers around high-tech and multimodality as a means of excitement:

Technology is the key to the motorcoach of the new decade. Turbine-powered, comfortable with low noise levels and pneumatic suspension systems, adjustable seats, lounge areas, galleys, stewardess service (for special events), even taped stereo and foreign language programs—all are part of today's motorcoach. Professionalism also characterizes this mode of transportation, with well-trained personnel, thoroughly researched tours, experienced drivers, lecturers, and guides; in total, a composite of classy coaches and people dedicated to making the highways and attractions in this country the ultimate level experience for travelers.

Intermodal travel is, for example, one of our major thrusts in the eighties. When a client can fly into a given area, be transferred by motorcoach, be given a special sightseeing tour in a limo, then flown over the destination in a helicopter for some spectacular picture-taking, then coach-transported again to a narrow-gauge railroad for a two-hour ride up the mountains, and finally swept down to an awaiting coach via tramway—that has to be a satisfied customer! And that's intermodality, as it will exist in years to come.

We are introducing a number of intermodal tours combining air, rail, coach, river rafts, jeeps, limos, cruisers, mule trains, campers, safari-wagons, and any other form of transport you can imagine. It's an exciting time, and can be one of the great rewards for travel agents and other sales personnel who "get on the motorcoach" and appreciate its versatility and profit potential in the travel product mix.

GRAY LINE AND THE NEAR-TERM

Up until 1980 the travel industry was on a fast track, breaking records at every turn, but the new decade brought some changes—high inflation and escalating fuel costs—that caught the 300 billion dollar industry off stride, and almost caused a stall.

More of the same is lined up for the near future, according to Sheridan. A new temperate approach to travel will appear because of heavy attitudinal transitions, he suggests. "Six out of ten people are self-oriented today, but they still recognize the need for guiltless income disposition."

Gray Line, which operates 1,655 daily tours around the world, is in a good position to feel the pulse of travelers. Its tours run from under $5 to over $2,000. And despite economic pressures, Sheridan feels a vacation is almost an inalienable right, and Americans will take their holiday, maybe on a shorter schedule and with less frills. The average traveler has a family income of about $15,000 and feels society "owes" him a vacation as a means of rest and relaxation, escaping routines, recharging and exploring new places. Most trips are of less than eight-day duration, and not many families stray more than 500 miles from home. But a vacation they have!

Gray Line notes that a motorcoach tour, whether a 10-day romp through the Colorado mountains or a half-day sightseeing excursion of Manhattan, is still the best dollar-for-dollar travel buy. But Sheridan insists that "memorability" as well as value is the basis of pleasing customers. For example, in a tour from Phoenix to an old mining town, gunslingers are hired to capture the bus then take a prisoner for ransom. It's a spirited moment, not easily forgotten by passengers. And in one multimodal tour from Denver, visitors are given a special sightseeing tour by motorcoach, then flown over a destination by helicopter, transported by narrow-gauge railroad up the mountains, only to descend by tramway. This five-hour tour is an exercise in time-and-place engineering.

Theme and national parks represent a nice opportunity for the family to splurge together on a low budget. Disneyland and Disney World, Six Flags, Marineworld, Busch Gardens are among the leaders. On a typical summer Saturday, for example, motorcoaches bring about 8,000 people to King's Dominion, a theme park near Richmond, Virginia. Yellowstone National Park, the Grand Canyon, Jackson Hole and the Grand Teton National Park, are the most popular park destinations. Gray Line unloads around five million sightseers at these attractions in a summer.

MATURE MARKET

Sheridan notes the emergence of the mature market as a major source of new business for tours. "One out of five Americans is now between the ages of 45 and 64. . .and is a good spender. The person is in transition, between middle and old age, and there is plenty of discretionary time and income, with travel as a priority. These people are not retirees, but want to get in their share of living while they still have peak income." Gray Line has targeted a number of tour and discount programs in this audience.

With seventy years of experience, Gray Line has a pretty good focus on what makes people happy. Its seventy-one years of professionalism backed by a continuing flow of new products and services make it the most natural way for visitors to discover a city. As Sheridan says: "Once you visit your relatives in a city, the next best thing is sightseeing. . .and it will probably always be that way."

Reprinted with permission of *Travel Agent* magazine, August 30, 1982.

"How Eggheads Evaluate Tourism" provides additional insight in-to the psychology and sociology of tourism. The more marketers know about why people travel, the more responsive marketing pro-grams can be to traveler needs. When marketing travel services it is essential to understand as much as possible about the motivation of prospective buyers.

HOW EGGHEADS EVALUATE TOURISM
By Eric Friedheim, Editor

Although there are more than a billion holiday trips every year, this mass migration has been largely ignored by sociologists and an-thropologists.

There has been organized tourism for thousands of years: Chinese and early Romans journeyed extensively for pleasure. In Colonial Amer-ica, there was a thriving trade to spas for health and recreation.

But experts on social behavior and culture, like many governments, seem to have a blind spot when it comes to the significance of travel. The handful of social scientists who have bothered to explore the motivations for vacation trips generally dismiss them as a phenomenon that more often than not fails to meet the participants' expectations.

Their scholarly papers published in obscure academic journals are peppered with unflattering comments about recreational travel. They la-ment the superficiality of vacations taken by Americans with several arguing that the touristic experience can be meaningless, disappointing or worse.

These pedantic critics of the travel phenomenon obviously are en-gaged in posturing before their peers; while we have no information about their travel habits, it seems safe to wager that based on what they are writing none would be happy on a package tour or with indepen-dent sightseeing which they characterize as a ritual doomed to failure.

Fortunately, this narrow perspective of travel is not shared by all of their own colleagues. We are reminded of this by a splendid rebuttal ap-pearing in the *Annals of Tourism Research*, an internationally recognized publication that covers all aspects of tourism in depth.

An article by Alma Gottlieb, doctor of anthropology at the University of Virginia, contends that what the vacationer experiences is real, valid and fulfilling.

She concedes her conclusions are also theoretical, being based on interviews with both middle class and upper class tourists and from literary, popular and journalistic writing. She says this research has produced "folk" data, which is more likely to produce a realistic appraisal of whether people enjoyed themselves and had rewarding experiences while away from home.

While it has been our admittedly unscientific observation that a tourist is a tourist is a tourist the world over, Dr. Gottlieb confines herself to vacations by Americans. A vacation is defined as an activity that strongly contrasts with what is normally done in the daily life back home.

To dramatize her point, Dr. Gottlieb divides American holiday trippers into two general classes: those who vacation and become "Peasants for the Day" and those who become "Queens (Kings) for the Day."

Those categorized as temporary peasants are upper or upper-middle class Americans who relate to the lower class inhabitants on an equal basis as they never do at home, where they hold authoritative jobs.

They go into local bars, attend folk festivals, revivalist meetings, bullfights, cockfights, see cheap popular movies in native language which they will struggle to understand. At home, they have tickets to the opera and theater and never see such movies and despise local, lower class dialects such as Black English. They adventurously eat in local, cheap and dirty restaurants serving uncontrollable, spicy food at outdoor rickety tables and street stands, although back home they normally dine at expensive immaculate restaurants serving mild or mildly spiced fare.

"In general," says Dr. Gottlieb, "they play at getting with the lower-class natives as they normally don't at home."

"The other type of holiday," she continues, "Queen (King) for a Day, is converse of the Peasant. Here, lower-middle to upper-middle class Americans go on vacation to raise themselves to a position of social *superiority*. While back home they may be extremely practical and keep to stringent budgets, buying only essential goods and even those only on sale, on vacation they become wildly extravagant, paying inflated prices for luxury goods and souvenirs for which they may have little use when they return. But paying such high prices becomes a form of upward mobility, with the vacationers temporarily adopting the buying patterns of the upper class.

"While these vacationers were careful to choose a moderate house or apartment in America, abroad they stay in luxury hotels with features that make them feel like Kings and Queens with breakfast in bed, midnight champagne, perhaps satin sheets. Indeed, a recent vogue has been literally to live the life of royalty by staying overnight in actual castles once inhabited by the noble class and converted to guest houses.

"Back home, the Queen (King) for a Day vacationers are fairly polite to waiters, maids, bus drivers, etc., perhaps even having some of their higher ranks (plumbers, electricians, restaurant managers) in their immediate families and circles of friends. While abroad, however, they are convinced that they are according the host country and its natives the privilege of bringing their tourist money to them and consequently they expect revered guest status. Thus they become embarrassingly aristocratic, ignoring the 'Gentleman/Lady' ideal of such behavior and instead emphasizing the crass privilege of rudely demanding information and special upper class treatment."

Travel agents may not all agree with Dr. Gottlieb's appraisal of how their clients behave but it is interesting to see how some in the scientific and academic community view contemporary travel habits.

"Motivation—Cruising's Challenge" describes marketing opportunities created by growth of the cruise product. Carnival Cruise Lines is clearly one of the most aggressive in the industry, and its Vice President of Marketing, Robert Dickinson, stresses the importance of a more efficient travel agent distribution system in this article.

MOTIVATION—CRUISING'S CHALLENGE

By Robert Dickinson, Vice President of Marketing, Carnival Cruise Lines

By 1985, the cruise industry will have the capability of carrying over 1,900,000 passengers annually. Commissions are forecast to double last year's payout and exceed $600 million annually. The challenge the cruise industry now faces is the development of sufficient consumer demand to fill the newly available berths—a challenge made more difficult by the current recession.

The marketing problem is intriguing because, unlike virtually all other segments of the travel industry, cruising has a single distribution system for its products: ninety-eight percent of all cruise line sales are sold through retail travel agencies. (In our opinion, it has been this singular distribution system, the travel agency, that has been the principal reason for the tremendous success of the cruise industry to this point in time.) However, as we all know, past success guarantees nothing for the future. The cruise industry has already committed approximately one billion dollars in new tonnage. What's necessary now is not a *new* distribution system—as other segments of the travel industry are exploring. But, rather, a more efficient distribution system: simply put, we need to have *more* counselors in *more* agencies *more* comfortable selling cruises!

We have heard some people say that the cruise industry's plans for new tonnage are much too aggressive. Yet, when you look at the big picture, the facts suggest the opposite. Between 45 and 60 million people in the United States and Canada take a major vacation each year. By "major" I mean a vacation of three nights or more which would therefore qualify for entry-level cruise products. (Remember, about 30% of all cruise passengers take cruises of three or four nights' duration; in fact, 86% of all cruise passengers take cruises of seven nights or less.) In 1981, 1,279,000 passengers from North America cruised from CLIA line ships. This means that the cruise industry's share of the annual major vacation market in North America was less than 3%.

What we have here, in plainest terms, is an embryonic industry. The 50% projected capacity increase in the next four years will still mean that the cruise industry will carry only about 4 1/2% of the vacation traveling public if it filled all its berths in 1985. This hardly constitutes aggressive growth and it certainly should be attainable.

Notwithstanding, it is not automatic and a big marketing job has to be done. Why? The small size of the cruise industry has worked against us. Less than 3% of the population of the United States and Canada has *ever* taken a cruise; therefore, over 97% of the population have no direct experience with a cruise vacation. We know that people are creatures of habit; therefore, too many vacationers go into travel agencies suggesting vacations with which they are familiar. Virtually all other vacation alternatives which are commissionable to you the travel agent can be combined into two broad segments: resort vacations and sightseeing vacations. In both cases, they involve a hotel. People are used to hotels. There is no mystique about them. Therefore, a hotel vacation represents a lower perceived risk than a cruise vacation. Further, because cruising is not in the personal experience of most clients, it is not "top-of-mind." Yet, market research consistently indicates that when specifically asked to evaluate cruise vacations, prospective vacationers give cruising consistently high marks.

If the cruise industry is to continue its meaningful expansions, counselors must *suggest* cruising as a vacation and not just be content to sit back and "take orders." We know that those people who have actually cruised come back quite satisfied. In fact, the Gallup studies clearly show that cruising enjoys the highest customer satisfaction ratings of any vacation alternative. Because the backbone of the retail travel agency business is repeat clientele, it behooves travel counselors to suggest vacation alternatives that will guarantee high customer satisfaction. A satisfied customer is a repeat customer.

In order for a travel counselor to feel comfortable selling cruises, she or he must not only have an appreciation of the high customer satisfaction rating of cruising but must feel reasonably informed of the various cruise products to assure a good fit between cruise ship and client. Fortunately, the cruise industry is making this job easier. Consider the following:

- Typically, cruise brochures are among the easiest to read in the travel industry.

- All cruising today is one class—which tends to minimize the possibility of error, as most ships offer a product to a broad spectrum of taste.

- The CLIA reference manual provides sample activity sheets and menus of all 27 CLIA member lines—this gives a good insight into the ambiance on board as well as the variety of activities and type of cuisine.

- In recent years, individual cruise lines have placed more emphasis on the personalities of their ships, rather than merely informing agents where they cruise and what the price is. When in doubt, call the cruise lines and ask pointed questions—they'll give you honest answers.

While all this information is available, one should not get the idea that cruising is in fact a difficult sell. Virtually any counselor in a travel agency can comfortably sell a Club Med vacation. Most cruises in fact are kind of floating Club Meds. One class, they are an easy sell, there's one price for the total air/sea vacation and one phone call takes care of the whole booking. Like any other vacation alternative, as long as the ship and cruise experience are not oversold, your client will almost invariably come back very well satisfied.

The cruise industry must also place emphasis on the owners and managers of the agencies. Given the probable outcome of the CAB competitive marketing case, I believe more owners and managers will begin to seek out cruising as a viable alternative to improve their business mix. Even in the event that the retail travel agency community would retain its exclusivity in selling airline tickets for profit, the smart travel agents will focus on the fact that cruising and air/sea cruising represents the most profitable commodities that a retail agent can sell. The twin motivators of profit and high customer satisfaction (resulting in repeat business) should encourage more owners and managers to spend the time, effort, and money to have themselves and their counselors adequately informed and motivated to sell cruising comfortably. The smart agents will encourage participation in cruise line seminars, and port/ship familiarization tours. The time and effort spent will be paid back manyfold in increased cruise sales. Consider the fact that 80% of the cruise industry sales are generated by about 20% of the travel agencies in North America. What this really means is that the smart travel agents who are motivated to sell cruises sell *16 times as many* cruises as the nonmotivated agents. I can assure you, from many personal observations, that these agents do not walk on water and are not blessed with four-digit IQs; rather, they're just ordinary folks like you and me. The difference, in a nutshell, is motivation. A motivated agency can easily improve its gross profit by a hundred thousand dollars annually by making a determined effort to sell cruises.

The cruise lines individually (and collectively through CLIA) stand ready to assist any agency that wants to meaningfully put forth the effort to improve its cruise sales. In addition to the fine efforts of CLIA, travel agents can call on a sales force of more than two hundred trained, capable and efficient cruise lines sales managers to assist them in training and educating their staff.

If every travel agent in the country made just one additional cruise booking, each quarter, then the desired expansion of our industry would be assured overnight! Unfortunately, many agents still will not get the message—which means that the smart travel agent will continue to reap disproportionate profits and satisfied clients by selling more cruises. The choice is yours. As my father used to say—when your ship comes in, don't be at the airport!

Reprinted with permission of *Frequent Flyer* magazine, May 1983.

"A Hotel by Not Just Any Other Name" gives a good insight into the thought that goes into changing a business's name. The image of a hotel is very much affected by its name and reputation. Any decision to change this name is made with great care and usually with professional assistance.

The "case history" that follows the article enumerates the planning considerations that accompany such a change.

A HOTEL BY NOT JUST ANY OTHER NAME

By Barbara Sturken

"Good morning, the Fairf...er...the Ritz-Carlton," the hotel operator sputtered into the phone.

"Uh, then isn't this the Fairfax Hotel?"

"No," said the operator, regaining her composure. "We used to be the Fairfax. Now we're the (pausing to savor the effect) *Ritz*-Carlton."

Like many people in Washington last year, the hotel staff was trying to adjust to the fact that the venerable Fairfax Hotel had, overnight, acquired a new snob appeal.

The very name *Ritz* brings to mind old-world elegance and ostentation. One thinks of Hemingway sitting at the Ritz bar, or of F. Scott Fitzgerald's "Diamond as Big as the Ritz." But Ritz is a name that American frequent flyers are encountering more often in their travels than in literature. Not only has the Fairfax Hotel taken the name, but Manhattan's newly renovated Navarro Hotel has also become a Ritz-Carlton. By the end of the year, there will be as many as four more Ritz-Carltons in the U.S.

Many would argue that the firmness of the mattress is far more important than the name on the hotel stationery, but there is a large and specific group of people that disagree, people who are in the business of identity change. To appreciate the value of their efforts, imagine booking your next trip to Palm Beach on Allegheny instead of USAir.

Shedding an outmoded image is one thing, acquiring the Ritz seal of approval is quite another. Chicago hotelier John Coleman knows all about that. His fascination with the Ritz name dates to his youth in Boston, where the Ritz-Carlton Hotel was a legend. After making a fortune in investments, Coleman turned to the hotel trade. He bought the Tremont and the Whitehall hotels in Chicago, then turned them into elegant European-style properties. Next, the hotelier breathed new life (and untold millions) into the fading Fairfax in the capital's exclusive Embassy Row district. To top off his "collection of hotels" (Coleman disdains the word *chain*), he needed something in New York. What could be better than putting on the Ritz in what was the home of the grandest Ritz-Carlton of them all?

The original New York Ritz-Carlton opened in 1912 and soon became a synonym for luxury. Scene of countless society and celebrity gatherings, the Ritz survived until 1951, when it was torn down to make way for an office tower. The demolition was widely interpreted as an end to an era.

Thirty years later—last fall—the era of the Ritz was reborn on Central Park South. While the trend toward smaller, classier (and decidedly nonconvention) hotels was already well underway, the new Ritz-Carlton provided proof that the once-scorned "small hotel on valuable land" was again possible—and on some of the most valuable land on earth.

Cesar Ritz, the Swiss shepherd's son who opened Ritz hotels in Paris, London and Rome, would, no doubt, be pleased at the turn of events. It was he who imported the Ritz name to the United States, linking it up with the name of the hotel across the street from the London Ritz: the Carlton. The hyphenated result ultimately appeared on hotels in New York, Boston, Philadelphia, Pittsburgh and Atlantic City.

Ritz, however, might be somewhat bewildered by the business of marketing his name in the 1980s. It is a process that involves franchise rights, 800 numbers, teams of anonymous inspectors and even a White House pollster.

When John Coleman decided he wanted the Ritz-Carlton name on his hotels, he was guided by more than nostalgia. Coleman hired Richard Wirthlin, President Reagan's public opinion pollster, to conduct research on the name.

Wirthlin organized interviews with hundreds of customers of luxury hotels and restaurants. Not surprisingly, the Ritz turned out to be better known to upper-crust clients than the Fairfax. In New York, the survey found, the name Ritz was "an institution."

So Coleman knew that he wanted the Ritz-Carlton name, but before he could have it, the Ritz had to be sure it wanted Coleman. The keeper of the Ritz moniker is Boston real estate tycoon Gerald Blakely, owner of the city's Ritz-Carlton. Blakely is notoriously stingy with use of the hallowed name. Once granted, he enforces his exacting standards by sending out teams of disguised checkers every month to verify that everything is as it should be at a Ritz.

A Ritz "should make someone feel at home," he says, by providing attentive and unobtrusive service. Blakely also insists that a Ritz be individually owned and be located in a city with a vibrant business and social community. (Says Coleman, "You can't just announce that you're going to build a Ritz-Carlton in Rockford, Illinois.") Finally, Blakely insists upon a share of the profits any Ritz earns.

In the old days the name Ritz may have been enough to link grand hotels, but today something more is required: an 800 number. The three East Coast Ritz-Carltons (Boston, New York and Washington) will soon begin to use Coleman's central reservations system, as will the Whitehall and Tremont. Advertised under the immodest heading, "A number of spectacular hotels," the reservations system will differ significantly from the more familiar chain res systems: callers will be switched directly to the requested hotel to speak with the people who know the hotel best. The only other Ritz-Carlton, in Chicago, is managed by the Four Seasons chain and will continue to use that company's reservations system.

Blakely says that five more cities are being considered as repositories for the name Ritz, and that "three or four" of the name changes could be completed before the end of 1983. Blakely is keeping his silence about negotiations, but insiders tell *Frequent Flyer* that potential Ritz hotels are being considered in Los Angeles, San Francisco, Atlanta, Dallas and Houston. Blakely does say that no more than ten U.S. cities qualify for a Ritz. In Europe, Ritzes are found in Paris, London, Madrid, Barcelona and Lisbon; they are regarded as distant cousins of the U.S. hotels, with a loose association maintained between the two groups.

When a hotel changes its name, regular patrons aren't always pleased. In Washington, the Fairfax was already considered a superior address before it took the name Ritz. Its Jockey Club restaurant and bar was already one of the favorite gathering places for visiting and local celebrities. When the white-and-blue Ritz awning suddenly appeared, there was more than a little grumbling heard on the capital cocktail circuit. Washington taxi drivers still haven't gotten used to the new name. Says one of the hotel's neighbors on Embassy Row, "Some people will carry the Fairfax name to their graves."

But for every disgruntled dowager there are others who come just because of the Ritz name. The hotel's manager, Paul Seligson, says that the number of European guests has increased dramatically. However, Seligson describes his clientele as "mainly American royalty, the cream of the corporate world." On one recent day, the president of Paramount Pictures and former Secretary of Defense Donald Rumsfeld were seen checking in.

No complaints have been heard from New York denizens over the name change on Central Park South. The Navarro had become so run down, many New Yorkers had forgotten that it was there. But the Navarro had managed to keep a small following of loyal theater and music stars, most of whom are said to have adjusted to the name Ritz without too much pain. Opera star Luciano Pavarotti has decided to move into the hotel—which is a short walk from Lincoln Center—and pops by frequently to see how the interior designers are coming along with his personalized living environment.

Guarding the Ritz tradition sometimes means putting up with guests who have egos to match their expense accounts. Staff members tell bizarre tales: the Ritz-Carlton in Washington recently had to track down a circumcision kit for a visiting African doctor. Most guest demands are more predictable, however, and Coleman boasts that his staff can scare up a for-rent Lear jet as quickly as they can arrange a private buffet dinner.

Even guarding the very name Ritz is no easy matter. More than once Blakely has gone to court to defend his claim to the name. Years ago the hotel lost its most famous case when it attempted to force Nabisco to select another name for its little round cracker. But Blakely has been more successful in blocking use of the name by other hotels and by apartment developers. The full Ritz-Carlton name is now on the National Register and has been incorporated in twenty-one states for added protection.

While Cesar Ritz might have had his patience tested by eccentric millionaires, the modern Ritz owners have an advantage he didn't. The old tradition of maintaining guest histories has been computerized. The Boston Ritz has more than 110,000 entries, which were stored until recently on old-fashioned file cards. The information is now being turned into computer data.

Each morning Coleman receives a telexed list of all the guests expected at his hotels that day. If he spots a noteworthy name, he can respond. Thus, when Nancy Reagan recently checked into her $750-a-day suite at the New York Ritz-Carlton, she found the room filled with bananas, her favorite fruit.

A short walk down Central Park from the Ritz is another example of identity changers at work: The Plaza has always been the Plaza (and for thousands of loyal patrons that is more than enough), but now it is part of the Westin chain, née Western International (two years ago the company hired San Francisco-based Landor Associates, the world's best-known corporate-identity firm, to rid them of the name they no longer wanted).

Landor has guided a number of travel companies through the process, turning Allegheny into USAir and Air California into AirCal, among others. Landor president, John Diefenbach, knows what's in a name, and he can spot a dud when he hears it. Like Western International. "It didn't make any sense," he says. Not only was it nondescript, it was contradictory to call something western *and* international. After considering 200 possible new names, Westin—a contraction of the old name—was adopted.

"Companies are frequently stuck with names that are too limited," he says. "A name doesn't make the change, it reflects it." Western International, he says, needed a name that was shorter (so that it could more easily become part of each individual hotel's name) and didn't have *too* much personality (so that it could fit comfortably on the firm's diverse hotels and resorts). Unlike most other Westin hotels, the Plaza remained simply the Plaza: its identity was deemed too strong to be tampered with.

Another too-specific hotel chain name that has now vanished from the earth is Airport Marina Hotels, renamed Amfac Hotels by Landor. The old name was simply "lower class" says Diefenbach ("the 'airport' had to go"). Landor also gave the company a crisp new logo to appear on everything from awnings to bath towels.

Sometimes proposed name changes never get far enough for the chains to find out whether or not the public is willing to accept the change. At about the same time Western International became Westin, similar-sounding Best Western asked Landor for a suggested new name. The company had a reputation as an expressway-exit motel chain. But some of the properties were trying for a classier act. The Best Western name, they said, could be a lot better. Landor recommended calling the chain, simply, Best.

The company's board of directors liked the idea, as well as the flashy new logo that Landor had designed. At a meeting of the chain's franchisees, however, the name change was voted down. "When people travel they look for that Best Western sign," said one of the owners.

Other name (and image) changes are certain to come our way in the months ahead. SAS recently hired Landor to study ways to modernize its corporate image. Plans have not been finalized, but at the very least aircraft interiors will be redesigned and flight attendants will get new uniforms (designed by Calvin Klein). The SAS Hotel subsidiary may also get a new name. Says Diefenbach, "Who wants to eat 'airline food' in a hotel dining room?"

Skeptics might question how much difference uniforms or logos make to consumers. But according to Diefenbach, each element is part of a total corporate image. "It's all advertising," he says, "down to the last bath towel."

Reprinted from *Hotel & Motel Management,* April, 1983.

A CASE HISTORY:
WHAT'S IN STORE FOR A HOTEL CHANGING ITS NAME? PLENTY.

Changing a hotel or motel's name involves a lot more than simply putting up a new sign—as the HBE Corp. recently learned firsthand. The difficulties the firm encountered in bringing three Sheratons and an independent under its new Adam's Mark banner prompted it to submit this advice for lodging properties looking to change identities.

First, the firm warns, a property changing its name has to remember that the switch "involves hundreds of items and dozens of legal maneuvers," plus "a handful of considerations that often evade the most careful planning, or that require more planning than first apparent."

Among the latter considerations, the firm continues, are matters like:

•*Ordering lead times*—the often-frustrating amount of time a property has to wait before it can completely erase all traces of the old identity. "It's not the day-to-day items, but the one-in-a-lifetime items you want to search out," the company cautions. In particular, it says, the new exterior signage and lighting may take five months to reach the property.

•*Re-establishing good employee relations*—explaining the change to all staff members to prevent a wide-spread "revolt" or morale-sapping rumors. The firm recommends that the new management team immediately meet with the staff to let them know exactly what will happen, and when.

•*Re-establishing customer relations*—the steps needed to keep the property's source of business from being lost in the confusion.

"Travel agents, contract business and other groups may hear of the pending name-change before a formal announcement," HBE explains. "Questions of changing management, policy changes, honoring commitments, etc., will naturally cross their minds.

"Be prepared to answer customer questions before your formal name-change announcement is made."

•*Changes in advertising materials*—particularly for ad spots booked on long-term timetables. In particular, the firm warns that directories may be in production—with the old name—many months before being printed. Outdoor billboards carrying the old logo may also take a considerable amount of time to change, "with 'paints' scheduled at inopportune times."

•*Drafting regulations for signage*—a matter that comes into play, as it did in HBE's instance, when a new chain "of almost any size" is being formed.

A group of hotels connected in any way usually have a set of "traffic regulations," the company explains. Developing and putting into effect a new set of standards "can take many months."

"All Aboard Amtrak" shows an evolution of marketing themes since 1976. The themes attempt to parallel the growth of service of Amtrak—a relatively new entity in the travel industry. Not only is Amtrak relatively new (founded in 1971) but the organization has had to counter a very negative image. Amtrak now invites comparison with other travel modes—"the time is right for taking the train instead of the flight." Amtrak's development is a most interesting marketing study.

IT'S A SONG, A SLOGAN, A CHOICE: ALL ABOARD AMTRAK

By John F. McLeod, Senior Editor, Corporate Communications, Amtrak

Amtrak has a new slogan that is more than a slogan. It signifies a whole new feel and a new direction. At the same time, it underscores what we are today and what we will be for the future.

If you've paid attention to our ads on television and in print, you have seen and heard the slogan, which is simply "All Aboard Amtrak."

This replaces two previous slogans, which had their own significance in the history of Amtrak.

In 1976, we introduced the slogan "We've Been Working on the Railroad." It reflected exactly what was going on. What it said was that we at Amtrak knew that we were a long way from being perfect. But we knew what our problems were and we were hard at work solving them.

As many of you remember, Amtrak started with some severe handicaps when we took over the pieces of America's rail-passenger services in May, 1971, and began to structure a national system. Much of the passenger equipment we inherited was called "rolling antiques."

But by 1976, we had begun to acquire substantial amounts of new equipment, and the Northeast Corridor Improvement Project, for which Congress eventually authorized $2.5 billion, was underway, promising higher speeds and greater comfort to the half of our ridership that uses this vital, high-speed, Washington-New York-Boston corridor.

By 1979, it was obvious that much of our claim to be "working on the railroad" was paying off. We had acquired even more new equipment. The magnificent new double-deck Superliners were coming into service on our long-distance Western routes. Our research showed increasingly positive attitudes about our service. This new era was summarized in the slogan "America's Getting Into Training." Our song based on the slogan became one of the best-known jingles on radio and television. We did, however, still have service problems.

Now in 1983, we are entering yet a different era. "All Aboard Amtrak" doesn't ask for patience and understanding, as did "We've Been Working on the Railroad." It is a far more positive slogan than "America's Getting Into Training." What it now says is that we are a mature, competent national passenger system, one that serves more American places than all the major airlines combined—and that we do so with great comfort and style and on time. We are confident you'll like our service.

One of Amtrak's executives explained our new approach:

> In most industries there is a standard by which all others are measured. In the travel and transportation industry the airlines have been perceived as the "gold standard" for a long time. . . Now Amtrak has come along with a product good enough to exceed and surpass that perceptual standard. Those three little words, "All Aboard Amtrak," is a clarion call that positions train travel as a better choice.
>
> This phrase conjures up all the rich heritage of the railroad—a phrase that is a powerful call to action. We could have used it before, and many wonder why we haven't. The reason is that we are building a bond of trust with the traveling public. It wasn't until now that we could, in all honesty, tell them to get on board.

Amtrak's new, more assertive approach invites comparison with other travel modes. One jingle in the new advertising says:

> . . .the time is right
> for taking the train
> instead of that flight.
> . . .All Aboard Amtrak.

Amtrak's research, which preceded the new slogan and marketing campaign, revealed that many travelers will find the train more attractive than other modes because of a "freedom factor." On a train you're not strapped into a seat. You can get up and walk about. You don't have to wait until a captain tells you that you can light up a cigarette (there are whole cars reserved for both smokers and non-smokers). On a train you can get something to eat or drink without waiting until they're ready to bring it to you. On a plane you can't even lean back until the light goes off.

That's what people who love train travel mean when they say, "It's the only civilized way to travel." On the train you retain your freedom.

All Aboard Amtrak.

Reprinted with permission of *Frequent Flyer* magazine, March 1983.

"Team Playing, Airline Style," describes the coordinated marketing efforts of major, large , jet-oriented air carriers and regional airlines (formally called commuters). Both the major and the regional carriers gain from such cooperation. Regionals gain association with recognized larger carriers. The larger carriers gain traffic fed to them at major hubs by the smaller, regionally-oriented carriers.

TEAM PLAYING, AIRLINE STYLE
By David Martindale

In his 1954 novel, *Lord of the Flies,* William Golding wrote of innocents who, freed from the restraints that regulated their social order, lapsed into a savage struggle for survival and for power. Golding's contenders were schoolboys shipwrecked on a remote island. A 1983 attempt to explore such a vision of atavism and anarchy might well chronicle the recent history of U.S. domestic airlines.

They were nurtured in an environment of privilege, order and strict supervision; theirs was a secure world where wealth was distributed according to custom and everyone accepted his place. Then came the Airline Deregulation Act of 1978.

If carrier executives initially feared the loss of their snug little club, most of them ultimately came to relish combat. Competition to see who would emerge as lord of the skies began to resemble guerrilla warfare: cut-throat fare slashing and preemptive strikes on fellow carriers' most vital routes became part of a day's work; CEOs who had once hobnobbed on the golf course now routinely charged each other with attempted sabotage; once-restrained voices developed a shriek.

Anarchy does not rule absolute along the nation's air lanes, however. Following a heady period of every-carrier-for-itself competition, airlines are beginning to learn the value of allies, and of at least limited cooperation. In a potentially dramatic trend in airline marketing strategy, carriers are forming "teams," coordinating their sales efforts, ground services and schedules—sometimes even their corporate logos. It's a new kind of cooperation for the U.S. airline industry, born of competitive pressures rather than camaraderie. In most cases, airline teams are created by agreements between major carriers and smaller regional carriers. American, United and TWA still aren't on speaking terms.

So far, airline teams have been good for the frequent flyer. In the best of cases they mean the convenience and security of on-line connections even when interlining from a regional to a major team member. If the trend continues to its extreme, however, airline teams could greatly limit the travel options available to flyers to or from scores of small-and middle-size cities across the country.

In late 1981 Eastern Airlines signed a cooperative agreement with Bar Harbor Airlines (a regional carrier serving fifteen cities in New England and New York State) to coordinate schedules at Boston Logan and LaGuardia. Under terms of the agreement, Bar Harbor is required to schedule at least 80 percent of its flights to connect with Eastern services at the two airports. In return, Eastern agreed to handle Bar Harbor's reservations and share gate space and provide ground services at LaGuardia, Logan, JFK and Albany. Eastern also threw in a $5 million loan guarantee so that Bar Harbor could buy a new aircraft. For connection-frazzled frequent flyers, the agreement had its benefits: passengers flying between Worcester and Atlanta, for example, no longer have to trek from one end of LaGuardia to the other to change planes.

Except for the loan guarantee, the provisions of the Bar Harbor agreement are not unique at Eastern: the carrier recently signed similar agreements with Vermont-based Precision Airlines and Texas-based Metro Airlines. Nor is Eastern alone in its courtship of commuter carriers. Most major airlines and a few larger nationals have signed symbiotic agreements with smaller carriers aimed at closer interline cooperation at hub airports.

Although general interline agreements exist almost industrywide, between majors the arrangement represents an uneasy peace, at best. And competition may yet bring down the interline system. Major/commuter teams, however, involve much more than a willingness to accept the other's ticket stock.

Among the majors, the degree of involvement in commuter partnerships varies considerably. United and American each have formed teams with at least twelve commuter lines; Northwest has signed no such agreements.

There are no strict ground rules for forming an airline team. Each is tailored to the unique needs of the two partners. Certain features are commonplace in the industry, however. Among them:

• *Schedule coordination*. "If an aircraft comes in, and it doesn't connect to anything, it's going to be a loser," says Richard S. Nelson, manager on interline sales for American. "And no one wants to run an airplane that loses money." For this reason, both partners usually trade preliminary flight schedules and agree to rearrange flight times whenever possible in order to maximize connection opportunities.

• *Shared terminal facilities.* "A critical part of these agreements is joint facilities at hubs," says David Kunstler, Eastern's marketing vice president. "That's what makes it convenient for passengers." Once banished to isolated terminals far removed from the airport core, many commuters now park their planes right beside their major airline partners. Some examples: Mississippi Valley Airlines shares Gate F-11 at O'Hare with United; Pilgrim Airlines flights at JFK operate from American's terminal; and Ransome Airlines shares gate space with Delta at Philadelphia, Boston, Hartford and the three New York City airports. Although space restraints sometimes prevent such airport proximity, at least one major has gone out of its way to provide its commuter partner with adequate airport accommodations. Recently, TWA built not only an entire terminal facility and operations center for Golden West Airlines at LAX, but a 44,000-square-foot hangar, as well. Golden West leases the facilities at a favorable rate from TWA.

• *Joint reservations.* Under the terms of many team agreements, the major carrier agrees to handle the commuter's reservations. In addition, the commuter partners of American and United receive preferential displays in automated reservations systems.

• *Joint fares.* While the major carriers continue to maintain a variety of joint fares with a large number of commuter airlines, particularly attractive joint fares are often negotiated with commuter partners. For example, passengers who fly aboard Pacific Coast Airlines from Santa Barbara or Bakersfield to Los Angeles pay only ten dollars for the trip if they connect to a Western flight at LAX. The connecting flights are free to passengers traveling first class on Western.

• *Joint marketing programs.* For both the major and the commuter airline, a joint sales/advertising campaign is a key ingredient to a successful partnership. "Joint advertising is an effort to bring the message to a community that may not be familiar with American Airlines," says Nelson. "That message is: 'Hey, this carrier is an extension of American Airlines into your community. And by getting on them, you can reach a major hub in the national transportation network. From there, you can go to just about any place you can think of.' "

Without question, team arrangements have helped commuter lines thrive. They save money by eliminating the need to operate and staff a computerized reservations system. At hubs, the majors help reduce their costs by providing reasonably priced ground services and gate space. Sometimes the majors throw in other cost perks, as well.

Because it buys jet fuel in greater bulk quantities, Western is able to trim the fuel bill of one of its commuter partners by a full twenty cents per gallon. What's more, such close associations with the majors generally trigger a significant increase in passenger traffic for the commuter. At the same time, the partnership allows smaller carriers to develop a marketing link to major airlines—carriers that boast nationwide consumer confidence and name recognition.

As the majors acknowledge, altruism is not what motivates them to be so generous to commuter partners. "We're not in the business of helping regional carriers just for the sake of helping them," says Republic's director of regional airline affairs, Jim Basinger. "We've got to be very honest about it—we want to work with regional carriers because they feed us traffic, but on the other hand, we want them to give us some traffic, as well."

Although the extent of feed varies between partners, the majors are generally pleased to receive 20 to 30 percent of all passengers carried by their commuter partners into a specific hub.

The volume of feed tends to increase as a partnership matures. For example, in June 1982 Western's partners at Salt Lake City—Trans-Western Airlines and Sky West Airlines—provided $100,000 worth of connecting traffic to Western. By December, the figure had leaped to $160,000—or approximately $1.9 million per year.

Partnerships are not without their drawbacks, however. Says Western's director of interline development, Bill Nielsen, "One disadvantage is that our passengers may board a commuter flight and think the carrier is part of Western Airlines. These services have to be good, because if they're not up to standard, then the passenger's not going to travel on them, and it's going to hurt us."

Jeff Warner, staff vice president of passenger sales for TWA, agrees: "We have to carefully select the commuters we want to have joint marketing efforts with," he says, "so that these carriers will not diminish TWA's reputation in any way."

Despite the advantages that accrue to a commuter from a partnership with a major, the regionals see potential drawbacks to such close relationships—drawbacks directly linked to the size disparity between the two partners. Even though the regionals that participate in the

Allegheny Commuter system are pleased with their relationship with USAir, most commuter airlines do not want a similar all-encompassing involvement with a major. Instead, they prefer to retain total control over their own operating affairs. And rather than subordinate their name recognition to that of their big-league partner, most also insist upon maintaining their own corporate identities.

For now, most of the majors seem willing to allow the commuters to maintain both their independence and their identities. "Yes, we could put our name on the side of their planes," says an American spokesperson. "But we'd much rather give these people as much leeway and independence as possible. We want to be their partner. We don't want to take them over, because frankly we don't know how to run their business as well as they do. We want to keep them strong and vibrant, because the more *they* grow, the more passengers we have a shot at."

Jim Basinger of Republic agrees. "We want their growth and their relationship with us to be complementary," says Basinger. "We feel that if the control is too tight, the commuter is probably going to have to break away and go out on its own."

For its part, Eastern doesn't rule out the possibility of painting the planes of its commuter partners in Eastern colors. Yet, Kunstler adds, "It would only be as a way to illustrate the close working relationship, not a way of exerting control over the commuter."

One airline that does paint the planes of its commuter partners in its own colors is Air Florida. Since October 1980 the Miami-based national carrier has been attempting to set up a tightly controlled, Allegheny Commuter-style network of its own. The move was initially spearheaded by then-Air Florida chief C. Edward Acker. Since becoming chairman of Pan Am in 1981, Acker has pushed to develop a similar commuter network for Pan Am, as well. So far, neither Air Florida nor Pan Am has come close to imitating the success of USAir's commuter involvement, or even many of the other major carriers, for that matter.

Unlike USAir, most of the majors do not contractually prevent their commuter partners from entering into similar agreements with other major airlines at other hubs. "I think we have to realize that if a regional carrier is operating into two hubs," says Basinger, "we may be the dominant carrier in one hub, but have very little service in the other hub. We have to be willing to accept the fact that regional carriers may have to work with a different major carrier in another hub."

Not every regional wants to team up with a major, but there is growing evidence that at least some are being forced into choosing mainline partners. Consider Rocky Mountain Airways, the largest regional carrier serving Denver. At the present time, Denver is the site of an intense three-way battle for traffic by United, Continental and Frontier. Although all three carriers are of approximately equal strength at Denver, each is seeking to dominate the market.

Not surprisingly, Rocky Mountain Airways is being courted by all three airlines. According to Dennis Heap, vice president of customer sales and services, Rocky Mountain would prefer to work on an equal footing with United, Continental and Frontier. Yet Heap predicts that within the next year Rocky Mountain will have no choice but to team up with one of the three leading carriers at Denver. "Basically, what we're being told by the major carriers is either we're going to have to work with one of them or somebody else," says Heap. "We simply aren't given the option of working in the old world of normal interline anymore."

Rocky Mountain hopes to hold off selecting a partner until a shake-out occurs in the Denver market and a clear-cut victor emerges in the three-way battle. "Whoever we go with, the other carriers are going to be shunning us," Heap predicts.

"If you work exclusively with one airline," explains Rick Russell, vice president of marketing for Golden West, "you put yourself in a precarious competitive position. You're forcing the other large airlines to look for another source of feed. You also have less control over your own destiny if you link yourself up too closely with another airline."

Even the majors concede that teams pose a dilemma for the regionals. "I think there's a delicate balancing act for the commuters," says TWA's Warner. "If they align themselves too closely with one carrier, then they can expect another major to try to go out and find another guy to work with." "I'm not sure the trunk carriers will allow the commuters to continue working with everybody," says United's manager of regional and commuter airline marketing, Marty Kloska.

The implications of such a development could be far-reaching. If competitive pressures reach the point where majors begin "booking away" from commuters aligned with competitors and "booking toward" their own partners, the commuters could become the majors' pawns in the war for market share. And instead of providing their passengers with the most convenient interline connections, the majors could begin to deliberately divert traffic to their commuter "friends," no matter how inconvenient the connections.

As it stands now, no major airline actually owns a commuter airline, and there is some question whether antitrust laws would permit such a purchase. However, Pan Am recently considered purchasing Golden

West. Offering hefty payments as enticements to sell, what would happen to the commuter industry if a major carrier began gobbling up its commuter partners? In the knee-jerk, me-too environment of the present U.S. airline industry, wouldn't the other majors feel compelled to purchase their own commuters just to remain competitive? And if a major collapsed and filed for bankruptcy, wouldn't its former commuter routes consequently go unserved?

Even in the absence of outright commuter ownership or commuter franchises, some observers wonder whether the dozens of "mom and pop" commuters that now blanket the nation can continue to survive if their routes are challenged by large regionals backed by the majors. Will commuter partners thrive at the expense of the smaller regionals, leading to a reduction in the number of airlines serving the nation's smaller communities?

Ultimately, the marketplace will determine whether such speculation becomes a reality tomorrow. In the meantime, it seems certain that more and more regionals will be wooed by the majors.

Provided such partnerships remain relatively unchanged in the future, frequent flyers stand to benefit. The passenger acceptance of the Allegheny Commuter system attests to the popularity of the airline-team concept by air travelers. And even though most U.S. airlines do not now seek as comprehensive a relationship with the regionals as USAir has with *its* commuter partners, the fact that major/commuter teams are proliferating is especially good news for frequent flyers concerned about air service to smaller cities. According to RAA, roughly two-thirds of all traffic carried by the regional carriers is business-related. Aware of this fact, many of the majors are even permitting passengers to apply mileage accrued on their commuter partners toward the majors' frequent flyer bonus programs.

Clearly, major/commuter partnerships remove much of the hassle from connecting at hub airports. Frequent flyers can only hope that by trying to further facilitate such interline connections with their partners, the majors will refrain from discouraging or impeding travelers from connecting to other regionals—carriers that are either nonaligned or married to a different airline.

The case study of the Ala Moana Hotel in Honolulu shows how a hotel must recognize its shortcomings and market its strengths. The case is a good example of the use of strategic planning in a marketing environment.

MISSION STATEMENT
ALA MOANA HOTEL, HONOLULU

The Ala Moana is a first-class hotel located between Honolulu's business section and the Waikiki tourist area. There is no first-class hotel closer to the business section and Honolulu's special event areas. The hotel is adjacent to Hawaii's largest shopping center with 155 stores.

To be successful, the hotel must be No. 1 to Honolulu's business traveler, airline crews, Japanese special campaigns, Kamaaina individuals, and Kamaaina groups. These markets should be supplemented by Japanese package series business, government employees, special events, and one-shot group business.

The Ala Moana must have authentic Hawaiian atmosphere, entrance, decor, and uniformity. It should be known for its Hawaiian style service (language, dress, fruit, flowers, and special touches).

When Japanese and U.S. F.I.T. demand slackens in the Waikiki area, the hotel is vulnerable to competition and loses significant business to the first-class Waikiki hotels. During these periods, it must depend on its major market segments and get one-shot group business. The hotel's rooms product must be designed and maintained to meet the needs of its four major market segments. There is a potential F.I.T. market of frequent Hawaii visitors and stopover business.

Because of the hotel's difficult competitive position for tourist room business and its high vulnerability to tourist fall-off, the food and beverage outlets offer the only major opportunity for revenue growth. These outlets must appeal to its local community; however, they must be flexible enough to meet its room guest requirements as well.

The Ala Moana must be known by its employees as the "best hotel in Honolulu to work in." Its employees should have the Aloha Spirit and should communicate that spirit to each other and to the guest.

Financial Goals

	Occupancy	Avg. Rate	Room Revenue
'83	86.4%	$30.16	$11,357,300
'84	87.0%	32.14	12,186,000
'85	87.0%	35.00	13,270,400

	Food Revenue	Beverage Revenue
'83	$5,757,000	$2,194,000
'84	6,670,000	2,632,800
'85	7,670,000	3,036,000

Assumptions:

1. *Major Market Segments*—The sales and marketing efforts of the hotel are geared toward the following market segments:
   a. Airline Crews
   b. Japanese Special Campaigns
   c. Yes We Cana
   d. Government
   e. Kamaaina
2. *Rooms Rehab Program* will continue as planned.
3. *Food & Beverage Department*—A master plan to reconceptualize total Food and Beverage outlets is being prepared in order to update and gear the operation towards the markets identified. This effort in connection with increased sales and marketing efforts will increase the growth in the Food & Beverage Department over the next several years.
4. *Room Supply*—Additional hotel rooms in the area are planned as follows:

   1983
   440 Rooms   Hotel A
   1984
   650 Rooms   Hotel B
   360 Rooms   Hotel C
   495 Rooms   Hotel D

STRATEGIES AND OBJECTIVES

Rooms Business, Ala Moana 1983
Market Segment: *Special Events*

Definition: Any one-shot event taking place in Honolulu in a city, state or public facility or area; i.e., state fair, high school/college or professional athletic events and trade shows that creates a demand for lodging for either the participant or spectator.

Objective: The Ala Moana Hotel will be first choice because of location, facilities, service and price.

Person Responsible: Group Sales Manager.

Quota: 3,100 Room Nights

Jan.	300		July	500
Feb.	200		Aug.	450
Mar.	250		Sept.	150
Apr.	150		Oct.	450
May	150		Nov.	150
June	150		Dec.	200

KEY STRATEGIES

1. Develop leads through the following facilities:
   a. Aloha Stadium
   b. Blaisdell Center
   c. University of Hawaii
   d. Department of Planning & Economics
2. Maintain list of special events in the city. Source: Newspapers, HVB (Hawaii Visitors Bureau), monthly activities at Blaisdell Center.
3. Cultivate key personnel within these facilities to insure that we get the leads.
4. Identify and work the five key promoters using these facilities: (In the Strategies worksheet, names of five key promoters are listed at this point, with affiliations and telephone numbers).
5. Identify and solicit the major studios and producers filming in Hawaii: (In the Strategies worksheet, the names of five producers are listed at this point, with major movie studio affiliations). Use other sources—newspaper (close-in business).

MEASUREMENTS

1. Source of Business Report.
2. Site inspection quotas met.

"Marketing a New Hotel" provides an excellent case study of the development of a total marketing program. While the checklist provided at the end of the article is specifically designed for a city hotel, parallels can be drawn for all parts of the tourism industry.

MARKETING FOR THE EIGHTIES

One of the most professionally marketed chains in the world is Marriott Hotels. In this article, you will see, step by step, how they successfully opened the Washington Marriott on March 3, 1981.

"Marriott has developed a successful formula for opening its new hotels," said Elizabeth D. (Biffie) Meyers, vice president advertising and market research for the chain. The basic plan:

- Research
- Positioning
- Advertising Strategy
    Objective
    Target Market
    Basic Selling Proposition
    Support for Selling
    Proposition
    Tone (of the advertising)
- Media Plan
    Media Objectives
    Strategy and Rationale
    Budget
    Media Flow Chart
- Sales Strategy
- Public Relations Strategy
- Promotion Strategy
- Total Marketing Budget

The opening of the new 350-room Washington Marriott provides a case study of how the planning process works and how the corporate marketing department works with the hotel's director of marketing. When the Washington Marriott opened, the hotel's director of marketing was John J. Hyland. He is now off to open another new hotel.

Hyland reported to the hotel's general manager, Hugh Walsh. The advertising agency is Ogilvy & Mather. Their vice president and (Marriott) account supervisor is Henry (Hank) Ferris, who is based in the New York office.

RESEARCH AND POSITIONING

Marriott had six other properties in the Washington area. "So we had a lot of market data available to us," said Meyers. "We were able to quickly identify the customer mix we should go after and how to reach them. We knew the transient business traveler was our single most important market segment and we set our priorities accordingly."

The Washington Marriott was being built at 22nd and M Streets in the heart of Washington. Therefore the positioning agreed upon by Meyers, Ferris and Hyland was:
"...the most convenient quality hotel in the Washington area for the business traveler."

The sales effort followed directly from this positioning. Said Hyland: "We secured office space next to the site nine months in advance and hired four sales people. One person concentrated exclusively on transient business travelers..."

Hyland set up sales coverage of all offices in the downtown area. The sales team signed up secretaries and travel department managers in the Marriott 100 Club, which offers swimming privileges, discounts in the gift shop, and many other benefits for those who book executives into the Washington Marriott. The goal was to set up eighty top-volume bookers, but the sales team hit one hundred. Members were given a special reservations number which bypasses the switchboard and rings in the hotel's reservations department.

DEVELOPING ADVERTISING STRATEGY

Once the positioning was determined, the agency and client worked together to develop the advertising objective and strategy. First, the objective was agreed upon:
"To convince the target market that the new Washington Marriott is the finest hotel in the heart of town."

They defined the target market as the transient individual business traveler in the northeast and the middle income local professional. The business travelers were important for obvious reasons. The local professionals were important for these two reasons: (1) they book incoming clients and corporate executives; and (2) they are primary customers for the dining room—the Atrium—the lounges—the Court Lounge and Gambits—and the function rooms and ballrooms.

A "basic selling proposition" was then prepared to set forth the reason why a customer should select the hotel. Note that while the objective was stated in terms of what the advertising hopes to achieve, the selling proposition is stated in terms of consumer benefits:

"*The Washington Marriott is the most convenient quality hotel in the Washington Area.*"

When a benefit is promised, it must be supported by facts. The support for this selling proposition is as follows:

—the reputation of the Marriott Hotels

—excellent location

—deluxe facilities including an indoor pool, hydrotherapy pool and sauna.

The tone of the ads, it was agreed, should reinforce the quality image of the hotel.

CREATING THE FIRST AD

Once the account team at Ogilvy & Mather had the preceding information, they turned it over to the writer and art director team. The creative team was also given basic guidelines regarding media selection. For the Washington Marriott, it was decided to use a 600-line ad in local newspapers and one-page black and white ads in business magazines. The writer and the art director, said Ferris, decided four things:

1. The campaign must be consistent with the corporation's national campaign, which features President Bill Marriott as spokesman.
2. They would trade on the fact that the Marriott has six other hotels in the D.C. area and has gained a reputation for quality.
3. They would emphasize location, since this is one of the most important factors in a business traveler's decision.
4. They agreed that two separate ads were needed: one for the business traveler in the Northeastern United States, and the second for the local D.C. market.

They wrote the following headline for use in both ads:

"I'm proud to announce the opening of my seventh Washington Marriott Hotel—the first to be squarely in the middle of town."
—Bill Marriott, President, Marriott Corporation

But the body copy differed greatly. For the business traveler, the copy said:

"When the people at Marriott do it, they do it right. They knew Washington, D.C. already offered a large selection of convention hotels. So they built a luxurious 'personal' hotel."

(The rest of the ad features location, dining facilities, a special floor, and both local and toll-free reservations numbers.)

The ad for the Washington resident, by contrast, began as follows:

"A large part of the new 350-room Marriott at 22nd and M Streets was built for out-of-towners. But the rest was built for the residents of greater Washington—for you."

(The rest of this ad mentions the dining room, lounges, meeting rooms and weekend packages. The only telephone number listed is the local one.)

PRE-OPENING MEDIA PLAN

Because Marriott has a substantial corporate advertising campaign, the budget for each hotel's own media plan is usually set at about 1% of estimated room sales. For most hotels, especially independent properties, the advertising budget runs 2% to 3% the first year.

The media planner at Ogilvy & Mather was provided with three types of information by Hank Ferris and the account group: the target market including the cities where the target customers live, the opening budget (determined by the client), and the creative considerations (advertising objectives and strategy). From this, the media planner decided the most efficient and effective way to deliver the advertising message.

To reach the business traveler, it was decided to use the *Wall Street Journal's* eastern edition; *Business Week; Nation's Business* in the New England and Middle Atlantic Regions; and *Dun's Review,* the eastern edition.

In order to afford a two-month introductory campaign to build quick awareness, it was decided to use a quarter page ad in the Wall Street Journal for three consecutive weeks in March (the month of the opening) and full-page black and white ads in the business magazines for March and April.

Said Meyers: "We identified this as a 60-day announcement program to be followed by an on-going advertising program."

For the association market, advertising was placed in *Association Trends*, and for the travel trade, advertising was used in joint participation with other Marriotts in directories and meetings publications.

For the local market, the original plan called for three ads each in the *Washington Post* and the *Washington Star*. This would have given the hotel coverage of 77% of the metro area. But the agency and client agreed that most of the target customers were covered by the Post. Therefore they decided to drop the Star and add an additional insertion in the Post. The resulting schedule was one ad each week for the first four weeks in March, thereby building frequency against the local prime prospects.

PRE-OPENING SALES PROGRAM

John Hyland's sales team had been marketing the Marriott 100 Club nine months prior to the introductory advertising. They did so by a combination of direct mail and the sales calls discussed earlier. Hyland sent a letter, application form, and a color rendering of the new hotel to the prospect list. A newsletter was sent to the Marriott 100 Club members periodically and a party was thrown for them at the hotel the day after opening.

Next, Hyland targeted efforts toward the tour brokers, to develop much-needed weekend business. "We sent over a thousand letters which I personally signed, mentioning features that would be of interest to a tour broker: special weekend rates, parking for buses, indoor pool and sauna, and the fact that the hotel is adjacent to Blackie's House of Beef. I know it's a bit unusual to mention a competitive restaurant, but Blackie's has been a favorite of the tour operators for years," said Hyland, "and we saw it as a strong attraction." Lists for the mailing were culled from NTBA (National Tour Brokers Association) and sources from within the Marriott organization.

Once the primary prospects for midweek and weekend business had been covered by direct mail and follow-up phone calls, the sales team concentrated on association business. Said Hyland, "Our national sales director, Skip Boyd, came up with an idea for a 'hardhat luncheon' next door to the construction site. Association executives were invited. After lunch, our general manager, Hugh Walsh, conducted a tour. The involvement of Walsh is one of the reasons for our success. Customers want to meet the general manager."

The "hardhat luncheon" idea was so successful it resulted in about 4,000 room nights being booked prior to opening. Forty-nine percent of all group bookings into the hotel came from associations.

Hyland's sales team also sent letters to all tourist inquiries received by the Washington Convention and Visitors Bureau, promoting a 50% discount off the rack rate for weekends and holiday periods. A return reply card was enclosed along with a color rendering of the new hotel.

Hyland became active in the Washington Society of Association Executives (ASAE), Meeting Planners International (MPI) and other local group-producing organizations. He also enlisted the support of all available Marriott sales people in the Washington area for a three-day sales blitz of the area.

Other sales efforts included:

—mailings to chambers of commerce in major cities throughout the U.S., informing them of the hotel opening.
—sales trip to London to tap the inbound British traveler
—familiarization trips in conjunction with airlines, following the hotel opening
—promotion through direct mail to existing Marriott accounts, of the "Marquis Level" floor with special services at a premium price.

PRE-OPENING PR PROGRAM

There are six times during the construction of a new hotel that publicity can be obtained to generate awareness prior to the first ad running. They are:

—when construction plans are announced
—at the groundbreaking ceremonies
—at the topping-off of the building
—when the management and sales teams are hired
—at a pre-opening press party, a week or two before opening
—at the grand opening party.

The objective of the publicity should be to communicate the same points agreed upon in the advertising "basic selling proposition."

HOW MUCH TO SPEND

There are no industry averages to compare for pre-opening budgets, as there are with on-going marketing budgets. Because the expenses are generally capitalized along with construction costs, they don't usually show up on an operating statement.

Hotel pre-opening marketing budgets will range generally from 50% of an ongoing year's marketing budget to as low as 25%. But the best way to budget for the pre-opening period is to use the zero-based budget. In other words, decide what is needed to open the hotel; don't just arbitrarily spend a fixed amount.

The first expense will be a director of marketing. Then the sales team will be added. Advertising in the group or meetings publications will begin as much as a year prior to opening. But advertising to the consumer/business traveler will not begin until the month before opening. Temporary brochures, from the architect's renderings, should be produced as far in advance as possible, along with the hotel's logo, stationery, mailing labels, business cards, meeting planner fact sheet, press kit covers or news release paper, rate cards, flyers, etc.

Chain hotels can rely on the national and regional sales offices for much of the pre-opening sales effort, and will therefore have relatively low pre-opening expenses. An independent hotel, on the other hand, has a much bigger task (see checklist).

THE MARRIOTT FORMULA

The Marriott formula, as indicated by their advertising, is, "If Marriott does it, they do it right." So it is with their marketing a new hotel. They have the advantage, of course, of the national sales department, Biffie Meyers' corporate marketing department, and Hank Ferris and his colleagues at the agency.

But if you are general manager or marketing director of an independent hotel, you might have to do more yourself than you would at a chain hotel. Thus, we have included in this article a checklist designed for the independent.

Marketing Checklist for Opening a Hotel

Designed specifically for an independent hotel located in a city.

- *12 months in advance*
  Hire Director of Marketing. Retain advertising agency and public relations firm. Establish tentative rate structures. Affiliate with rep firm, international reservations systems, etc. Begin

market research on sources of business, competition. Submit listings to all directories which close prior to opening of hotel (examples: Hotel & Motel Redbook, Hotel and Travel Index, Yellow Pages and White Pages of local telephone directory, Convention & Visitor's Bureau publications, Chamber of Commerce publications, tourist map companies, meetings and association magazines annual directory issues, inplant agency and corporate travel association directories). Join local ASAE, MPI and other organizations for client contacts. Enter into agreements with any tour brokers or wholesalers whose programs/brochures you want to be in. Obtain mailing lists for all corporate, association and tour/travel clients who produce business for the area. Send press release to media to update them on progress of hotel and staffing.

- *9 months in advance*

Finalize positioning, advertising, media, sales and P.R. strategies. Finalize pre-opening marketing budget. Have full sales team in place. Begin sales coverage of accounts which are top priority for your hotel (such as corporations' travel departments and secretaries who book incoming business). Place heavy concentration on advance booking of association and corporate group business into the first three-six months the hotel will be open. Schedule advertising in the meetings and association magazines. Print all pre-opening sales material including four-color architect's rendering. Make any necessary revisions in rate structure.

- *6 months in advance*

Intensify sales coverage of corporate transient accounts. Adjust rates if necessary. Continue direct mail to corporate accounts, meeting planners and tour operators; update them on hotel progress. Continue press releases to local media, travel trade and meetings magazines.

- *3 months in advance*

Release advertising to consumer magazines and trade magazines to meet closing deadlines. Begin sales and direct mail blitz of travel trade. Continue updating corporate and association customers, giving them "hardhat" tours of hotel, including sample furnished room. Begin local, regional and (if appropriate) national publicity effort for hotel, including tours of hotel, personal interviews with general manager or owner. Finalize hotel rates for next 15 months.

• *The last 30 days up to opening day*

Release advertising to local media for introduction beginning the week prior to opening. Finalize plans for Grand Opening party, ceremony, etc. Hold opening press conference. Intense telephone sales blitz of all corporations in area for inbound business. Continue sales blitz of travel agents. Increase inspection tours by meeting planners who can book short term business. Hold receptions opening week for top corporate accounts and, separately, for local travel agents.

The following article, "BWI Promotion Pays Off," demonstrates the marketing needs of today's airports. With the current ability of airlines to enter and leave markets at their own discretion, it has become necessary for airports (especially where there is more than one in a region) to promote their facilities to the airlines.

BWI PROMOTION PAYS OFF

By Ann Cooper

In its quest to draw more passengers to Baltimore-Washington International Airport, the state agency managing the facility has given away bumper stickers and ballpoint pens, entered a float in the Preakness Parade, recruited children to sing Christmas carols and staged celebrity look-alike contests (last year's winner was a ringer for M*A*S*H character Radar O'Reilly).

Is this any way to promote an airport, a place where passengers are unlikely to care about much beyond whether they can get a flight and how far they have to walk to the departure gate?

The State Aviation Administration officials who run BWI think it is, and they say they have the numbers to prove it. In 1982, 4.6 million travelers used the airport. That was 20 percent more traffic than in 1981, representing the biggest jump in passenger growth in the airport's 33-year history.

BWI managed that increase in a recession-plagued year, when airline passenger traffic nationwide increased only 3 percent. Most major airports around the country posted traffic gains much smaller than BWI's, and a few reported declines during the year. In 1980 and 1981, years when traffic declined nationwide, BWI passenger levels stayed about even.

The airport did not fare as well with cargo traffic, which usually fluctuates more from year to year and declined by more than 5 percent at BWI in 1982. State officials blame the decrease on the general economic recession, which contributed to a 3.2 percent drop in airline cargo traffic nationwide and also hurt companies that haul cargo by rail, truck or ship.

Counting airport traffic is more than just an exercise in record-keeping. A growing airport can be a key tool in promoting an area for economic development, according to airport industry officials.

"When you have a thriving airport, you have a thriving community," said Richard Horstmann, manager of technical services for the Airport Operators Council International, a Washington trade group.

Airport services are on the checklist most businesses use when considering whether to move or expand in a community, said T. James Truby, state aviation administrator. "If you can't fly there conveniently these days, that's a negative mark on that community," he said. "The more convenient we can make Maryland to fly into or from, the easier it's going to make it for state and local economic development officials to sell Maryland."

When it comes to promoting BWI, "We're opportunistic," said Carroll H. Hynson, Jr., director of information and trade development for the airport. "We're in parades, we go to shopping centers. We're very heavy promoters here."

While BWI's contests and gimmicks are aimed primarily at building a high profile with potential passengers, the airport also spends time quietly courting new airlines and encouraging those already at BWI to expand their services.

"If you don't have the flights, there's no reason for (passengers) to come," said Mr. Truby.

In recent years, BWI has successfully filled in some service gaps that Mr. Truby said were sending potential business elsewhere. Last year, nine passenger airlines and two cargo companies began new operations at BWI. Commercial traffic in and out of the airport increased from 365 flights a day to about 400.

The airport still lacks frequent service to the West Coast, but "fewer people find it necessary to drive past the door to go to (Washington National Airport) for a more convenient flight," said Mr. Truby.

In addition to seeking more flights, state officials visit airline reservation centers and travel agencies, encouraging them to book more passengers through BWI. In these visits, the state stresses the "W" in the airport's name, arguing that many passengers bound for Washington and vicinity will find BWI just as convenient as the area's two other commercial airports, Dulles International and Washington National. Both of those airports are run by the Federal Aviation Administration.

Promotion efforts and $175,000 worth of advertising scheduled for 1983 should help BWI post increases of at least 6 percent in both cargo and passenger traffic, Mr. Truby predicted.

Piedmont Airlines' January announcement that it will make BWI an operations "hub," increasing its daily flights here from 6 to 30 by the end of the year, bolsters that prediction. Airlines use hubs as a central point for flight connections to other cities they serve.

While confidently predicting growth for BWI, state aviation officials acknowledge that other airports—including competitor Dulles, 26 miles west of Washington—are beginning to realize that they can't just sit back and wait for airlines and passengers to come visiting.

Industry officials say BWI was a pioneer in airport promotion, but the competition is getting stiffer. Virginia officials recently took a major step to beef up promotion efforts for Dulles, which could draw some traffic away from BWI.

Marketing has been a top priority ever since the state bought BWI from Baltimore city in 1972, according to Mr. Truby. But at other airports around the country, little attention was paid to promotion before 1978.

That year, the federal government relaxed rules that had made it extremely difficult for an airline to move in and out of new markets. Before the government-mandated deregulation, airports didn't have to worry much about losing service. Now, an airline can come or go at will, with relatively short notice to the airport.

With their new freedom, airlines have become highly competitive in the search for lucrative new markets. Airports, anxious to hang on to the service they already have, as well as add to it, find they have to compete, too.

"Airlines, particularly Piedmont, have encouraged competition among and between airports," said Mr. Truby.

In order to compete, "You can decrease your (automobile) parking rates. You can have a decreased landing fee. There are all sorts of promotional things you can do at an airport to attract either airlines or passengers," said Deborah Lunn, spokesperson for the airport operators council in Washington.

Mr. Truby said BWI has not tried landing fee discounts, though a financial break for airlines with a large number of flights is being considered. However, a discount program must be weighed against the fact that the airport is meant to be a profit-making enterprise. BWI had a $3 million operating profit last year, but it is behind in recovering the cost of capital improvements the state has made to the facility, Mr. Truby said.

Two years ago, Dulles eliminated fees traditionally charged for airline use of landing strips and mobile lounge services. The fees were reinstated this year, and Dulles officials said it is unclear whether dropping them had helped the airport retain or expand service.

Last fall, a new nonprofit Washington Dulles Task Force was established with the backing of local businesses, marking the first major promotional effort for the 20-year-old airport. Virginia has promised the group an annual contribution of $175,000 and business contributions are being solicited. Some of the steps planned by the Dulles group will echo marketing strategies already in use at BWI.

"BWI was one of the first airports in the country to have an aggressive marketing effort," said Thomas Morr, president of the Dulles task force. Mr. Morr's group will hire an advertising agency and publish a monthly guide to all flights available at the airport, two steps already taken by BWI.

The task force, still in its fledgling stage, was not able to persuade Piedmont that Dulles would make a better hub than BWI. Mr. Morr said Dulles was one of several contenders in that competition, but the federally-operated airport couldn't promise Piedmont officials "anything at the $21 million magnitude."

That figure refers to Maryland's promise to build a $21 million pier at BWI, adding 12 new gates to handle Piedmont's expansion. The state will pick up most of the tab for construction, already in the preliminary stages and scheduled for completion by the end of the year. Construction costs will be recovered over the next 25 years, through rent Piedmont pays for use of the facilities.

Mr. Morr and others involved in the competition said BWI won the coveted Piedmont operation with its aggressive marketing and the financial commitment. "The state (Maryland) made a decision to use taxpayer dollars and other funds to attract that. The federal government, the FAA, didn't have that flexibility" at Dulles, said Mr. Morr.

At National Airport, there is no outside promotional task force and no organized marketing effort by the federal officials in charge. Of the three area airports, National was the only one where passenger traffic declined—by 6 percent—in 1982.

However, National's 13.3 million-passenger load last year was almost twice as many as the total served at BWI and Dulles. A federal regulation bars National from handling more than 16 million passengers a year, and the airport has come close to hitting that limit in recent years.

Notorious for its congestion, National is a frequent target of attempts to curb or eliminate its operations. But its large roster of flights and convenient location—just across the Potomac River from Washington—provide it with plenty of defenders.

One recent study indicates that National would lose traffic to both Dulles and BWI if those two airports could win additional flights at their facilities. According to a survey done last year by the Metropolitan Washington Council of Governments, about a million passengers a year would abandon National if they could board the flights they wanted at Dulles and BWI.

Dulles would add about 900,000 departing passengers a year, while

BWI would add 200,000, according to the survey, which was based on questionnaires filled out by nearly 28,000 passengers catching flights at the three area airports.

The study indicates Dulles, 26 miles west of Washington, has greater potential for passenger growth than BWI, 30 miles northeast of the capital. Dulles is more convenient to the Virginia suburbs west and south of Washington, which Mr. Morr described as the fastest-growing parts of the Baltimore-Washington region.

Mr. Morr said Dulles and BWI serve different markets and are not directly competitive for most passenger traffic. Assuming area airline traffic grows in the future, "I think they're both going to do well," he said.

Mr. Truby agreed that his airport, BWI, will grow in the future, but said, "I think Dulles has some serious problems. It is not sitting between two metropolitan areas." BWI's location between Washington and Baltimore helps it draw traffic from both cities, he said.

In fact, drawing from Washington and its suburbs is essential for the growth of BWI, according to Mr. Truby. The Baltimore area—the city and its five surrounding counties—has about 40 percent of the Baltimore-Washington region's population. But the area accounts for only about 16 percent of the region's airline traffic, he said.

"When I talk to airlines about adding service here, I couldn't begin to sell them on coming to BWI simply on the basis of traffic available in the Baltimore region," Mr. Truby said. About 30 percent of BWI's passenger traffic now comes from the Washington area, up from about 18 percent in the mid-1970's, he said.

While BWI is a distant second to National in passenger traffic, it handles about 60 percent of all cargo shipped by air to and from the Baltimore-Washington region. Despite the drop in cargo traffic last year, a private developer this spring will open a new 60,000-square-foot facility, built on airport land leased from the state, to handle expected growth in BWI's cargo traffic.

The effort to expand both passenger and cargo traffic is an important part of development around BWI and elsewhere in the state, Mr. Truby said. Land around airports, unsuitable for residential development, can be attractive to businesses and industries if the airport offers convenient cargo and passenger service.

Half a dozen business and industrial parks operate close to BWI, and more are scattered at Anne Arundel county sites convenient to the airport. Local developers said the area is considerably busier than it was several years ago, but there is room for substantial new developments.

When work began in 1974 on the Baltimore Commons Business Park at the airport's western border, most of the area nearby was "virgin ground with very little development around it," said Robert Arnold, president of Parker Frames and Company, Inc. Parker, an industrial real estate brokerage, markets the 300-acre business park.

In recent years, development has increased, enhanced by the state's $70 million renovation of the airport facility in 1979. "It's still only beginning to reach its potential. But the improvement in the airport should help accelerate that pace," Mr. Arnold said.

In a privately owned company, leadership and marketing often go hand in hand. The Harley Hotel Company is not small, but it is privately owned, and Leona Helmsley, president, is in the forefront of both management and marketing activities. She is truly a "leading lady" in the industry, with a very personal style of management.

The advertisements shown here and on the next two pages use Leona Helmsley's personal style as the theme for a coordinated ad campaign. Her attention to detail and insistence on quality provide the theme for a campaign directed at two distinct segments of the market—hotel customers and the travel agents who book them. The first three ads appeared together in the same issue of Frequent Flyer *magazine, as well as in various combinations in such other periodicals as* Business Week, New York Magazine, *and inflight magazines for major airlines. The last ad, using the same thematic approach, appeared in* Travel Weekly.

Not only the theme but the pattern is the same in each of the ads. A very positive assertion from Mrs. Helmsley appears at the top of the ad; body copy on the right side below that expands on the quotation and tells where to call. A photograph provides interest left of the body copy, and the ad finishes with a slogan.

"The Lure of a China Experience" is an excellent example of the failure of salespeople to properly qualify or advise clients. What clients ask for is not always in their best interests. A salesperson must know all aspects of the travel product, including physical requirements for tour programs. Don't let the "mortuary rush season" include your clients.

THE LURE OF A CHINA EXPERIENCE

By Edwin M. Reingold, Time-Life News Service

The lure of a China experience brought an army of 50,000 American tourists to this once off-limits land last year, and this year the number is expected to swell to 70,000.

Because China is remote and because it wants foreign exchange badly, it is expensive to tour China. Naturally, those who can afford the trip are often people in their 60s and 70s.

But it is...strenuous. For many it is hazardous to health, and for at least 20 visitors in the past two years, it has meant death. In fact, three American tourists, all in their 70s, have died in China in the past four weeks.

One American who must deal with the deaths and often with illness, injury and just plain dissatisfaction, is the American Consul in Peking, Bruce Gray.

"Not all the hills need to be climbed by these older people," insists Gray. "Some could be viewed from an air conditioned bus. But people seem to want to do everything on this romantic China tour. They've paid for it. But many pay for it in ways they didn't intend."

Gray is the man who must seal the coffins, contact the relatives, recommend courses of action and sometimes explain to distraught tourists that medical facilities in China are by any standards primitive. The food can be greasy and loaded with monosodium glutamate and salt, the hotel facilities are at present second or third or 10th-rate at best, transportation is erratic. Sometimes the facilities tourists complain about are the finest available at this primitive stage in China's attempt to modernize.

And the costs are high, even exorbitant. But then, what else could you expect in a country where the family of an executed criminal must pay for the bullet used to kill him?

In their grief, families have learned that the average cost of returning a body to the United States is between $5,000 and $7,000. Embalming is rarely available, so families are cautioned to consult their local morticians before viewing the remains.

Many people come to China even though they have medical conditions that would give them pause were it not for the magnetism of China, says Gray.

"The tour guides tell me the average age of their clients is well over 65. Not one of the people who have died here in the last two years was under 60, most were over 65 and a third were over 70," says Gray.

Gray and others concerned with the problem feel that travel agents ought to be more explicit in explaining conditions in China to prospective tourists.

"They should know that emergency medical care of the type accessible to most rural Americans is literally not available here," says Gray, recalling the story of a 72-year-old woman who slipped and broke her hip at the Great Wall of China at Badaling, a two-and-one-half-hour drive north of Peking.

"They brought her to Peking on the back of a flatbed truck. When she got to Capital Hospital (where foreigners are treated) the doctors refused to operate on her, afraid she would die. So we decided to med-evac her."

This required purchasing an army field stretcher, sawing off the handles, buying quilts at the friendship store to pad the canvas, and putting it aboard a Chinese airliner bound for Tokyo. Payment of four first-class fares was required. Because of Chinese airline regulations, she had to be moved painfully on each takeoff and landing at two intermediate stops before arriving in Tokyo.

"Miraculously," says Gray, "she survived and wrote me about her experiences."

The ailments that should preclude a trip to China are precisely those that many of the aged tourists suffer. Says Gray, "emphysema, asthma, hypertension or any heart condition, all of these are conditions that we find in those who died."

One tour guide says that although the travel company requires a statement of health from each prospective traveler, the applicants are so eager to come that they lie.

In some cases where a tourist finds himself in the hospital—or writhing on the couch in Gray's office as one woman did recently, with blood pressure of 240/150—Gray calls the family physician. "I wish I had a nickel for every time I've had a doctor tell me 'I begged him not to go.'"

"The minimal comforts and facilities Americans can expect are simply not available in China," says Gray, who has served in Denmark, Taiwan, and Hong Kong. "Things like hand railings, heating, air conditioning, drinking fountains, sanitary rest rooms, things we are accustomed to in most tourist spots in the world. One woman told me she was so cold last winter she opened her suitcase and put on all her clothing."

"One man called me to complain that he was being cheated and had been taken to a bad, over-priced restaurant. I had to tell him he was taken to one of the best Peking had to offer."

Airline schedules are erratic, flights are sometimes cancelled, trains are overbooked, hotels are switched. Gray admits that statistically almost all American tourists survive the experience and arrive home with interesting stories to tell, but many have hurt themselves physically in doing it. Tour companies set a blistering pace for the tour groups with almost no concession to the age of the clients.

An elderly chain-smoking woman from Boston complained of the pace: "We got there last night and barely had time to change clothes before they took us to see the Peking opera. Most of us fell asleep in the first 10 minutes."

Gray recommends that elderly people who have pre-existing medical conditions go to Taiwan or Hong Kong, where tourist facilities are better, less expensive, safer and medical help is accessible.

"If they really must see the Peoples Republic of China," he says, "they can take a day trip from Hong Kong to Canton."

In view of the existing problems, one can only shudder at the suggestion made last week by Vice Premier Chen Muhua that China should develop ethnic tourist facilities so that travelers can live in Thai-type bamboo houses in steamy, humid Hunnan province and in yurts (felt tents) when they visit the primitive Inner Mongolian Desert.

Tourism is on the rise, according to Chen, and by 1983 Peking is expected to be able to handle 430,000 visitors a year in 3,600 hotel rooms—5,600 rooms by 1985. New hotels will also go up in Xian, Hangzhou, Suzhou, Wuxi and other scenic areas which are sorely lacking in tourist facilities, but which take many thousands of tourists nevertheless.

The Chinese view of the importance of tourism was frankly revealed in a memorandum lately circulated within the China travel service which pointed out that tourism is the fastest way for China to get foreign exchange, and urged agents to keep this in mind when dealing with tourists. In the last three years China has earned $1.3 billion from tourists, including some 12 million overseas Chinese who have come "home" for a visit.

As American tourists contribute to that increase, Gray and his colleagues are knocking on wood because while this is the height of the "mortuary rush season"—more black humor—there hasn't been a death for several weeks.

As for China's development of tourist infrastructure and the hope that tourist facilities will reach world class standards soon, one Peking wag puts it succinctly: "China is the country of the future," he says. "It always has been, and it always will be."

"Muse Air Breathing Easier," describes how a marketing gamble paid off. Lamar Muse and his son Michael turned an apparent trend in the personal habits of the American population into a marketing advantage for the carrier. By being the only "nonsmoking" airline, Muse Air established an immediate identity. In addition to the advantages for nonsmokers, Muse Air gained another benefit—lower maintenance costs. Muse Air's marketing success has now encouraged others to try similar programs. Thrifty Rent-A-Car (another small company in an industry dominated by big ones) is finding its nonsmoking fleet successful and a number of hotels (in Houston, Dallas, Tulsa, Midland/Odessa, and Los Angeles) are also providing nonsmoking rooms.

MUSE AIR BREATHING EASIER AS NO-SMOKING GAMBLE PAYS OFF

The no-smoking policy on all Muse Air flights was strictly a marketing decision. "It supported an idea whose time had come," says Michael Muse, president.

But there must have been some crossed fingers when the policy was extended to include not only the less-than-an-hour flights around Texas and Oklahoma, but also trips halfway across the country from Houston to Los Angeles.

Would smokers accept this restriction? Were there enough nonsmokers to fill the seats?

Muse insisted it would work, but when the new nonstop service was inaugurated in early October, the skeptics still expressed doubts.

Apparently Muse was right. The airline now says that only about three percent of the passengers on the long-haul complain about the restriction. And many of them admit that they had not known in advance about the no-smoking policy. Either the travel agent did not tell them, or they bought their tickets over the counter and did not pay attention.

And now, only four months from start-up of the service, Muse is doing a bit better than breaking even on the long haul, an indication that the public has no intention of ostracizing the company for its no-smoking rules.

Michael Muse and his father Lamar Muse, chairman of the board, did not make the original decision lightly. It was based on solid research. They had watched the smoking sections on major airlines getting smaller and smaller, often as little as 20 percent of the seats being ear-marked for smokers.

They heard no-smoking passengers express approval of the Texas service. And they listened to the comments that even in non-smoking sections the tell-tale smell drifted through the cabin. Air conditioning could only do so much.

Lamar Muse, already known for courageous and calculated decisions, appointed a research team. The team reported that for every airline passenger who requested the smoking section on flights of less than one hour, five others asked for non-smoking seats, and that even a significant number of smokers preferred the no-smoking section.

This indicated a majority vote. Muse admitted that a few confirmed smokers, who would spend an hour in church on Sunday morning without smoking, might go to the competition because of the flight restrictions.

"But," he added, "for every one of them, we believe there are 10 travelers who will switch to Muse Air for our no-smoking policy. It sure won't take long to find out."

And it didn't. Muse Air did just fine when it introduced the Houston-Dallas service in July 1981. In May of 1982 it expanded to include Tulsa and Midland/Odessa.

So the company decided to gamble on keeping the policy for the long haul, a gamble that appears to be successful.

Passengers like the clean, fresh-smelling airplanes. They appreciate not having to inhale someone else's puffing in an enclosed environment, a stand strongly supported by the American Lung Association, which reports twice as much tar and nicotine in second-hand smoke.

PASSENGER LURE

The Muse duo, father and son, have made it very clear however that they are not crusaders against tobacco. They are airline men, marketers who saw a competitive opportunity. They figure to attract more passengers than they lose because of the no-smoking policy.

Still other benefits have resulted. Lower maintenance and cleaning costs on their McDonnell Douglas Super 80 aircraft were a part of the decision too.

A visual display presented at the inaugural ceremonies for the Los Angeles service compared two air filters. One was from "somebody else's" plane. Its screen was thick with a brown sticky covering.

The second screen, reportedly used for many hours on a Muse plane in the Texas service, looked almost spotless with only a light covering of dust filtered from the inside air.

Has no smoking proved to be a problem for the passengers on the long haul? Not a serious one. In a few instances a chain smoker, unable to cope with his nicotine urge, has sneaked into the lavatory, taken a couple of quick drags and thrown the butt into the commode to hide the indiscretion.

Recently 25 travel agents from the Los Angeles area, about half of them smokers, made a weekend fam trip from LAX to Houston. None found the restriction difficult, maintaining that since no one on the flight was smoking, the urge to smoke themselves was less.

Said one agent, "It's like the old adage, monkey see, monkey do. If you don't smell it, you don't need it." All indicated that they had no reservations about selling the service to clients, smokers or non-smokers.

Muse marketing people have also come up with a new tool to help sell the no-smoking concept to dyed-in-the-wool smokers. Flight attendants give them a smile and a little handout entitled "Making Flying Beautiful." It contains a few sticks of gum and some tasty hard candy to help dull the urge for tobacco.

It also contains a promise in writing that, if the troubled smoker uses the second half of his roundtrip ticket on Muse Air and still can't get used to giving up cigarettes for three hours, "The return trip is on us." The passenger can send in his flight coupon and the cost of the return trip will be refunded.

Sales reps too are now equipped with handouts to give to top accounts when a client argues that he won't even try Muse Air and its anti-smoking philosophy.

"Try it. You might like it," urges the sales rep. "And if you don't, after all, you get half your money back." A lot of people just might take that gamble.

Other marketing gimmicks have worked, too. One year, during the Great American Smokeout, Muse Air distributed the Smokeout pledge along with its own "Break the Habit" coupons which entitled the holder to a free return trip on Muse during the next month if they signed the pledge. The coupons encouraged them to treat themselves to "Clean Air on Muse Air" while they stopped smoking for a day.

"Breaking the old habit of flying other airlines fit in very well with breaking the smoking habit," said Michael Muse. "The decision to be a no-smoking airline has given us a definite marketing advantage."

This year's newest promotion has been the announcement of a coordinated effort between Muse Air, Thrifty Rent-a-Car and major hotels in

Muse market cities to provide complete no-smoking travel arrangements.

Travel agents can book the cars and the hotel rooms when they make the flight reservations. Thrifty has designated 10 to 15 percent of its fleet in those cities as non-smoking cars, guaranteed not to smell like a dirty ash tray.

The hotels offering no-smoking rooms include: the Lincoln Radisson in Dallas; the Inn on the Park and Houston Center in Houston; the Directory and the Excelsior in Tulsa; the Executel at the Midland/Odessa Regional Airport and the Hyatt Regency on Sunset Boulevard in Los Angeles.

Both Doug Harrison, vice president of operations for Thrifty, and Ed Lang, vice president of administration for Muse, regard the action as a response to a national trend among the traveling public, the majority of whom are now non-smokers.

GOOD PUBLIC RELATIONS

The policy has also produced some public relations benefits. Both the American Association for Respiratory Therapy and the American Heart Association have made official public presentations of commendation for Muse Air.

The American Cancer Society went even further. It sent TV and movie personality, Dennis Cole, the honorary California chairman for the 1982 Smoke-out, to participate in the rollout ceremonies inaugurating the Los Angeles service.

No-smoking may have started as a marketing decision, but it has also produced other worthwhile benefits: lower maintenance costs, great public relations, and most of all, happy and healthier passengers.

Reprinted with permission of ASTA Travel News, April 15, 1980.

Qualifying the client is one of the most important parts of the sales process. "How to Eliminate Shoppers Who Don't Buy" provides additional information on identifying the noncustomer so that sales time can be concentrated on potentially profitable customers. Successful selling requires early identification and the elimination of those who are not truly prospective buyers.

HOW TO ELIMINATE SHOPPERS WHO DON'T BUY

By Lawrence J. Frommer, CTC

When is a customer not a customer? Frequently. The fact that a lot of people knock on our doors may be good for the ego but not necessarily for the pocket. Of every 10 people who phone or visit our offices, eight do not book—some because we don't do an effective job of selling, but most because they really aren't potential customers anyway.

Try this experiment that our agency conducted several years ago: In a given week, record the names of anyone other than established customers who phone your office or walk in requesting information and collecting brochures. Then, in 60 days check the list to ascertain how many actually booked. You may be amazed at how few.

When you get right down to it, only a small portion of a travel agent's day is actually productive because it is monopolized by comparison shoppers, curiosity-seekers, armchair travelers, impulse callers, boredom-breakers, habitual reservation-cancelers and various other time-wasters. Yet we devote as much time—if not more—to the pseudo-prospects as we do to actual customers.

Incredible, isn't it, how much we give for so little?

To be sure, all businesses have their "non-customers" who flit in and out of their offices or stores without buying. But unlike most businesses, a travel agency's basic products are time and expertise. Thus, in our business, the non-customer virtually devours the merchandise.

IDENTIFYING THE NON-CUSTOMER

The question is, what can we do about them? What methods and strategies can we employ to gracefully filter them out so that we can get on with more profitable transactions?

There are no simple solutions. Instinct, ingenuity, diplomacy, discipline and a substantial amount of chutzpah are needed to make successful sales. But first we must recognize that not everyone who knocks on our doors is a potential customer. For if we are to effectively ferret out and deal with the profit-losers we must admit that such people exist.

Then we must learn how to identify the typical non-customer, to recognize the tell-tale signs, the characteristics and peculiarities that distinguish this individual from the authentic customer.

One obvious indication that a prospect lacks serious purpose is his reluctance to offer a name. Nothing is more tentative than a person who begins a conversation with, "You don't know who I am, but I'd like to get the roundtrip APEX fare to Barcelona." Shoppers and other casual inquirers do not like to be identified because they are a long way from making any kind of commitment and prefer to play games under a cloak of anonymity.

Another clue is when a caller seems to possess a wealth of information, indicating that he has tested the waters extensively before contacting your office. As I pointed out in my article, "How's Your Salesmanship?" (ATN, October, 1979) ". . . he has already digested the prices and knows that a specific hotel is sold out for the dates he wants. . ." You can bet that he is using you either for comparison shopping or to reconfirm information he has already.

There is the terribly indecisive prospect, the one who phones you five or six times, engages you in lengthy conversations but remains unbooked. He may come around eventually but experience has demonstrated that he usually decides not to go at all.

Needless to say, prospects who hold duplicate reservations on airlines, steamships and/or hotels from other sources should not be taken too seriously. In most cases they are protecting themselves by playing the field.

Also be suspicious of the caller who is unusually impatient, who demands to know everything immediately, who can't wait until the person who can answer his queries with greater authority returns from lunch and who threatens to book with another agency if you can't help him pronto. I have found this type of caller very unreliable. His impatience usually stems from either compulsion or impulse that often evaporates as quickly as it surfaces. I've discovered that the most impetuous are the ones I had to phone the most frequently for decisions, and in most cases, they didn't go.

There is the former customer, the one you haven't heard from in at least five years although you have reason to believe he has traveled. Out of the blue he contacts you, invariably when space is tight, prefacing his requests with a guilt-tinged disclaimer such as, "I haven't really traveled anywhere for a long time, which is why you haven't heard from me."

Chances are he is using you—you're just one of several cards up his sleeve, and if reservations were not so scarce it is unlikely that you would have heard from him at all.

Be skeptical of the caller who inquires about one destination and suddenly shifts to others that are totally unrelated. I conversed with one of these armchair globetrotters recently who initially requested data on Bermuda; before the conversation was terminated I had helped her research Chile, Pakistan, Haiti, Biloxi and Alaska. Total time of conversation: 50 minutes.

Among the callers not to be taken seriously is the one who starts the conversation by criticizing another travel agency. Often this person's request will be just as difficult for you to fulfill as it was for your competitor, but he goes from agency to agency to find one with a "special magic." How many times have you heard such callers remark, "The other agency is not doing anything for me"? Perhaps "not doing anything" means being unable to book a very popular Caribbean hotel in mid-February.

Learn to deal effectively with prospects who frequently book but never go. There are many well-intentioned people with hangups of one kind or another about travel who cancel when the moment to act arrives. I've had prospects who have booked as many as five consecutive trips but each time have come down with psychosomatic illnesses just a few days prior to departure. They are more to be pitied than scorned, yet we must recognize their patterns.

Be very leery of the person who phones you two days before he plans to travel, asking you to book hard-to-get flights and hotel reservations. In some cases this may be a legitimate last-minute booking, but far too often it is a case of someone who has frantically searched around without success or a caller who has a sudden whim.

Another potential profit-drainer is the person who confuses a travel agency with a government tourist office. He has little conception of how an agency operates and regards it primarily as a source of information, brochures and other travel data. I know at least four people who regularly visit our office to collect brochures and ask questions, but have yet to book a reservation in four years. We suspect that they are either vicarious travelers or are building a brochure library for their youngsters' school projects.

HOW TO DEAL WITH THEM

Having identified the profit-drainers, it becomes much easier to deal with them. Naturally you just can't come out and bluntly accuse someone of wasting your time and suggest that he take his foolishness elsewhere. But there are polite and subtle methods that can be employed to get the non-customer out of your hair more rapidly.

Travel industry consultant John Dalton of Columbus, Ohio suggests that when a customer doesn't offer a name, the agent should try to establish intent by saying something to the effect of: "Good morning. Let me introduce myself; John Dalton is my name. May I have yours?"

Dalton contends that the capricious caller has no interest in being identified and that the proffering of a name is too much of a commitment for him. "By asking for his name the chances are likely that it will be a short conversation," he adds.

A Washington, DC agency owner discloses that when a caller asks why the agency wants to know his name she replies, "When you ask me to send you brochures or are ready to book the reservation I won't have to bother you about it."

When a caller seems to have too much information, ask him if he has already tried to get what he wants and, if he has been unsuccessful, would he buy alternatives? Why go through a fruitless repeat performance for someone who has already contacted other agencies?

If an unfamiliar prospect phones a day or two before his trip, asking you to book flights or hotel reservations, insist that he come down to your office and put down a deposit before you can make arrangements. His reaction to this will indicate whether he is serious or just impulsive.

Concerning the prospect who holds duplicate reservations on carriers and in hotels, firmly insist that he make an immediate decision as to which set of reservations he plans to use.

The person who is disgruntled with another travel agency should be questioned immediately as to why he is dissatisfied. It may well be that you can't do any more for him than the other travel agency.

To the person who books elsewhere but consults you for supplementary information, you might politely suggest that he obtain that information from the booking firm.

For the constant canceler it might be helpful to establish a system of cancellation fees. The prospect might become piqued at the suggestion, but what do you have to lose?

For the person to whom "money is no object," it might be a good idea to give him an approximate price quotation early in the game. If he is going to defect let him do so before you have spent too much time with him.

To the person who pumps you for information on the street, suggest that he phone you at the office where you have all of your data on hand. If he doesn't, you know he really wasn't serious.

THE INDECISIVE PROSPECT

With the indecisive prospect who has already stolen much of your time, you simply have no alternative but to pin him down by: 1. asking for a deposit to cover any reservations to be made; 2. writing up an order in the presence of the person; 3. asking specific questions such as, "Should we inquire if space is available?" "If we can get this for you is this what you want?" "Do you prefer a morning or an afternoon flight?" "How do you wish to pay for this trip—credit card, cash, etc.?"

The former customer must be handled a little more gingerly than most profit-drainers. After all, he's been on your books before and you may reason that if you do a good job for him you might win him back. Unfortunately, it doesn't usually work that way. For one reason or another he hasn't seen fit to book through you for five years or more, and when his current booking crisis is history he is likely to return to his normal sources. You might give him a chance, but don't lose too much sleep over him if you can't get what he wants.

Now you might ask: isn't there an inherent danger in systematically trying to eliminate people no matter how politely it is done? Yes, fellow agents, I'm fully aware that once in a while you're going to blow one: the person who already has a lot of information may still let you book his reservation; the duplicate booker may release his space to your agency; the impatient caller might sincerely desire to go somewhere at the last minute; and the indecisive prospect may eventually make a decision.

But for every legitimate customer who gets away, you'll be discouraging a countless coterie of frivolous and unreliable people from wasting your time and energies. And in an age of escalating costs and marginal profits, that's a requisite to survival.

In his article on "Selling," Lawrence J. Frommer, CTC, provides another view of customer oriented selling. While his article was written for travel agents, his ideas apply to all segments of the industry.

MEMO TO: TRAVEL AGENCY STAFF
FROM: MANAGER
RE: SELLING

By Lawrence J. Frommer, CTC

You and your customers are different people. One of you in the office took a cruise recently. You loved it. You're excited about selling cruises to as many people as possible, and heaven knows I would be the last person to dampen your enthusiasm. But make certain that your next customer is the "cruise type" before you try to persuade him. Another of you spent a few days last month at one of those charming cottage colonies in Bermuda. You fell in love with the place. But is your next Bermuda customer the cottage-colony type or the high-rise-hotel type? Remember, it's not what you like; it's what your customer likes.

Never bluff. If you're fuzzy about the answer to a customer inquiry, don't bluff it. It's far better to say, "May I check this for accuracy and get back to you?" or "Someone in the office is more current on this than I am; would you mind if I talked with her for a moment?"

Recognition is the "game of the name." There's a lot of truth in that old cliché that nothing sounds sweeter to a person than the sound of his own name. And there's nothing deadlier, no greater put-down than not being recognized. Think of the times you have phoned a place of business and identified yourself, only to be greeted with a dead silence or a rather bored "yes." Kind of took the stuffing out of you, didn't it?

So put yourself in the customer's shoes. If, for instance, a Mrs. Smith visits your office, greet her with a "Yes, Mrs. Smith" or "Hello, Mrs. Smith." It's flattering. It's friendly. It's the sweet sound of her own name. During the course of the conversation, re-identify her. Repeat her name several times.

And try this on for size: Instead of the usual greeting—"May I help you, Mrs. Smith?"—how about "*How* may I help you, Mrs. Smith?" Obviously you can help her. That's why she's talking to you. By going a step further and asking how you can help her, you get into the selling posture much quicker, and it's much friendlier and more personal.

Don't let customers play the waiting game. It's not good business to keep a prospective customer waiting. First of all, don't let incoming phone calls ring more than four times without answering. Protracted ringing suggests operational sloppiness and the caller begins to get nervous. If you must put a customer on hold, try to get back within 60 seconds. Otherwise, it poses uncertainties in his mind. Have you forgotten him? Is he still connected? Should he call back and start all over again? Should he just forget it and call someone else? If you're going to be busy for a while, explain the delay and ask if you can call back.

But let the customer know approximately when you will be calling. Most customers expect an immediate call back. If this is not possible, you or someone else in the office should indicate so at the time, something to the effect: "You know, Mrs. Williams, it looks like I'll be tied up anywhere from 30 to 45 minutes. May I phone you as soon as I'm free, or is there another time more convenient for you?" This gives the caller the option of waiting for your call back or doing other things. Above all, the caller will know what to expect.

What are the alternatives? By its very nature, our industry demands more alternatives than most others. A person may want a particular brand of vacuum cleaner or make of automobile, but the chances are he can wait a few weeks for delivery if it's not immediately available. He doesn't have to have the product on a specific day. In travel, it is just the opposite. The customer is programmed to travel on a specific date. He's made arrangements to go then. In most cases, he has little leeway.

Boost certain customers up the ladder. Price is the most overworked word in today's travel vernacular, and "bargain travel" has become a household phrase. But there are clients whose lifestyle is inappropriate to bargain travel and who would be unhappy booking a package with less-than-deluxe hotels or a cruise ship that is below their usual standards. You will do this type of a client a service by suggesting an upgrade and a disservice if you don't. In this case, you're not trying to get the customer to spend more money per se, but rather to maintain his lifestyle. So next time such a customer says he's interested in some bargain he's read about in the newspapers, you might say to him: "You're accustomed to traveling better than this, Mr. Holmes. Why do you like this particular package?" or "Please keep in mind, Mrs. Johnston, that the ship you're interested in is not nearly as elegant as the one on which you cruised last year."

A toughie is the unspoken objection, the one you don't hear or feel. That's the one at work when the customer says, "I'll think about it" or "Let me go home and talk it over with my wife" or "I don't know if I can afford it.'' This kind of remark usually means that you haven't overcome all of the client's objections, that there are still a couple lurking that must be gotten out on the table. Certainly, at that point, a question such as "Do you need additional information?" or "Is there still a question in your mind that we haven't answered yet?" would be timely and appropriate.

The toughest type of sales resistance is when you get seemingly unrelated objections that don't ring true. No sooner do you answer one objection than you get another, totally unconnected to what has gone before, almost as if the customer is trying to throw as many roadblocks in your way as possible. This pattern often indicates that it is both painful and difficult for the prospect to make a decision and this is his way of postponing it. Sometimes this can be handled with a sense of urgency on your part, that is, by persuading the prospect that if he doesn't act now, it could work against him later. A comment like "This package is very much in demand and if we don't book it very soon it will likely be sold out" reflects this approach.

As you might have ascertained by now, we are in a perfectly illogical business, a business in which income is disproportionate to the amount of work invested. Pushing our products and services requires an extraordinary amount of time and talent. There are constant barrages of questions and answers, incessant changes, busywork, long conversations. There's rarely a quick transaction. There's always a lot happening with nearly every prospect we talk to.

Yet nothing really happens. . . until we close the sale.

INDEX